I0795750

The Campus History Series

CAMPBELLSVILLE UNIVERSITY

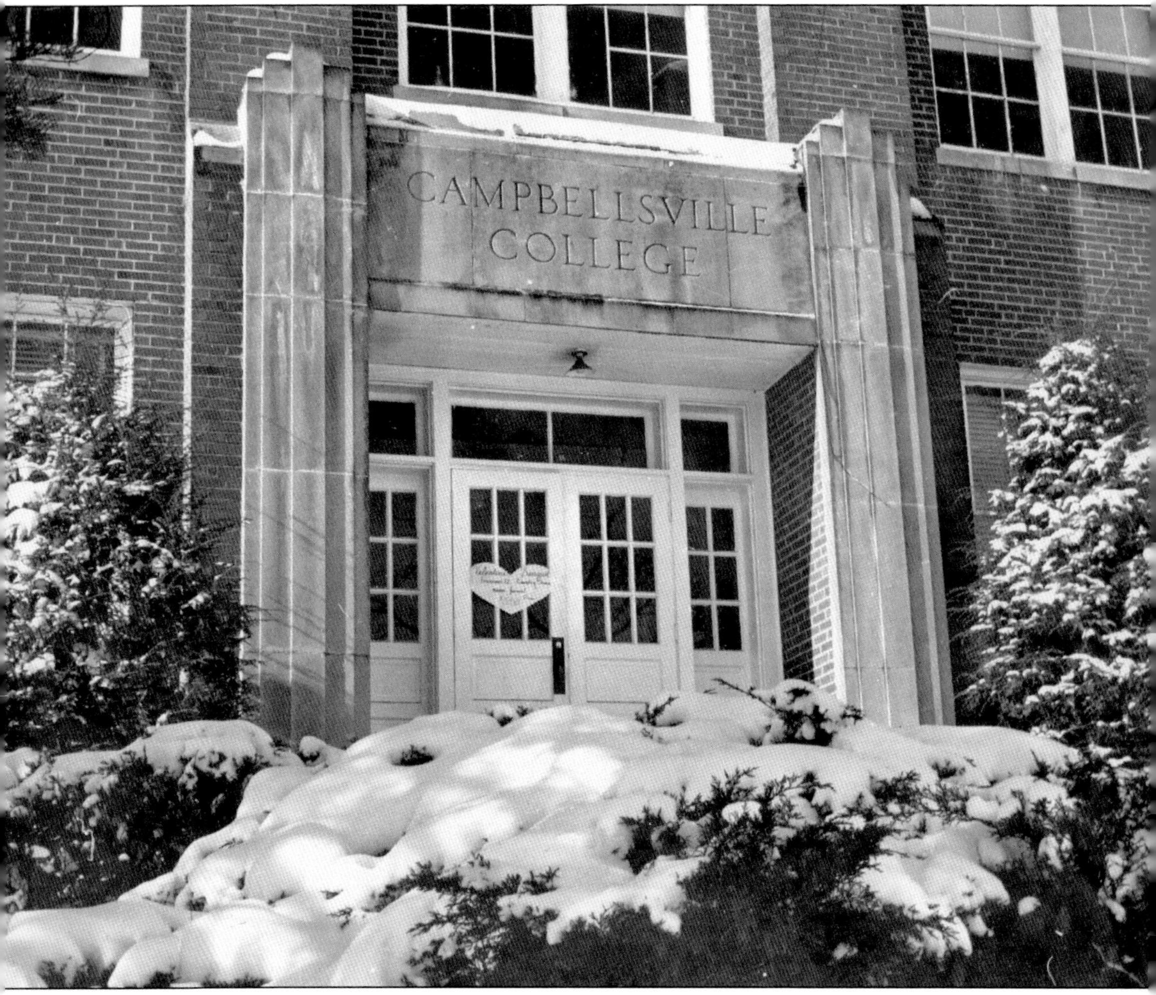

Photographed on a snowy February day, the main entrance to the Administration Building is as recognizable today to Campbellsville University students as it was to their predecessors at Campbellsville College. The only substantial changes over the years have been to the surrounding landscape.

On the Cover: Pictured are the members of the 1915 normal school class. Normal school training was one of the primary requirements to become a teacher in the Commonwealth of Kentucky. Another significant requirement was to pass a state-administered teacher-competency examination. Russell Creek Academy–trained teachers routinely passed the state test, which was a testament to the quality of the education provided by its faculty. (Photograph courtesy of A. B. Colvin Baptist Collection and Archives Room, Campbellsville University, Campbellsville, Kentucky.)

The Campus History Series

CAMPBELLSVILLE UNIVERSITY

JOHN R. BURCH JR. AND TIMOTHY Q. HOOPER

ARCADIA PUBLISHING

ISBN 978-0-7385-5288-7

Published by Arcadia Publishing
Charleston SC, Chicago IL, Portsmouth NH, San Francisco CA

Printed in the United States of America

Library of Congress Catalog Card Number: 2007926835

For all general information contact Arcadia Publishing at:
Telephone 843-853-2070
Fax 843-853-0044
E-mail sales@arcadiapublishing.com
For customer service and orders:
Toll-Free 1-888-313-2665

Visit us on the Internet at www.arcadiapublishing.com

In memory of Dr. A. B. Colvin, Dr. Edwin R. Montgomery, and Mrs. Ovaleta Montgomery

Contents

ACKNOWLEDGMENTS

A project of this scale cannot be completed without a significant amount of assistance; therefore, we must express our sincere gratitude to all those individuals who made this endeavor possible. First, at Campbellsville University, thanks are due to both Michael V. Carter and Frank Cheatham for the support and encouragement that they have provided over the course of this project. A great deal of credit is also owed to our colleagues at Montgomery Library: Patty McDowell, Sandra Riggs, Ted Schulz, Mary Street, and Regina Thompson. Deedra Bray also made contributions to the effort. Joan McKinney and the Campbellsville University public relations staff have been extremely helpful. This book would have looked very different had McKinney not given us total access to her files, which included many great photographs that she personally took. Access to photographs was also provided by Bryan Blair, Franky James, Frank Cheatham, Mary Street, J. Robert Gaddis, Alcingstone Cunha, and Eric Graves. We would be remiss not to acknowledge the obvious contribution of all the photographers who have documented the history contained within this volume. When possible, we have credited the photographers for their wonderful images. For historical accuracy and perspective, we have relied greatly on J. Chester Badgett's *History of Campbellsville University, 1906–2006* (Prospect, KY: Harmony House Publishers, 2006). At Arcadia Publishing, kudos is due to Kendra L. Allen for all of her assistance. Thanks are also due to all of Arcadia's employees whose work contributed to the production of this volume. Finally, thanks are also extended to those individuals who have been inconvenienced the most by this project, namely, Venita, Neil, Clay, and Glen Hooper and Idalia, Samantha, Morgan, Alexandra, Christopher, and Kayleigh Burch.

Unless otherwise indicated, the images found in this volume are from collections housed in the A. B. Colvin Baptist Collection and Archives Room, Campbellsville University, Campbellsville, Kentucky.

INTRODUCTION

With an enrollment of 2,384 students, Campbellsville University begins its second century as a Christian institution whose mission is focused on scholarship, leadership, and fellowship. The school currently offers more than 40 different areas of study, most of which lead to the acquisition of an associate's, bachelor's, or master's degree. Although a majority of the students attend classes on the 75-acre campus located in the heart of Campbellsville, Kentucky, Campbellsville University also offers educational programs in such disparate locales as Louisville, Kentucky, and Recife, Brazil.

In 1900, the Russell Creek Association of Baptists formed a committee that was charged with drafting a charter for the establishment of a school. In 1906, the dream of the committee came to fruition with the purchase of 10 acres of land from Charles and Georgie Hoskins that would comprise the campus of the Russell Creek Academy, which was officially established that same year. Construction quickly commenced on the Administration Building and J. S. Stapp Hall, which served as the residence hall. The Russell Creek Association School Committee selected W. G. Welborn to serve as the first principal of Russell Creek Academy. He held the post until 1912. Under his leadership, elementary and secondary school classes began to be offered in September 1907, as did normal school training for teachers.

From 1911 to 1913, Russell Creek Academy served as Taylor County's public high school. This situation was the result of a 1906 mandate from the Commonwealth of Kentucky's general assembly that required each county to have a high school. Since the county did not have the financial resources to construct its own facility, it turned to the privately owned Russell Creek Academy to serve that function. During the 1913–1914 academic year, the Russell Creek Academy's high school ceased to exist, although the elementary and normal school programs continued. During that academic year, Taylor County leased the academy's facilities.

The Russell Creek Association was at a critical crossroad. It could allow the school they founded to become Taylor County's public school, or they could keep it a strictly religious institution. This was not an easy decision because if they chose to remain a private institution, they probably stood to lose high school students to the soon-to-be-constructed county school system. The Russell Creek Association opted to ensure that Russell Creek Academy remain a private Baptist educational institution. Under the leadership of Rev. L. C. Kelly, who served as the pastor of Campbellsville Baptist Church, associational leaders traveled throughout Central Kentucky to raise the money required to operate their school. They also had to recruit a new principal and faculty, since a majority of the people previously serving in that capacity had left the institution at the conclusion of the 1912–1913 academic year. Fortunately, the Russell Creek Association was able to turn to Prof. W. G. Welborn to lead the rebirth of Russell Creek Academy's high school in 1914.

The year 1924 was pivotal for Russell Creek Academy because its final class graduated and Campbellsville Junior College was established. Thirty-three students were enrolled in the college for the 1924–1925 academic year. Despite becoming a junior college, the institution continued to educate elementary and secondary school students until 1941.

Although the Great Depression did not officially begin until October 1929 with the crash of the stock market, much of rural America had already been suffering through a severe economic decline for several years. Campbellsville Junior College was feeling the consequences of this decline by 1927. That year, each member of the faculty and trustees were asked to donate $100, but most were unable to comply with the request. In 1929, the board of trustees asked the faculty to donate one-tenth of their salaries to the institution but was rebuffed. With the faculty unwilling to give up part of their salaries, the trustees began selling assets, including a 52-acre farm with livestock and farm implements. The president's home was also sold during 1929. The monies that were raised failed to alleviate all of the institution's financial woes, so the faculty were told that they were going to be required to take a significant cut in pay in 1930. Rather than accepting a reduction in their salaries, many members of the faculty chose to resign on March 5, 1930. On April 7, 1930, the school's president, Warren F. Jones, resigned. Rather than taking the easy solution and closing Campbellsville Junior College permanently, the board of trustees quickly hired Denton J. Wright to serve as president. The remaining faculty members continued to teach despite having no guarantees that they would be paid. The school did not begin to financially recover from that era until the post–World War II boom that saw many veterans take advantage of their military benefits.

The difficult decade of the 1930s was capped by the April 14, 1939, fire that gutted the original Administration Building. The loss was particularly devastating because the building housed faculty and administrative offices, classrooms, science laboratories, and the library. As has been evident throughout Campbellsville University's 100-year history, rather than feel sorry for their plight, the entire campus community made sacrifices in order to raise the revenue required to replace the building. In an amazingly short amount of time, the new Administration Building was constructed and opened for use on January 2, 1940.

Campbellsville College became a four-year college in 1959. During the 30 years that the institution was a four-year school, the campus expanded significantly. The expansion of the campus was mirrored by improvements in student life. The athletic program grew, with the notable additions of men's football and numerous sports for the ladies. The campus's musical offerings were enriched through the establishment of a number of musical ensembles, including a marching band and a handbell choir.

This growth occurred despite Campbellsville College's continuing financial difficulties. In order to finance the growth of the campus's physical plant, as well as the expansion of academic and extracurricular activities for the students, the school operated under a tight budget.

The institution became Campbellsville University in 1996. The change, while reflecting the growth of the school, also allowed for the expansion of graduate programs. At the time of the status change, the institution had 1,097 full-time students. Since 1996, there has been tremendous growth of both the student body and the campus. Among the new buildings on campus are the Betty Dobbins Heilman House and the E. Bruce Heilman Student Center Complex, which houses the Winters Dining Hall and the Davenport Student Commons. The newest building on campus, the Ransdell Chapel, is a fitting and beautiful capstone to the first century of the institution's history. It reflects that present-day Campbellsville University still holds true to the value expressed by the Russell Creek Association of Baptists over a century ago: Christian values can be maintained while providing a high-quality education.

One

Russell Creek Academy 1906–1924

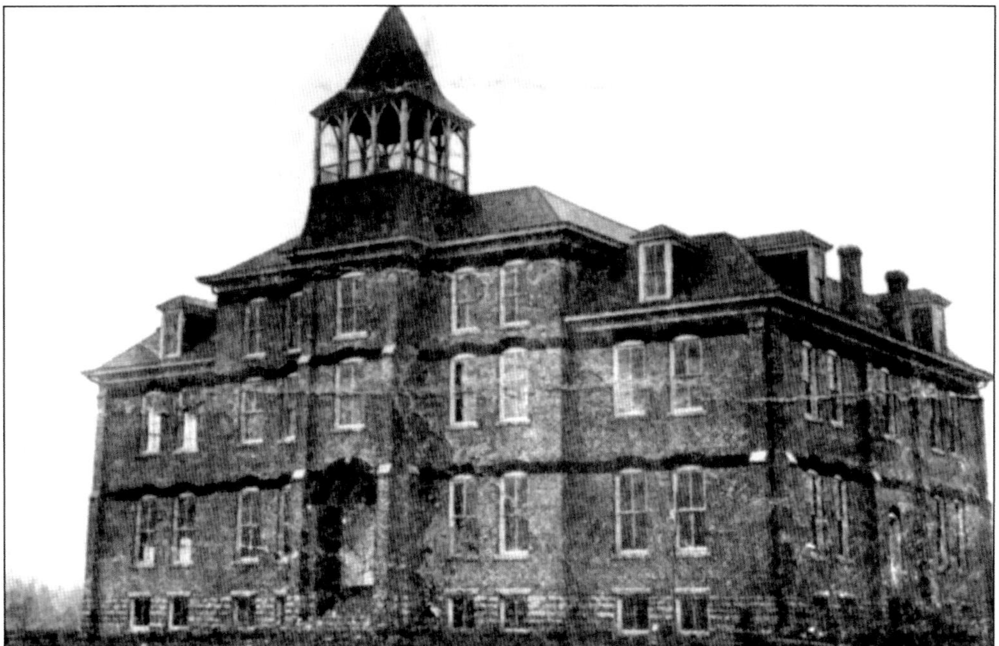

In 1907, construction on the original Administration Building was completed. It was a brick building that consisted of two stories and a basement. Initially housed within the building were eight classrooms, music and art rooms, a cloakroom, and administrative offices. The basement was utilized as a play area by the children during periods of inclement weather.

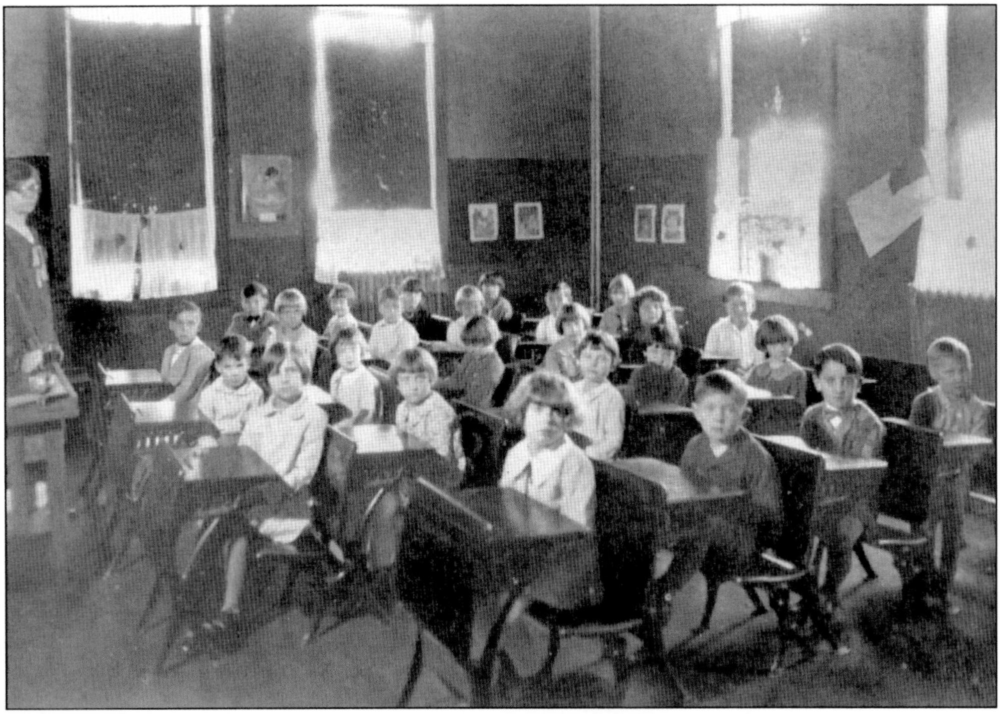

Primary school students attend class in one of the Administration Building's classrooms.

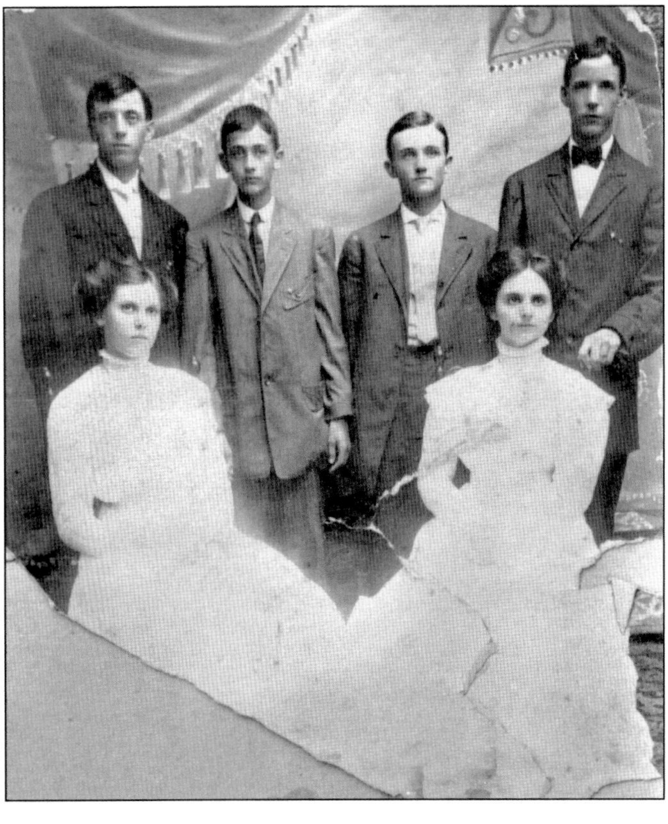

The members of the 1909 graduating class of the Russell Creek Academy were Jane Chandler, Harry Gatton, Carl Walling, Frank Buckner, Harper Gatton, and Myrtle Hendrickson.

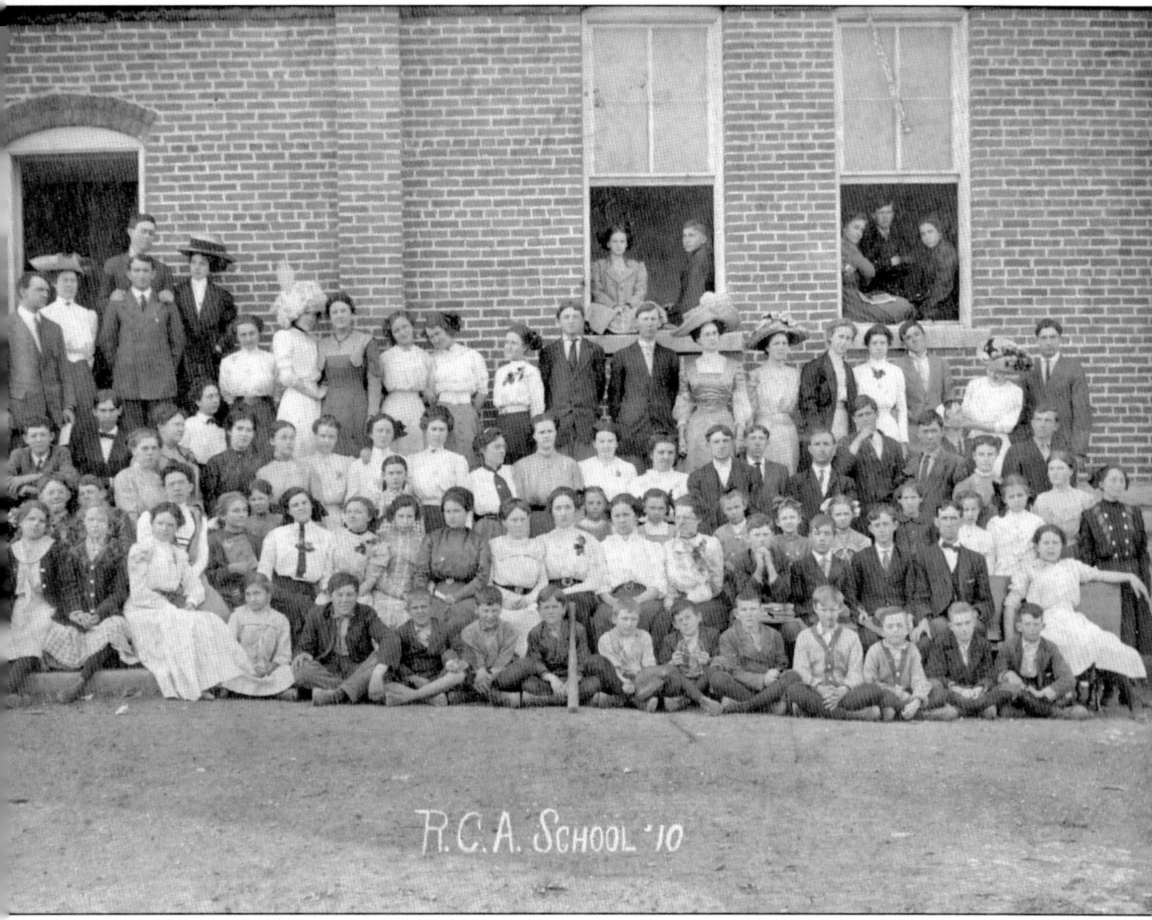

This portrait of the entire Russell Creek Academy community in 1910 shows a wide range in the ages of the students. Many students were enrolled in the primary school or the high school. Some of the older students were enrolled in the teacher-training program, which was offered through the Normal Department.

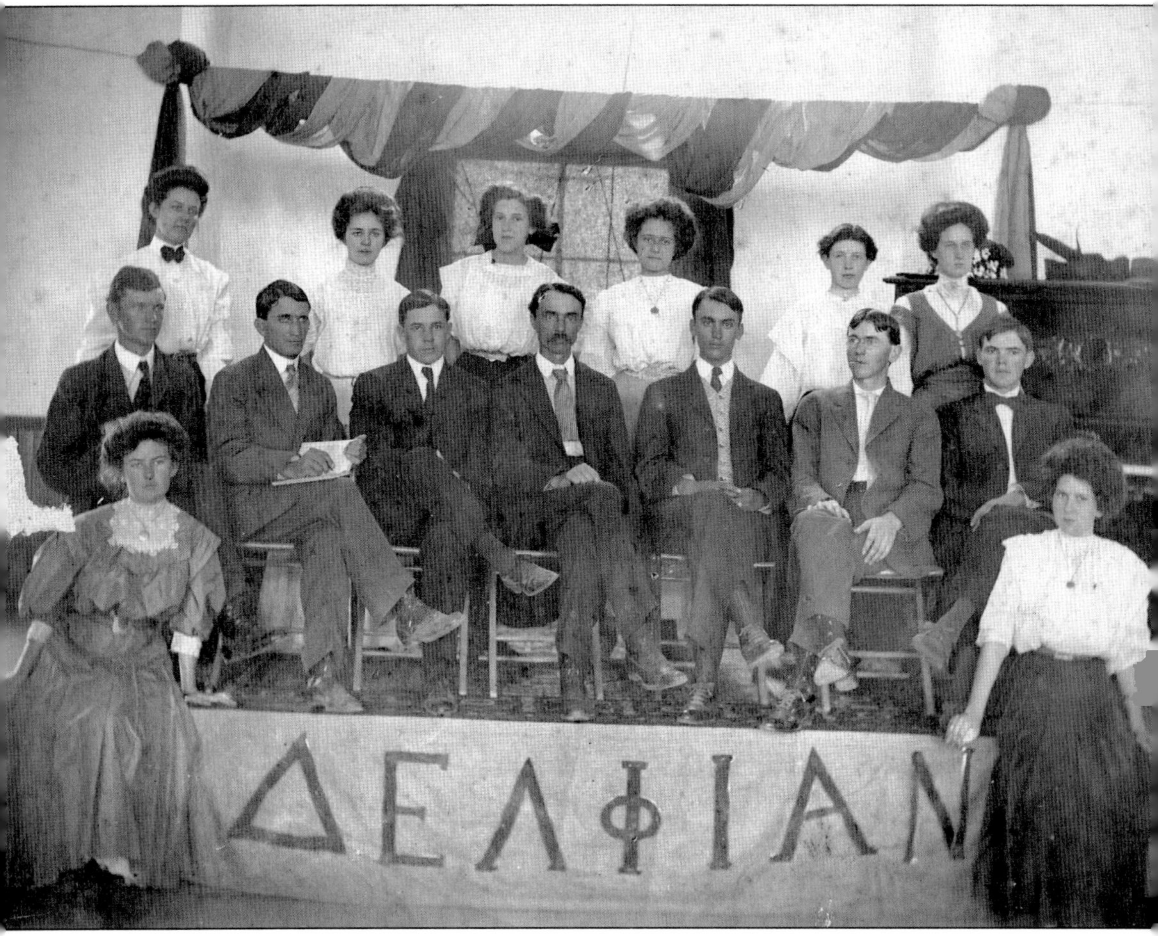

The members of the Russell Creek Academy's Delphian Literary Society are pictured *c.* 1910. The Russell Creek Academy's founders encouraged students to organize academic societies for the purpose of publishing periodicals. It was believed that such an endeavor would not only help students improve their writing ability, but would also allow for the development of journalism and business skills.

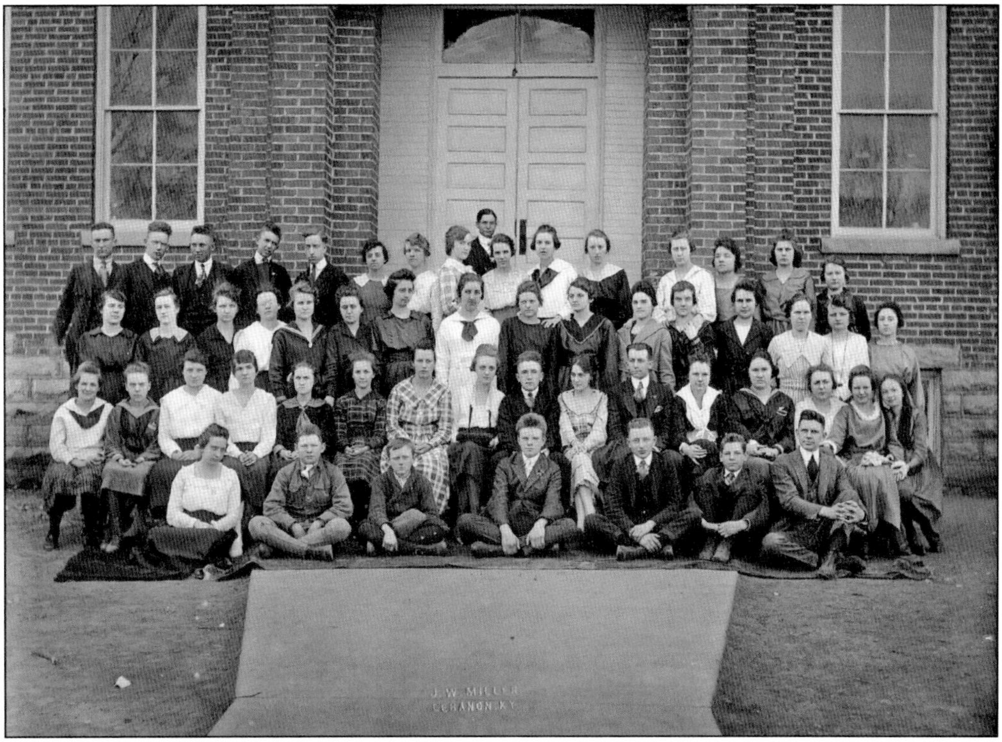

The Kappa Alpha Society (above) and the Sidney Lanier Society (below) were two of the literary societies created at the Russell Creek Academy. These organizations provided students the opportunity to apply the academic lessons learned in classes in a businesslike setting. The practical skills learned in the societies would prove invaluable to the students in their later endeavors.

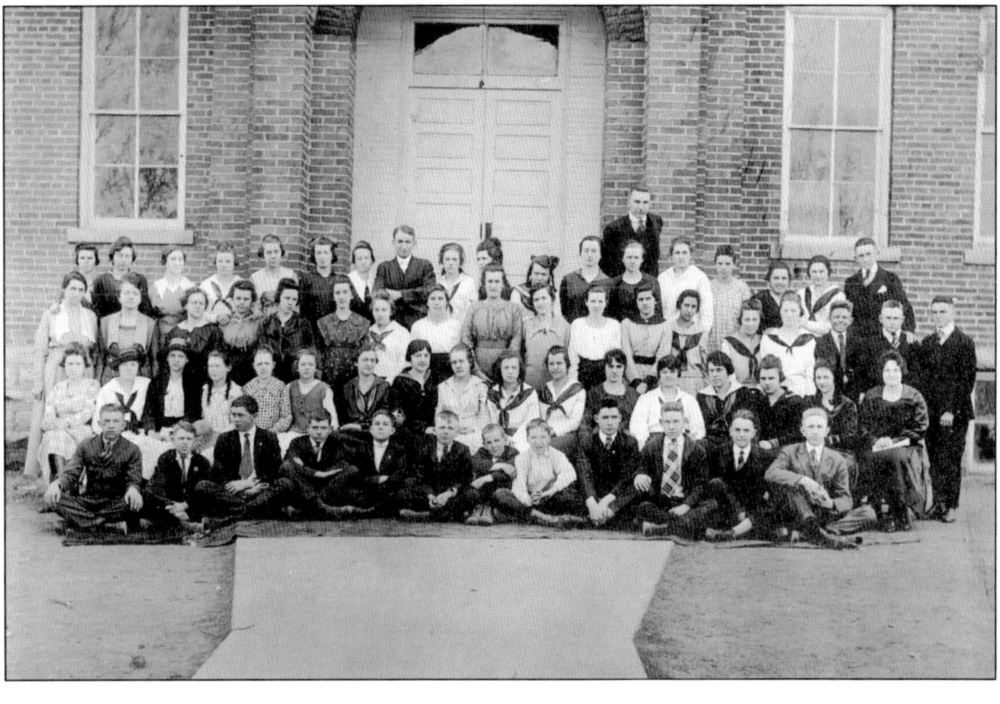

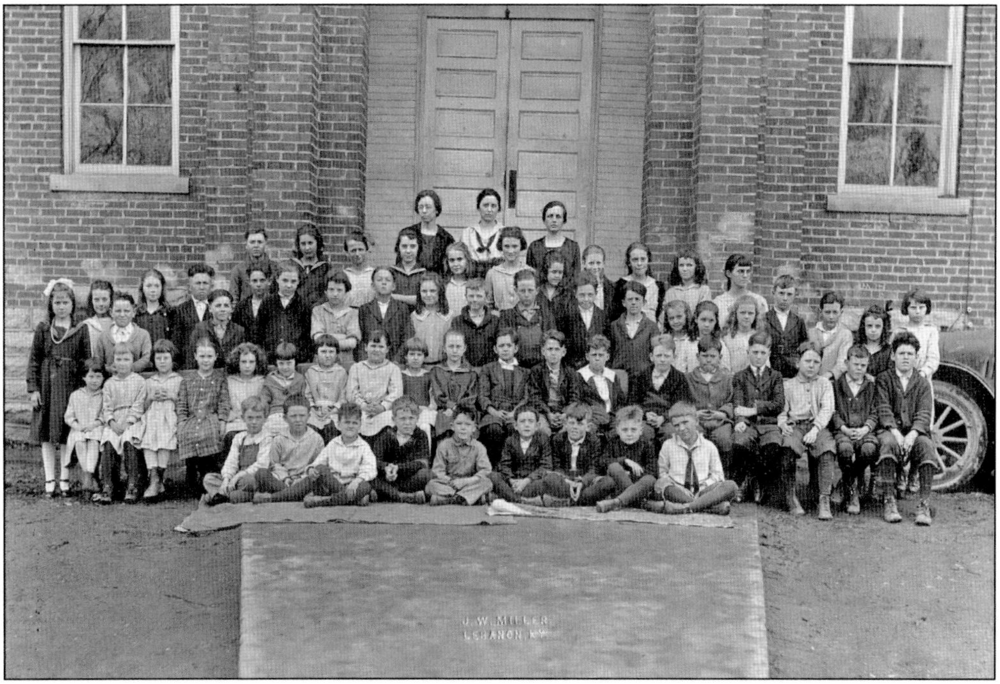

The Russell Creek Academy's elementary school students during the 1920–1921 academic year are pictured with their teachers. Some of the girls are wearing their official uniforms. Girls were required to wear light-blue uniforms during the summer months. During the winter, their uniforms were navy blue and white. In this picture, both uniforms are in use.

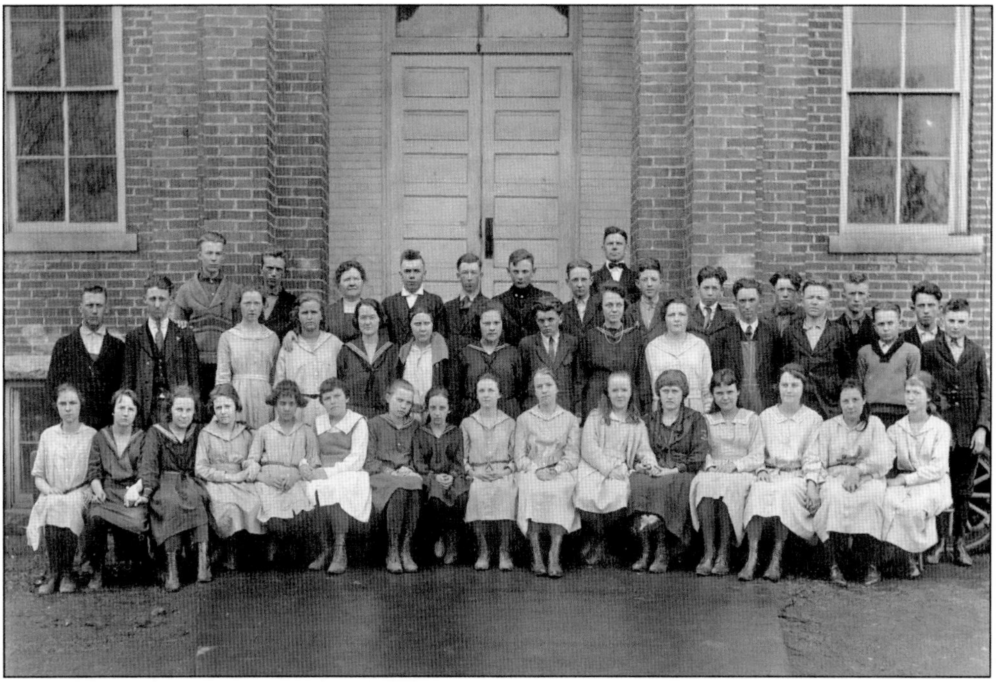

Maude Wade had the primary responsibility of teaching Russell Creek Academy's seventh and eighth graders during the 1920–1921 academic year.

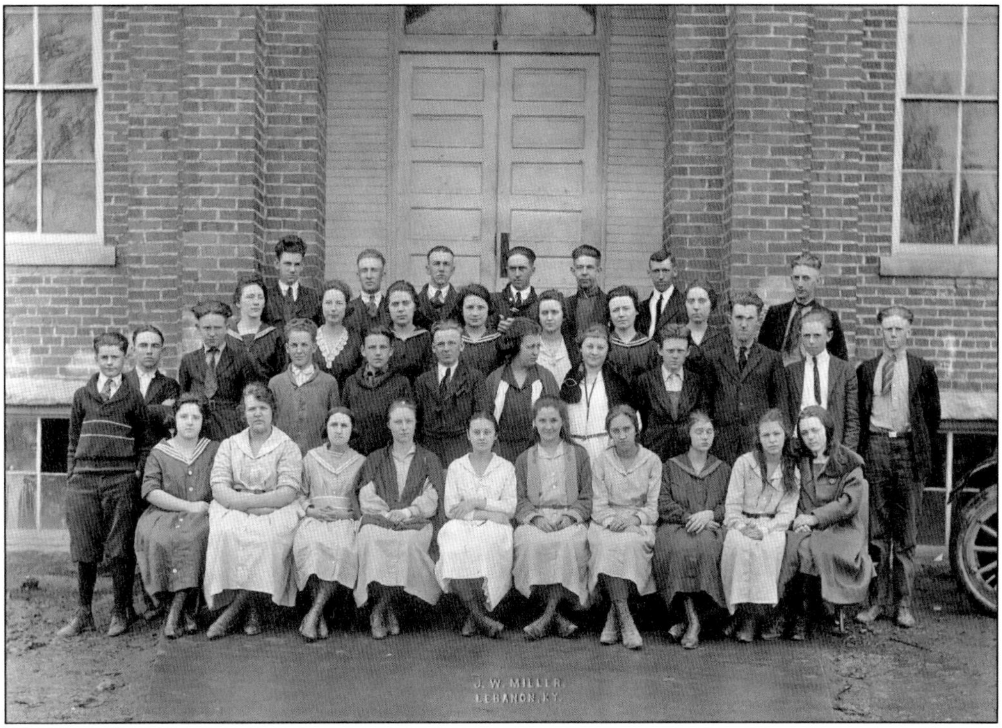

The members of the freshman class pose together during the 1920–1921 academic year.

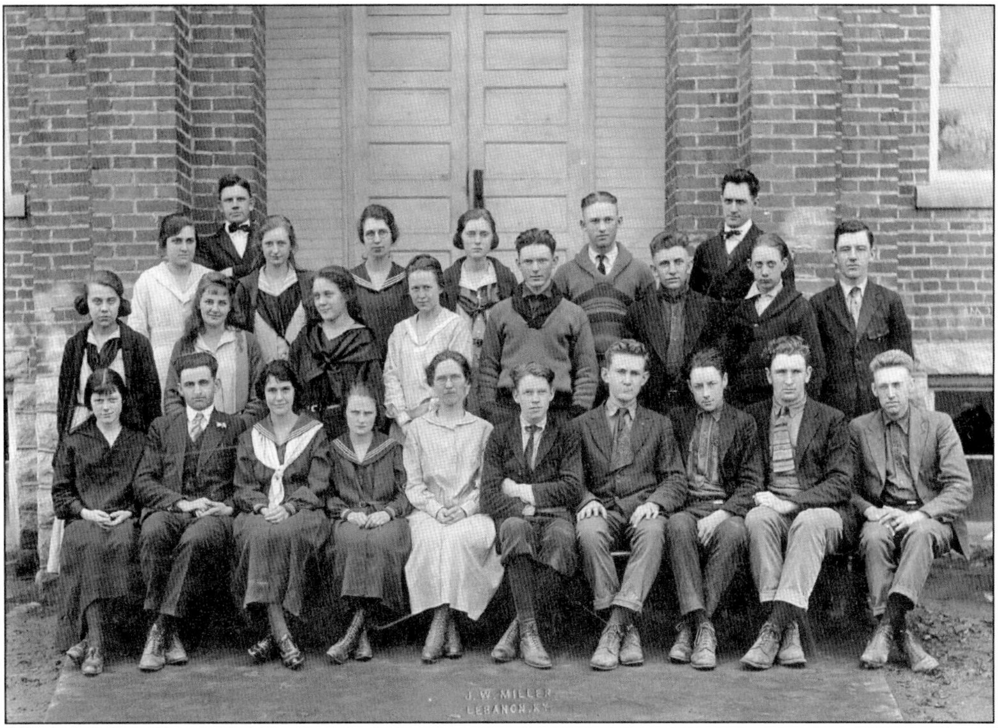

The members of the sophomore and junior classes are pictured during the 1920–1921 academic year.

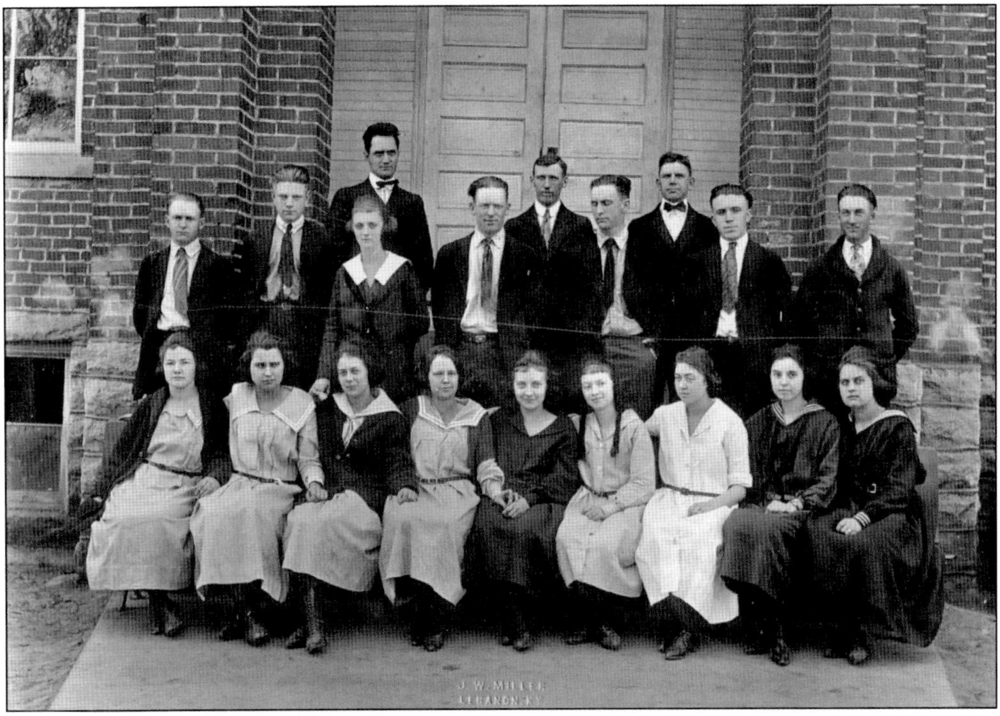

The members of Russell Creek Academy's class of 1921 are pictured together.

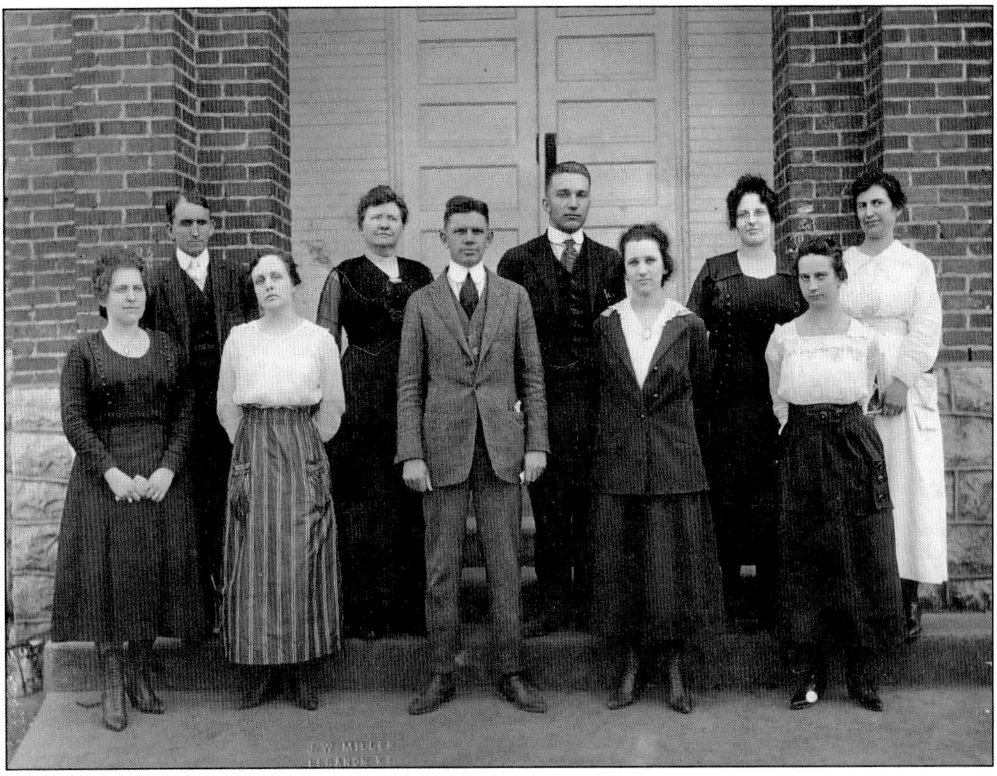

The Russell Creek Academy faculty is pictured during the 1920–1921 academic year.

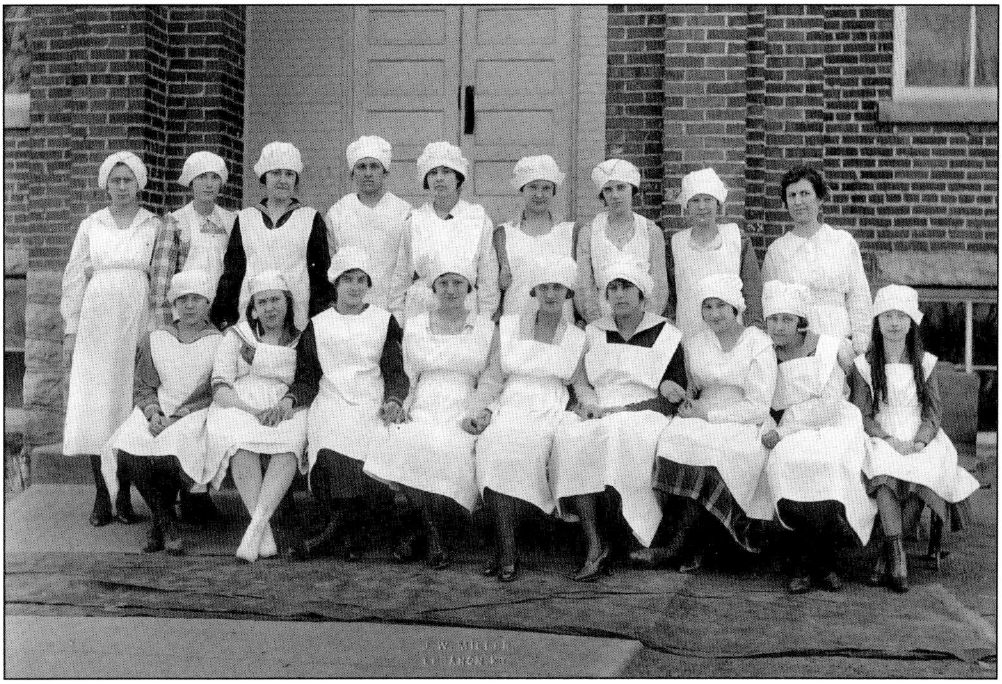

Teacher Eliza Burford (standing far right) is pictured with her home economics class during the 1920–1921 academic year. These female students were part of Russell Creek Academy's domestic science program, which was initiated in 1919. While the domestic science curriculum was designed to instruct young ladies in how to prepare nutritious meals, it also taught them how to be good hostesses or waitresses.

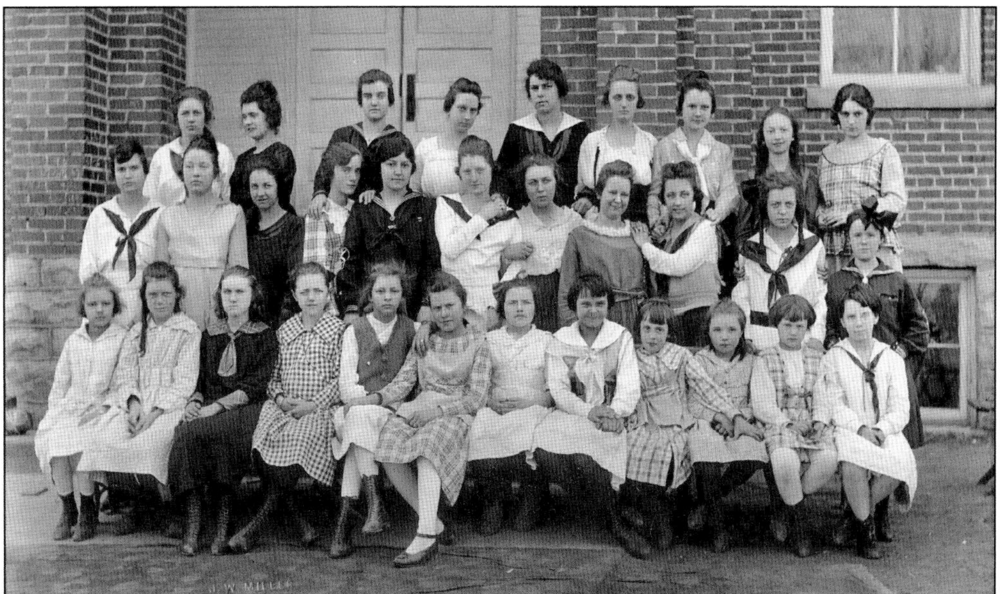

Students at Russell Creek Academy had the opportunity to receive a quality musical education in both piano and voice. The teachers who provided their instruction were often graduates of music conservatories.

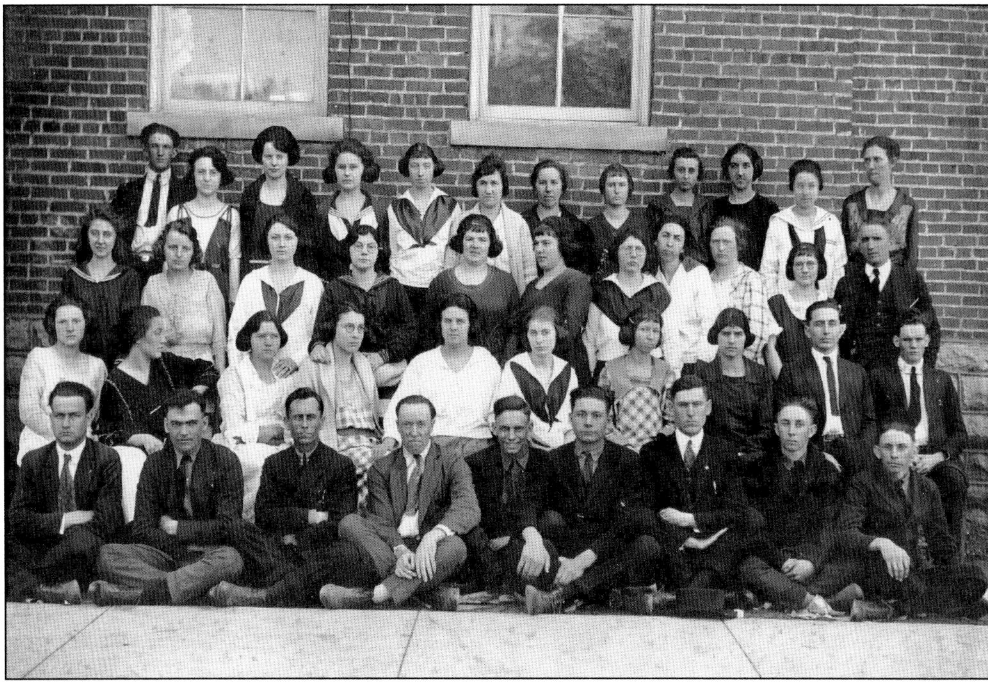

The class of 1922 poses for a photograph. These students graduated from the normal school at Russell Creek Academy.

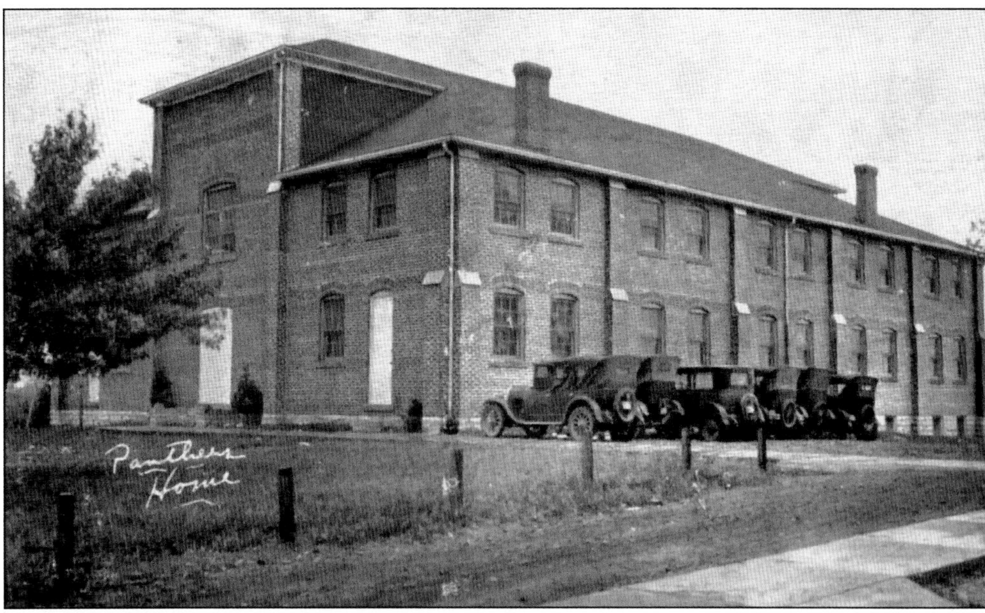

The Gymnasium is a brick building that was constructed during 1922 and 1923. The gym was used by generations of Panther and Tiger athletes, but with the construction of the J. K. Powell Athletic Center in 1969, the original building's usefulness was nearly at an end. By the late 1970s, Campbellsville College was using the building as a storage facility. In 1991, a renovation of the original building was completed and the newly dubbed Student Activities Center opened to the public.

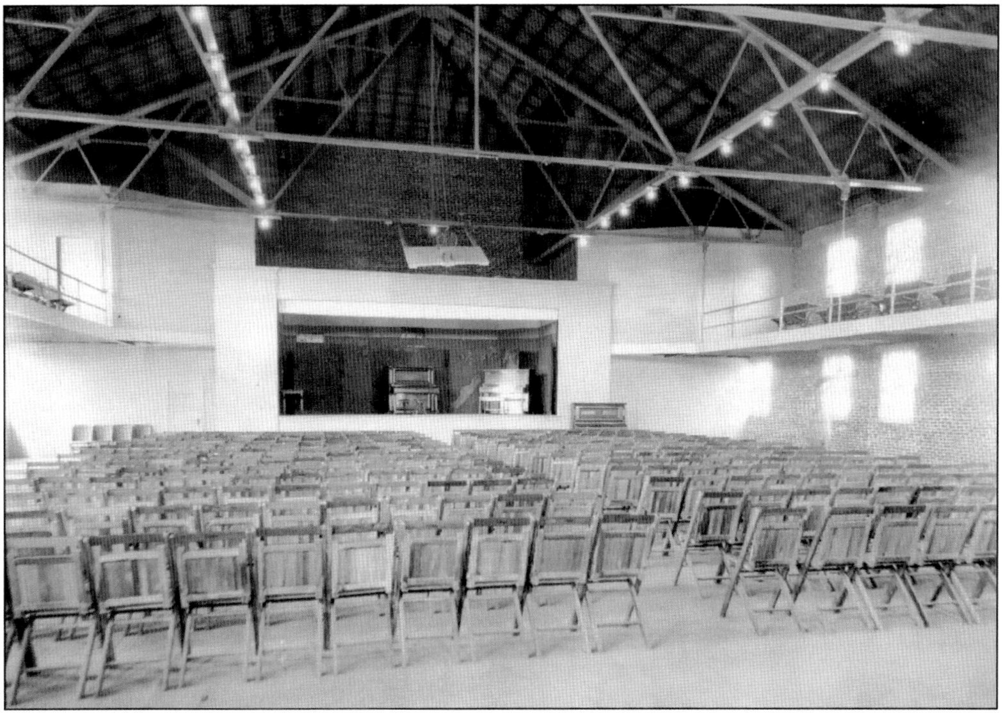

In addition to serving as an athletic facility, the Gymnasium was also used as Russell Creek Academy's auditorium.

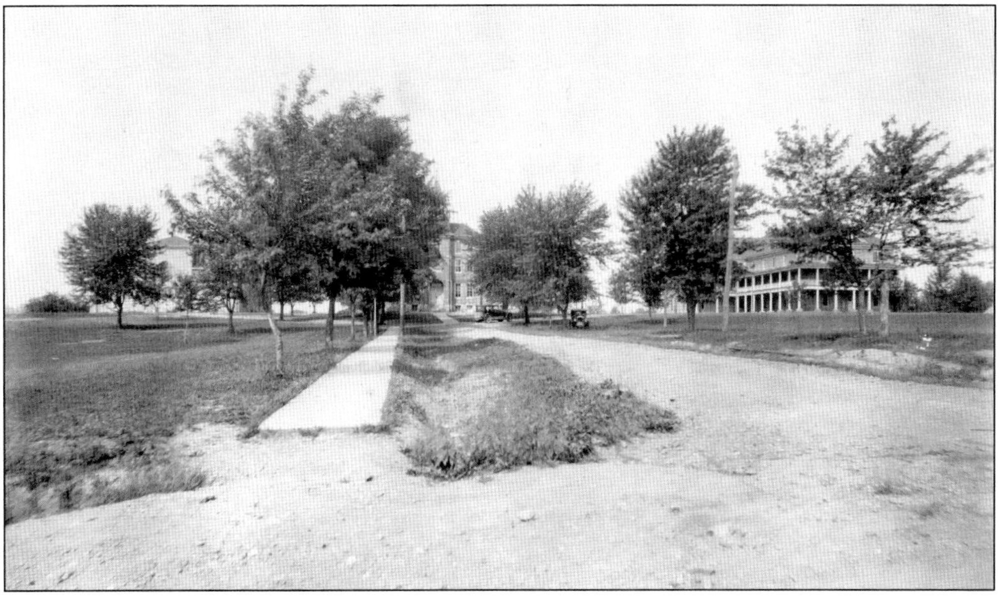

The installation of sidewalks that led to both the Administration Building and the Gymnasium greatly enhanced the physical appearance of the campus during the early 1920s. Students especially appreciated the addition of the sidewalks because, during rainy weather, the dirt road turned into an impassable mud pit. It is curious that the administration opted not to construct a sidewalk on the right side of the road, since J. S. Stapp Hall also needed to be accessible when it was raining.

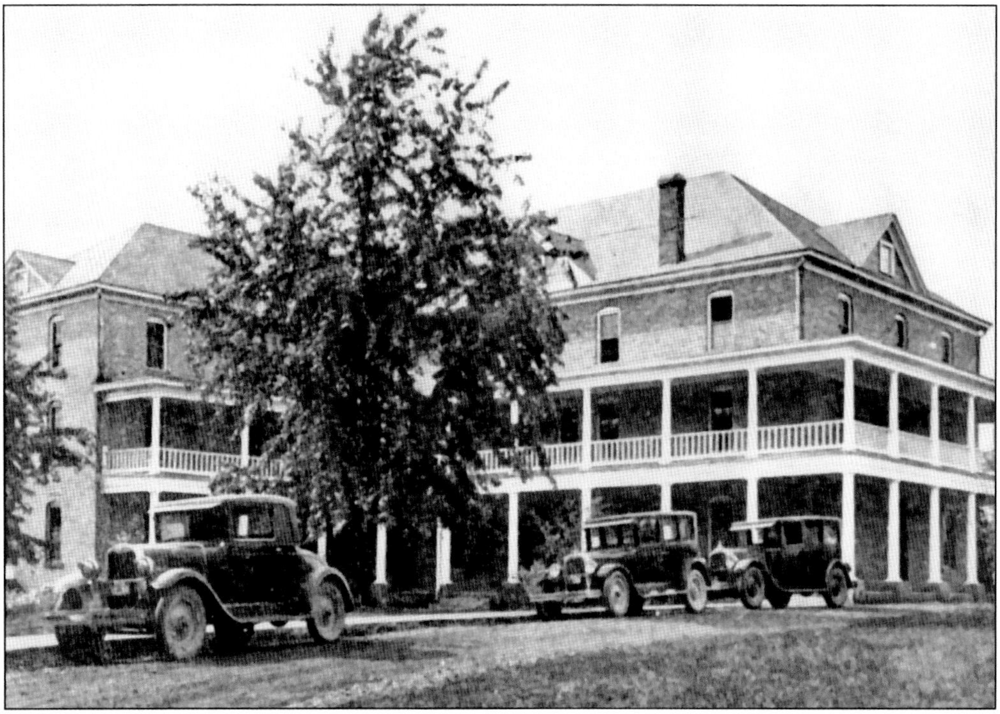

J. S. Stapp Hall was expanded during the early 1920s. The changes to the exterior included the additions of porches and white balustrades. The new annex also included lodging for an additional 60 students, plus a dining hall with a capacity of 150.

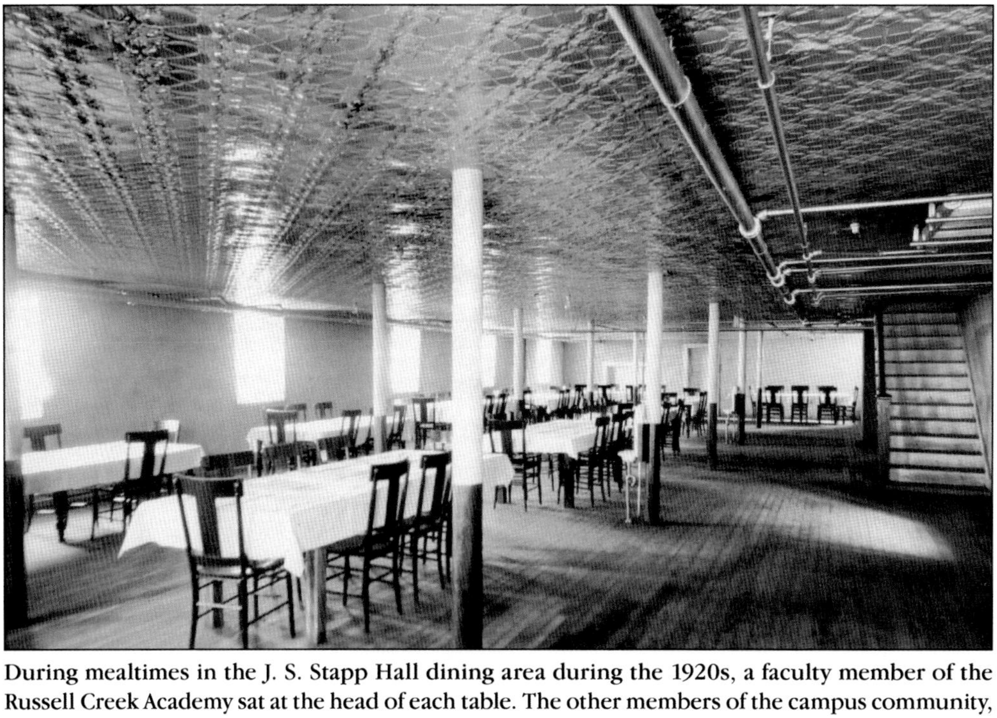

During mealtimes in the J. S. Stapp Hall dining area during the 1920s, a faculty member of the Russell Creek Academy sat at the head of each table. The other members of the campus community, primarily students, occupied the remaining seats.

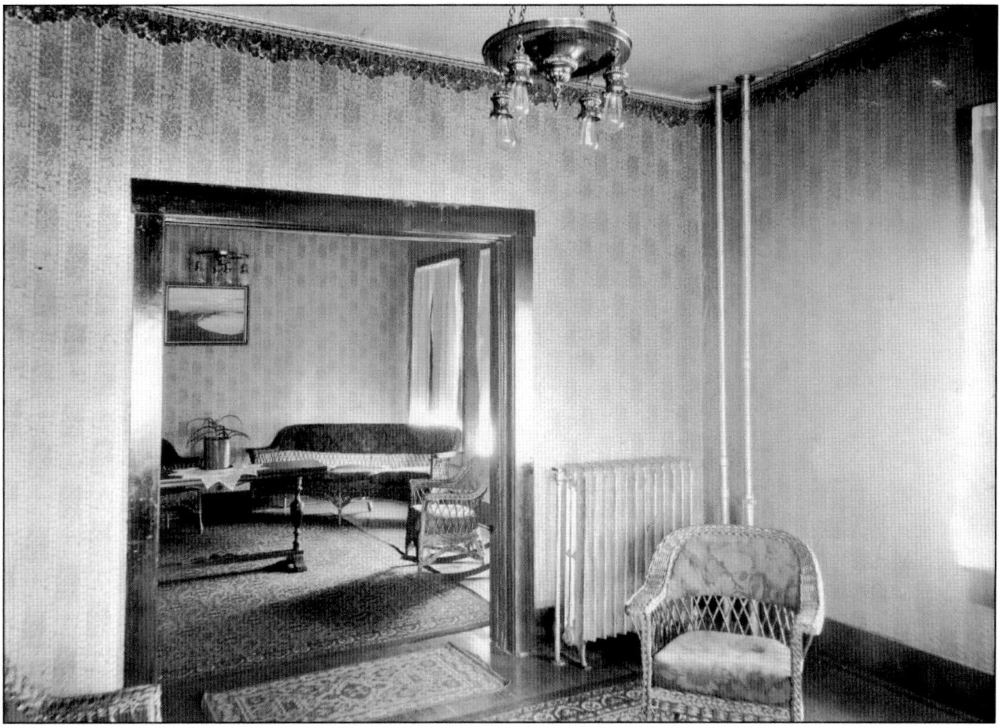

The parlor in J. S. Stapp Hall, which served as the girls' dormitory during the 1920s, was a place where the students could comfortably socialize with one another. The building featured electric lighting and used steam for heating.

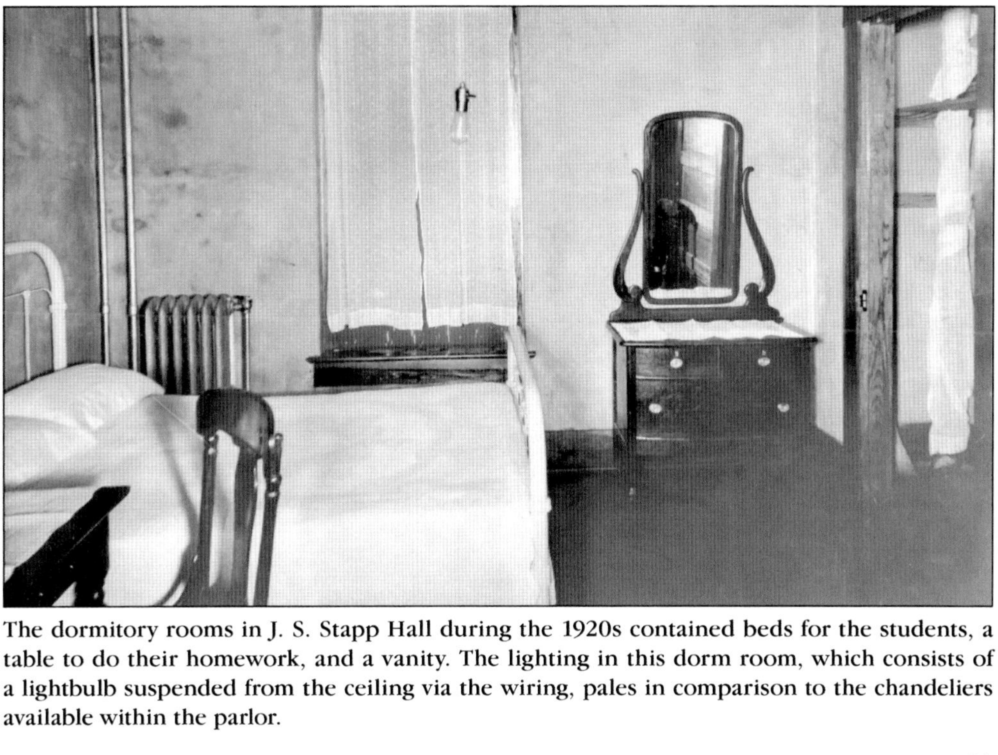

The dormitory rooms in J. S. Stapp Hall during the 1920s contained beds for the students, a table to do their homework, and a vanity. The lighting in this dorm room, which consists of a lightbulb suspended from the ceiling via the wiring, pales in comparison to the chandeliers available within the parlor.

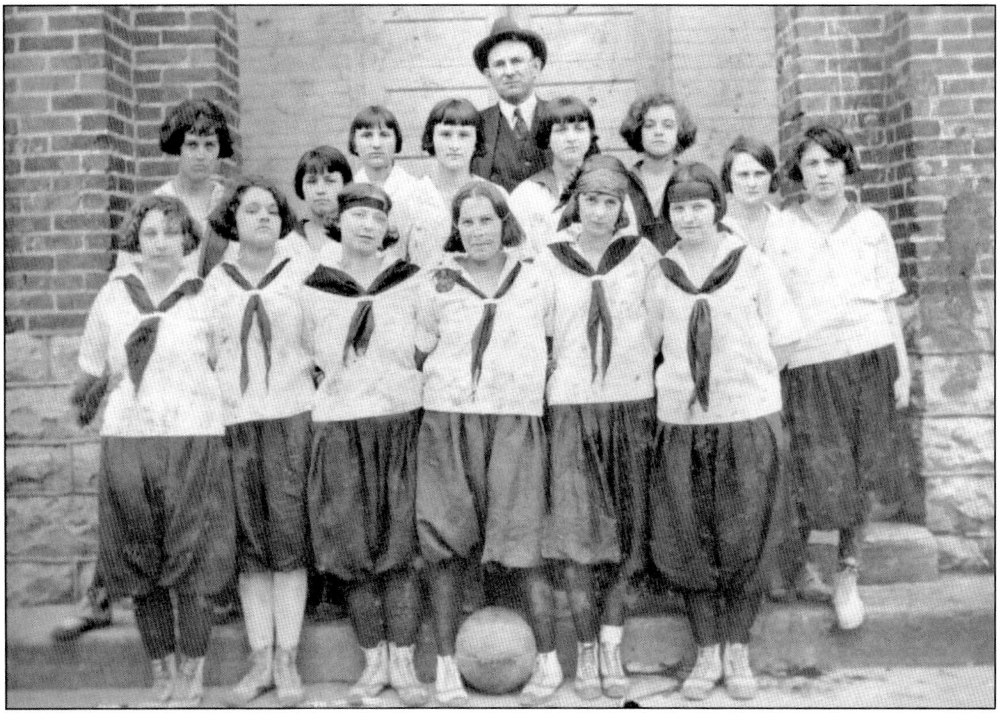

The 1923 Russell Creek Academy girls' basketball team is shown with their coach, John T. Neal.

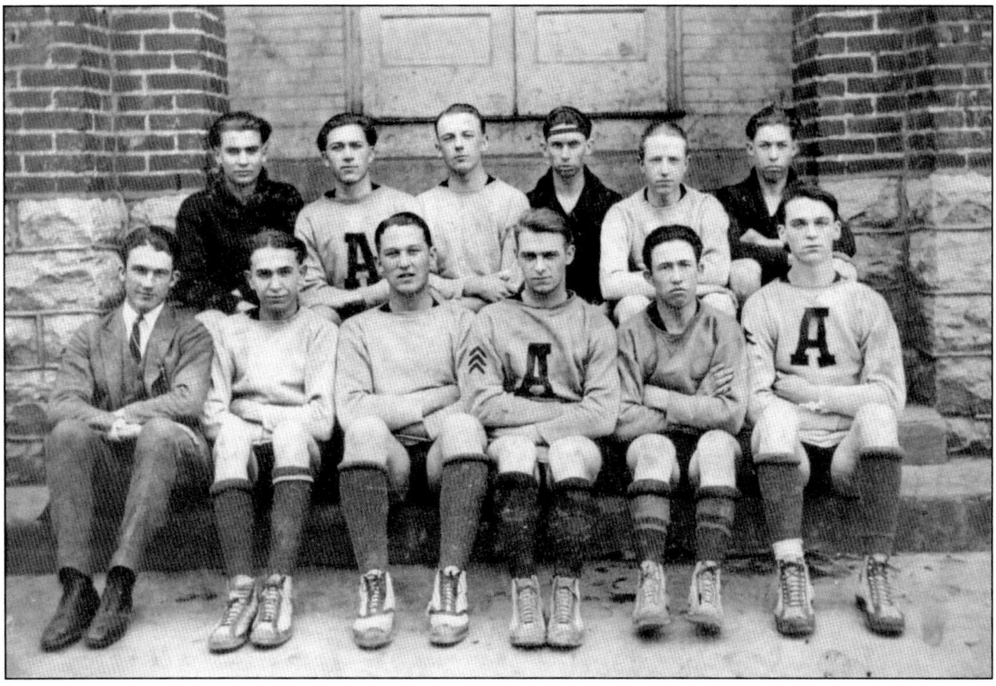

The members of the 1923 Russell Creek Academy basketball team are, from left to right, the following: (first row) Ivan Durrett, Owen Jefferies, W. W. Durham, Joe Wilson, Phillip Corbin, and Cambron Wilson; (second row) Lewis McCubbin, Lindsay Newton, Robert Borders, Charles Hill, John Walter Cloyd, and Howard Smith.

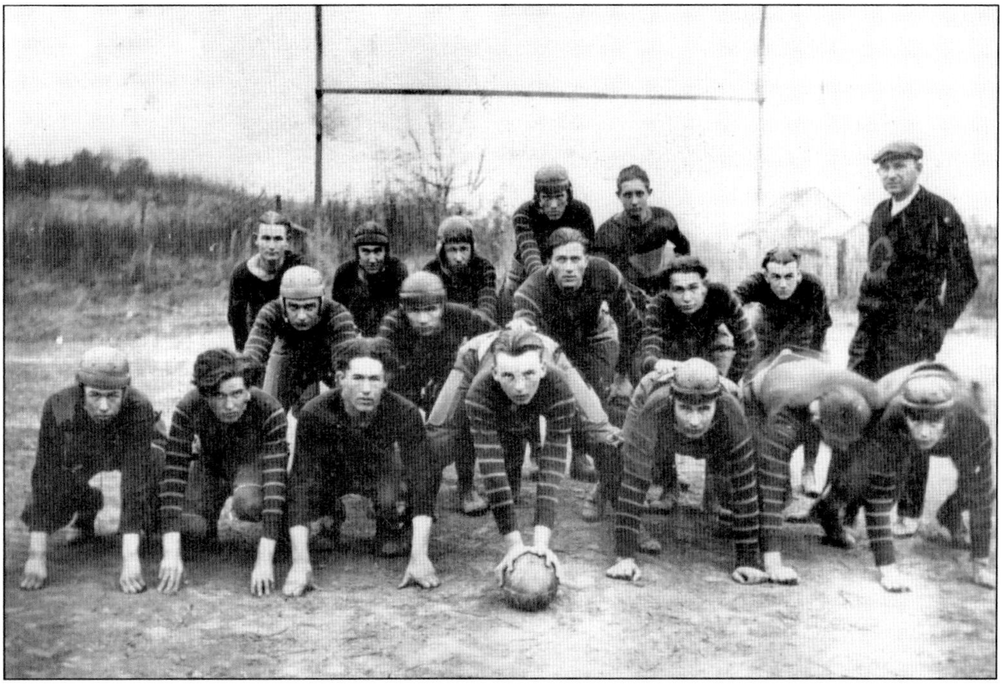

The year 1923 marked the creation of Russell Creek Academy's first football team, which was coached by John T. Neal. Because of the non-existent eligibility rules of the time, any male student who was enrolled in the academy, even part-timers, could join the football team. This resulted in significant age and size disparities among the athletes.

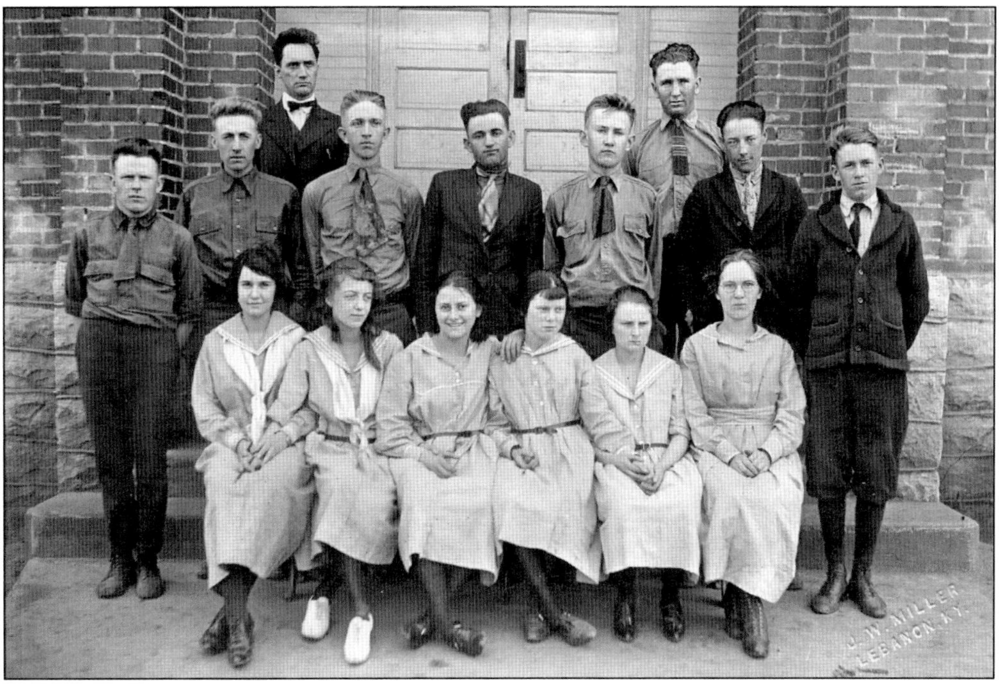

The young ladies sitting in front of their fellow graduates of the class of 1923 are pictured wearing their light-blue summer uniforms.

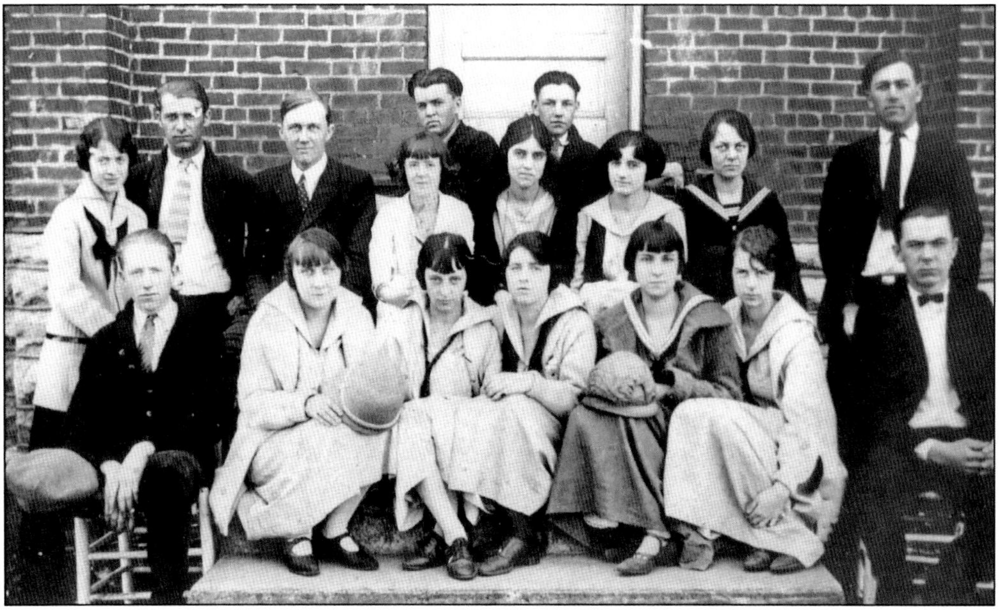

Muriel Martin (second row, fifth from left) began teaching Latin, French, and English at the Russell Creek Academy in 1923. After the school changed to Campbellsville Junior College in 1925, she continued to teach the same subjects until 1931.

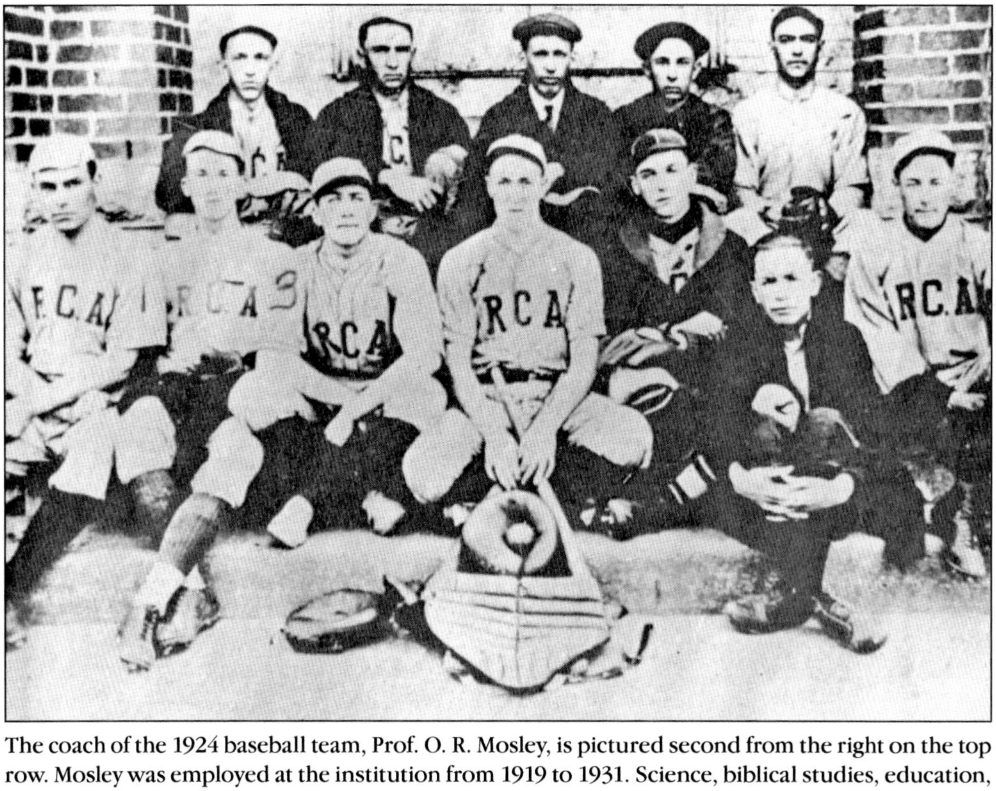

The coach of the 1924 baseball team, Prof. O. R. Mosley, is pictured second from the right on the top row. Mosley was employed at the institution from 1919 to 1931. Science, biblical studies, education, and psychology were among the subjects that he taught. He also served as both dean and athletics director during his tenure at Russell Creek Academy and Campbellsville Junior College.

Two

Campbellsville Junior College 1924–1959

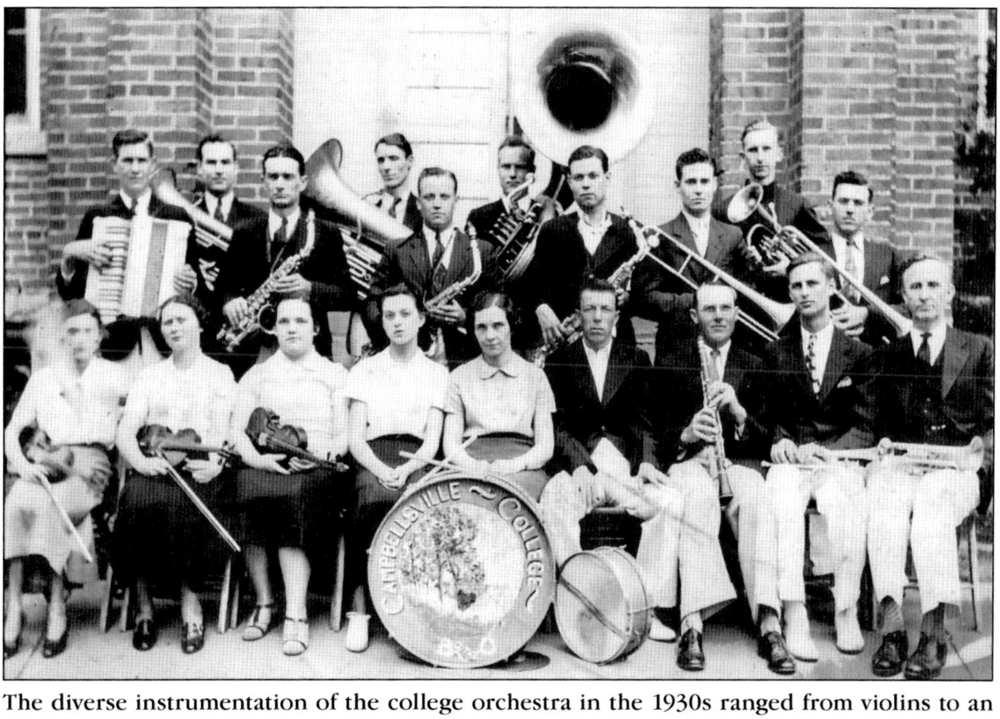

The diverse instrumentation of the college orchestra in the 1930s ranged from violins to an accordion. The inscription on the bass drum is misleading since that particular instrument was not used exclusively by the Campbellsville Junior College Band.

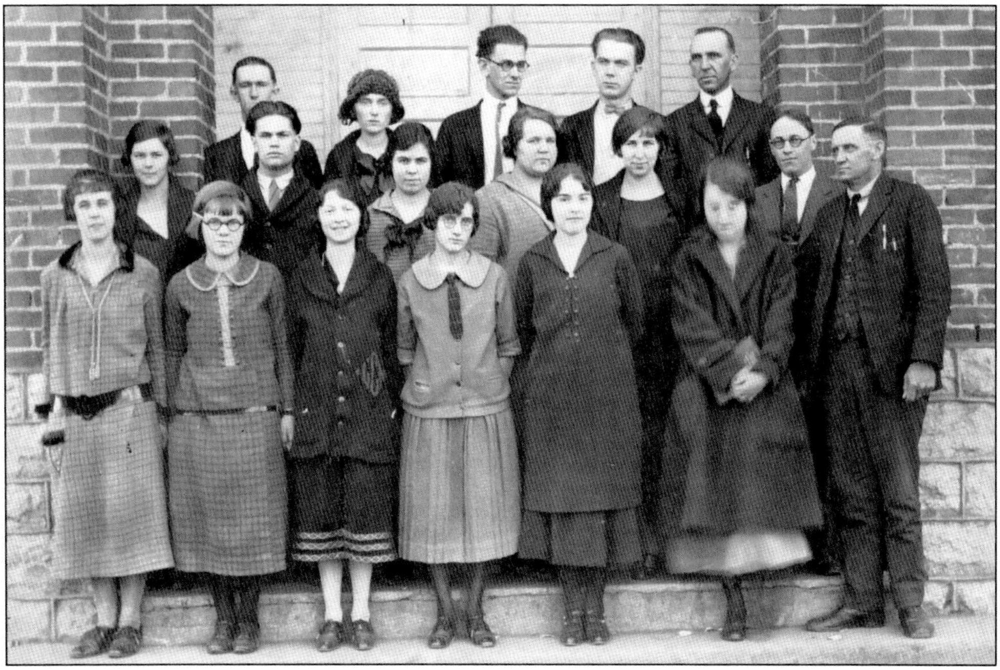

This group of students may be Campbellsville Junior College's class of 1925. It is apparent that the dress code for the ladies had been revised since 1924, since none of the students were wearing the old uniform.

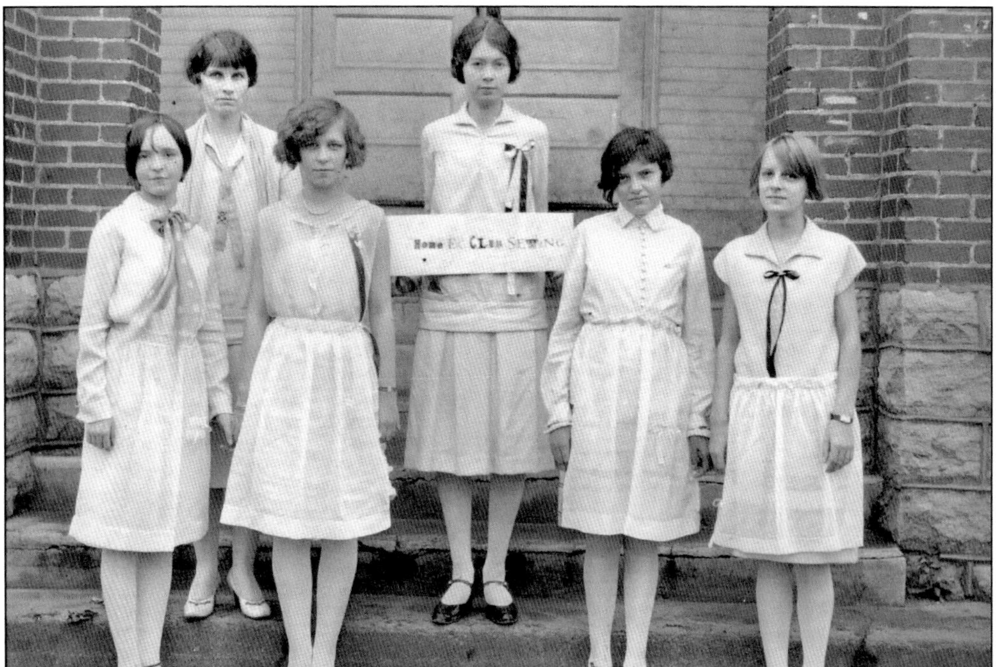

Eva McKendree was the sponsor of the 1927 Home Economics Club, which also included sewing within its scope. From left to right are Kizzy James Bell, McKendree, Helen Haynes, Elizabeth Smith, Virginia Seidell, and Martha McLin.

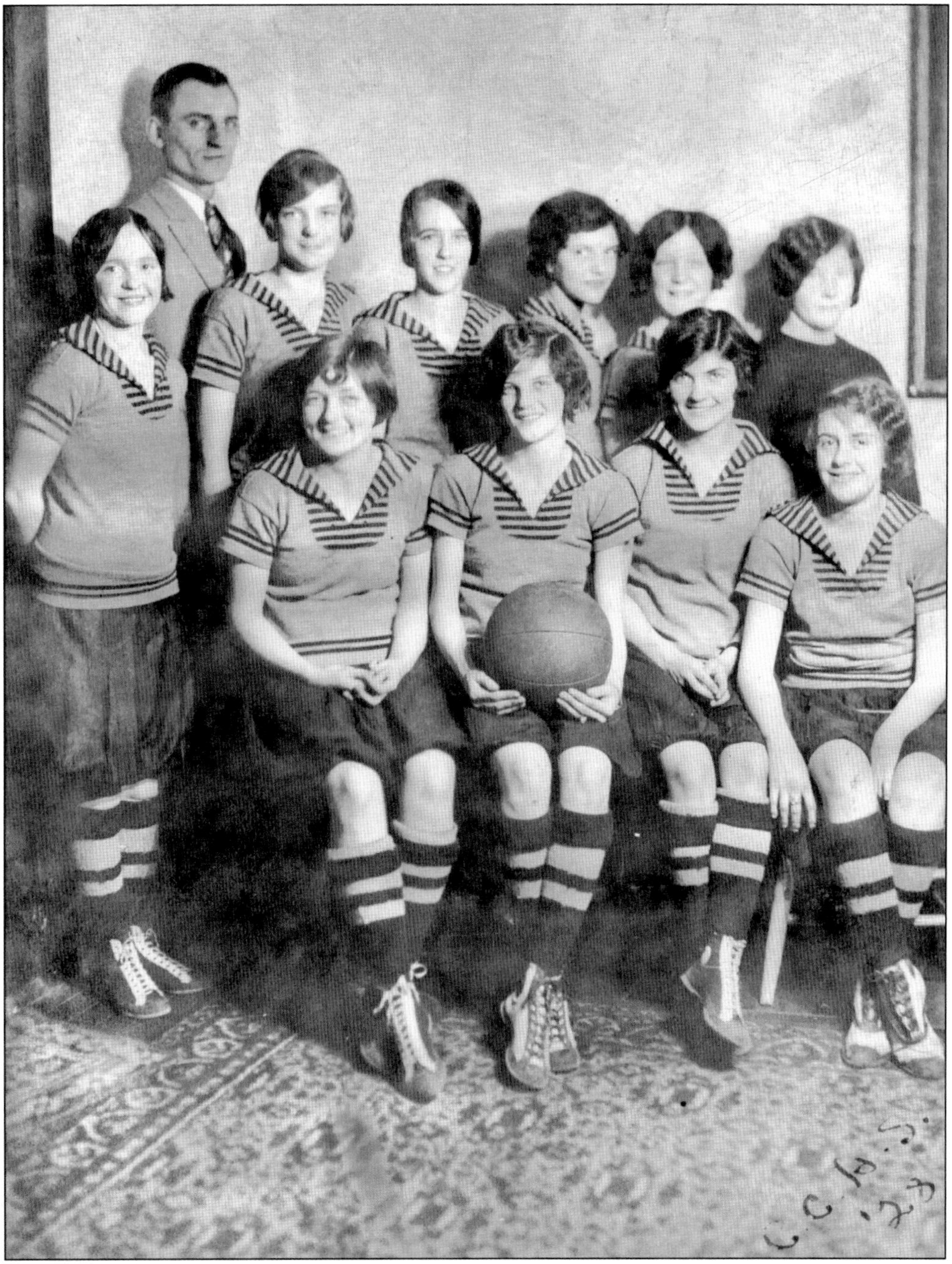

This photograph, taken *c.* 1928, shows the Campbellsville Junior College high school girls' basketball team. Despite the popularity of the girls' basketball program among the students, it was discontinued in the early 1930s. The program was a victim of cost cutting as the school tried to stay financially afloat during the Great Depression.

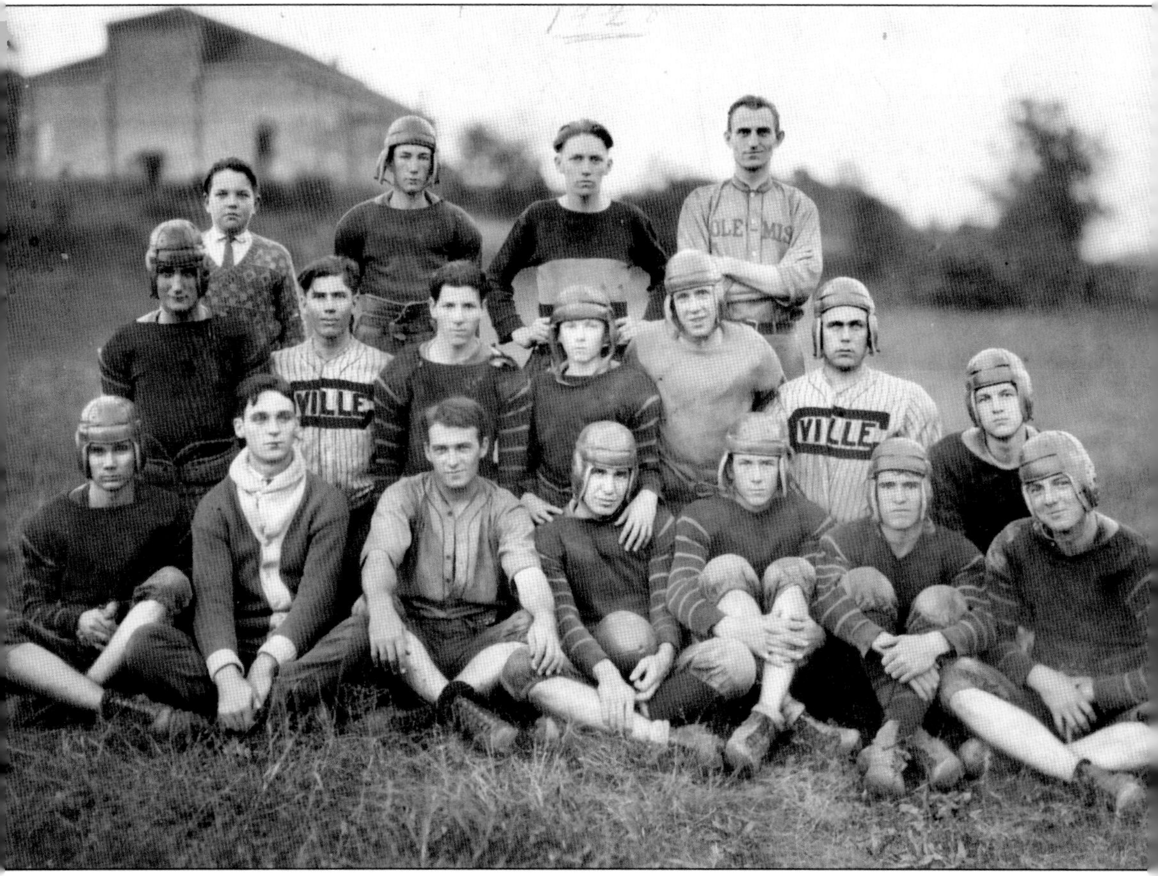

Coach L. C. Henderson stands at far right with his 1928 football team, the Campbellsville Junior College Panthers. It wouldn't be until the 1930s that Campbellsville athletic teams would be known as the Tigers. Henderson coached the team until March 5, 1930, when he joined the majority of the faculty in resigning his position over salary issues. The faculty had been informed by the trustees that the institution could not afford to operate without the entire faculty taking significant pay cuts. The institution's chronic financial difficulties eventually led to the dissolution of the football program sometime during the 1930s.

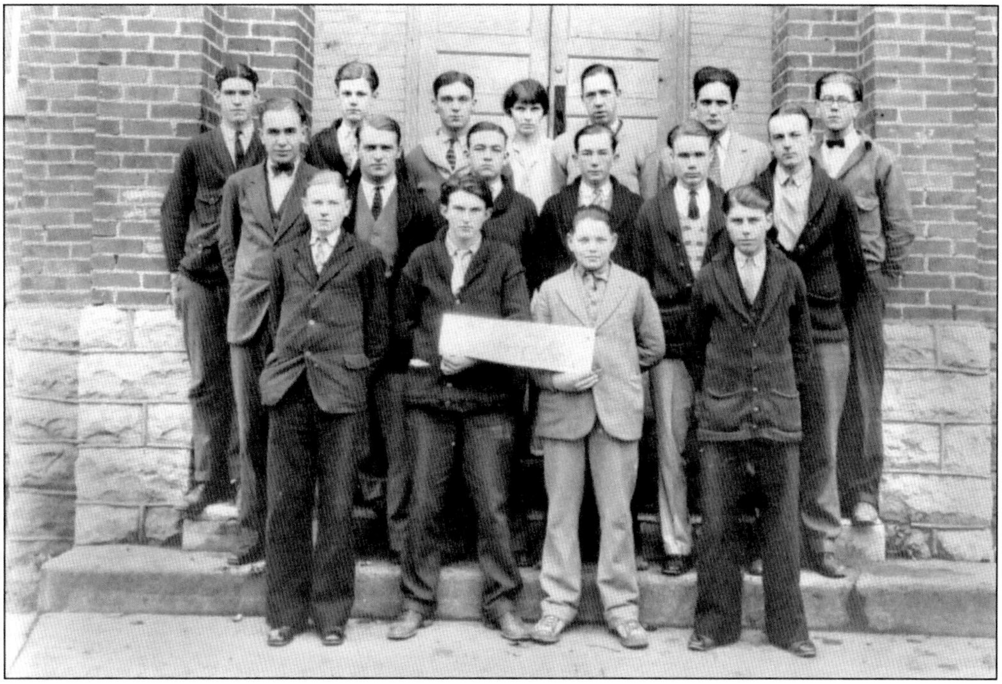

Campbellsville Junior College had two glee clubs during the late 1920s, one for young men and one for the ladies. These vocal groups were two of the many musical ensembles that were open to students at the school.

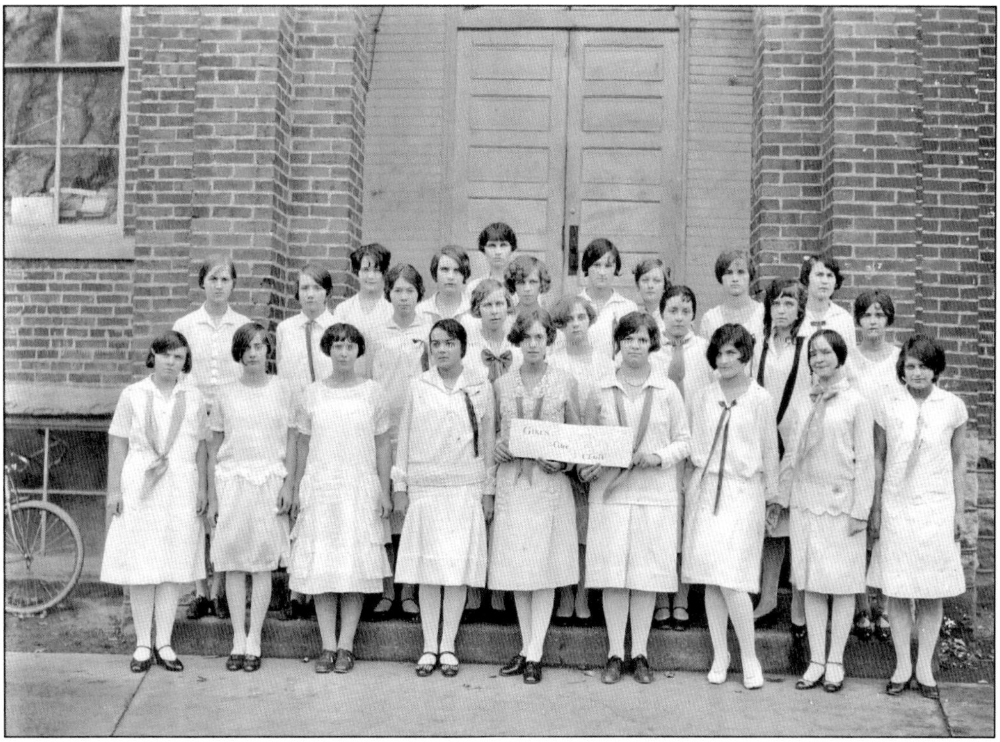

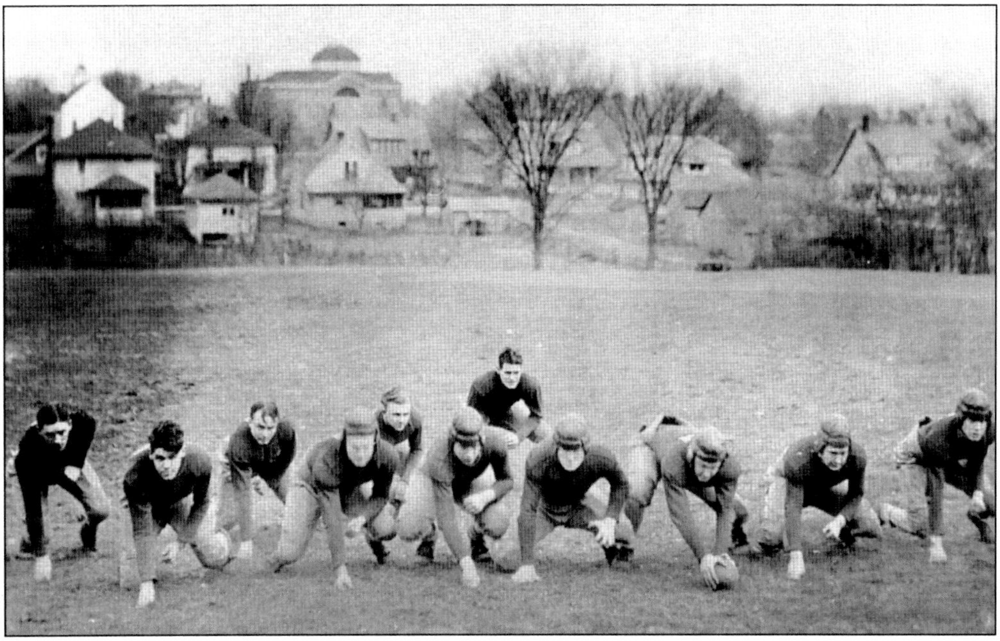

This photograph, taken *c.* 1929, shows the Campbellsville Junior College football team.

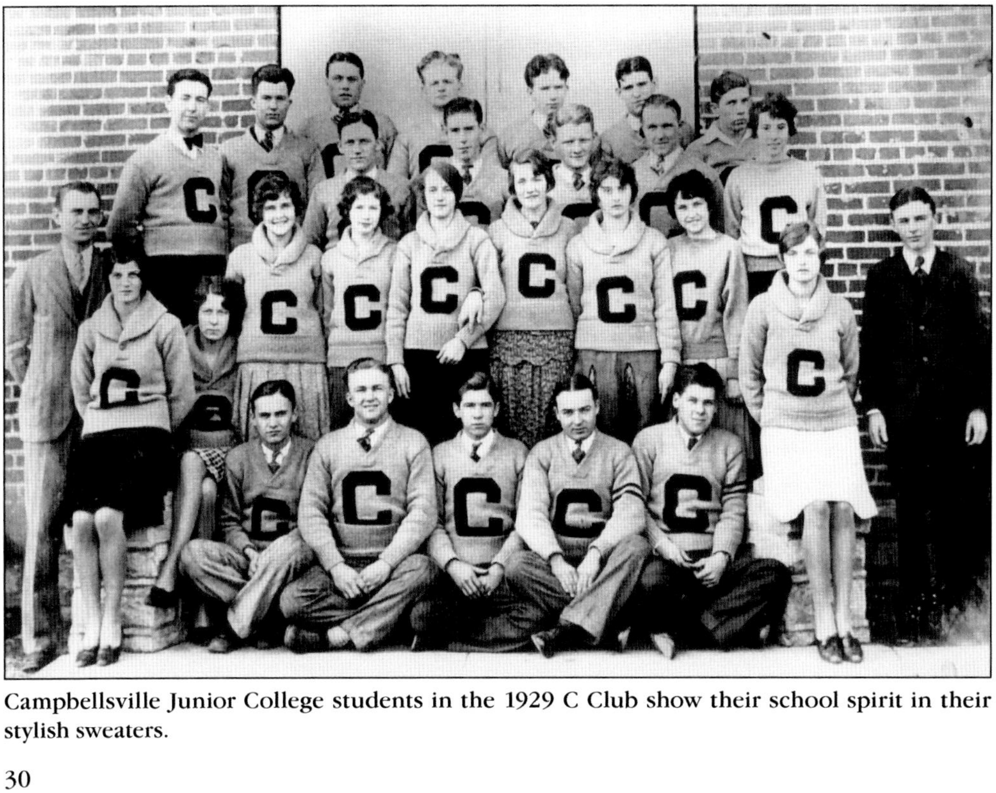

Campbellsville Junior College students in the 1929 C Club show their school spirit in their stylish sweaters.

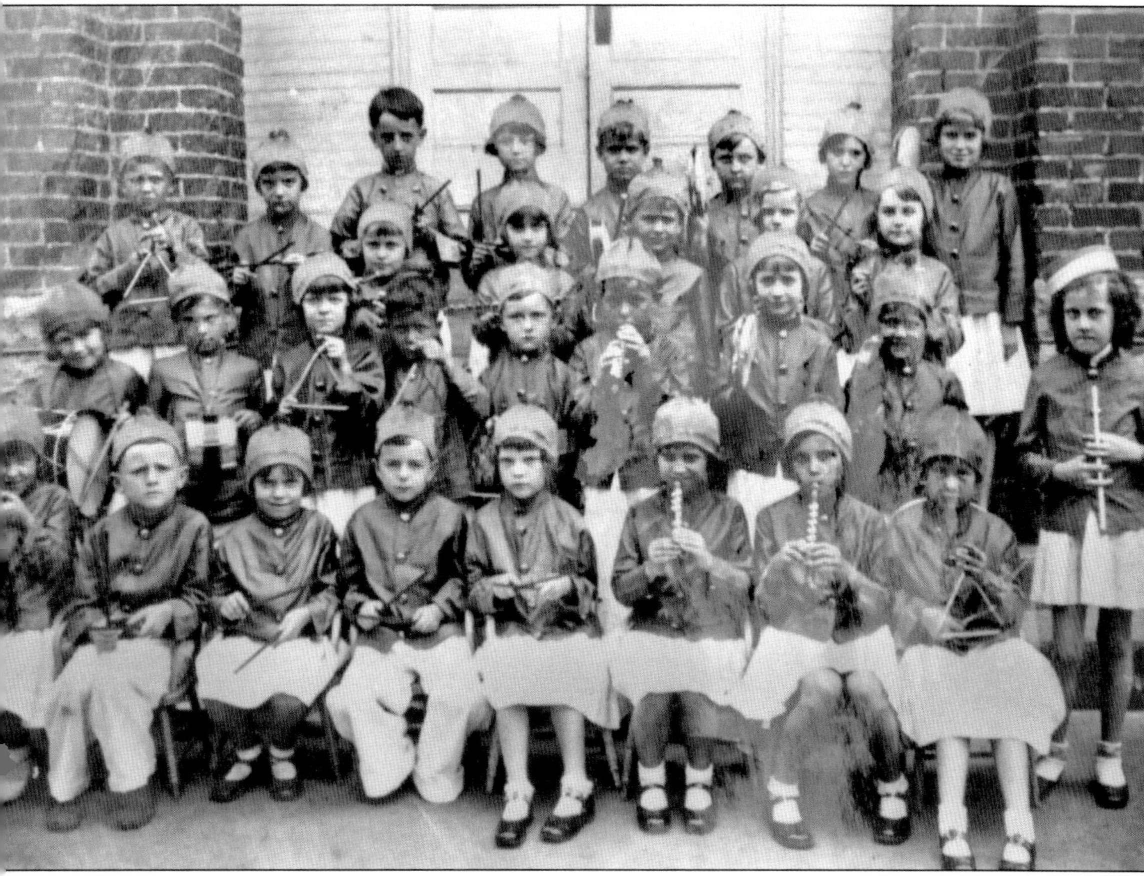

The members of the elementary school's band are pictured *c.* 1930.

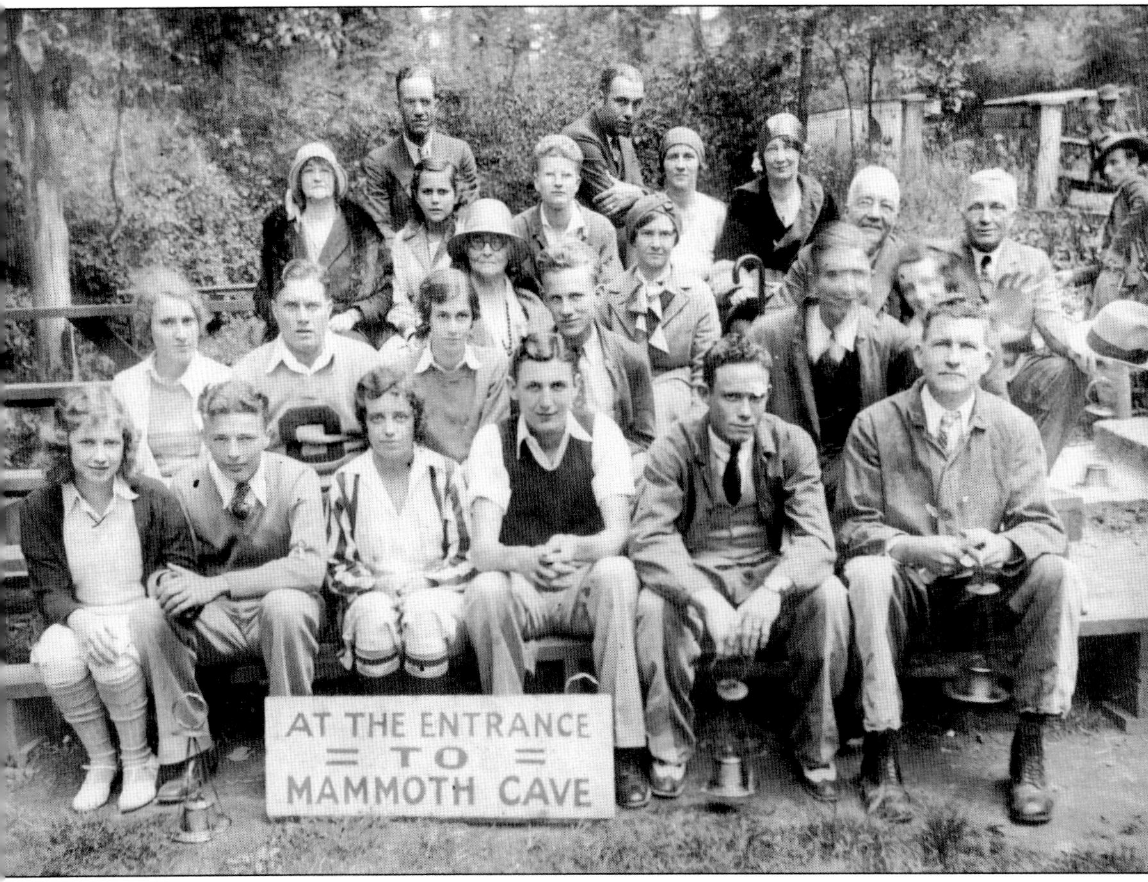

Virginia Mitchell and other members of the campus community visit Mammoth Cave.

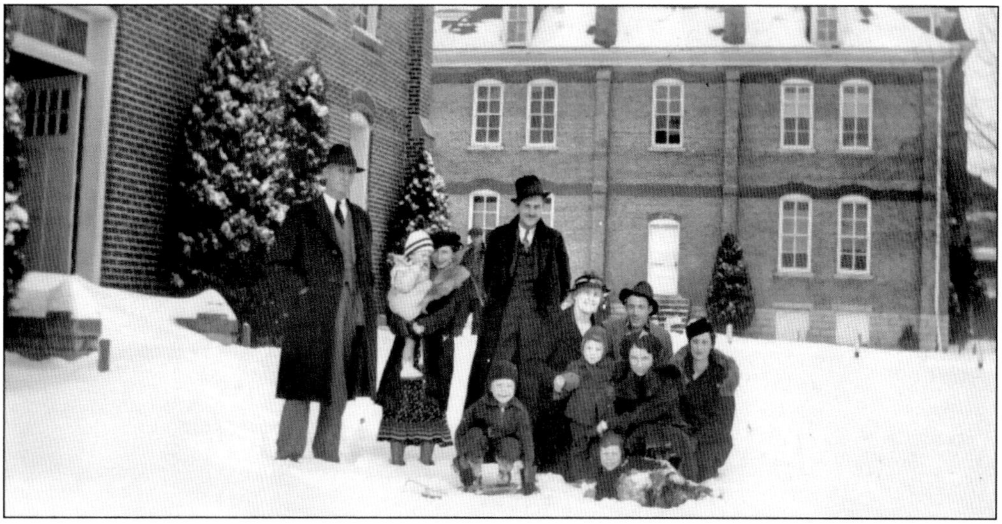

Prof. Homer Felts and his wife, Lula, pose for a portrait with the rest of their family in front of the Gymnasium in December 1935. Despite Campbellsville Junior College's precarious financial condition at the time, there must have been enough money available to pay heating bills since someone carelessly left the gym's door open in the middle of winter.

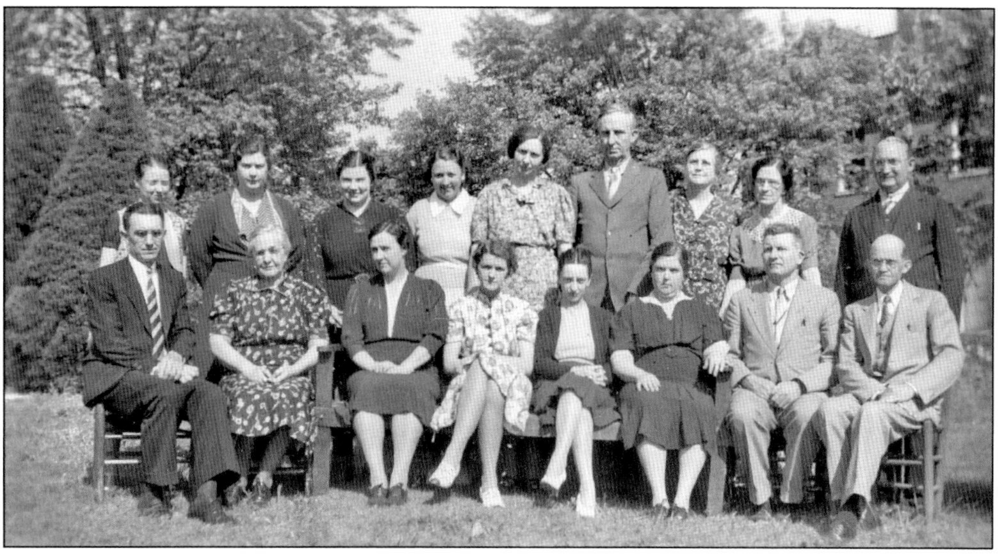

The members of the faculty sit for a portrait *c.* 1938.

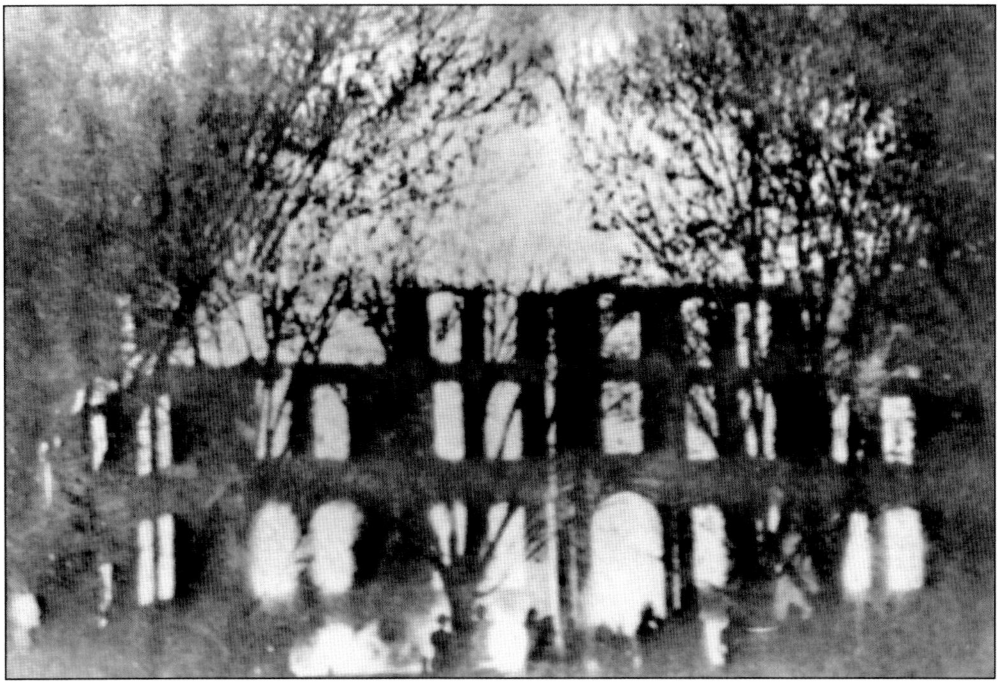

Maybe the greatest catastrophe in the history of present-day Campbellsville University occurred on April 14, 1939, when the original Administration Building was engulfed by fire. The negative effect of the conflagration to Campbellsville Junior College was obvious to all who watched the flames because the building housed administrative offices, classrooms, scientific laboratories, and the library.

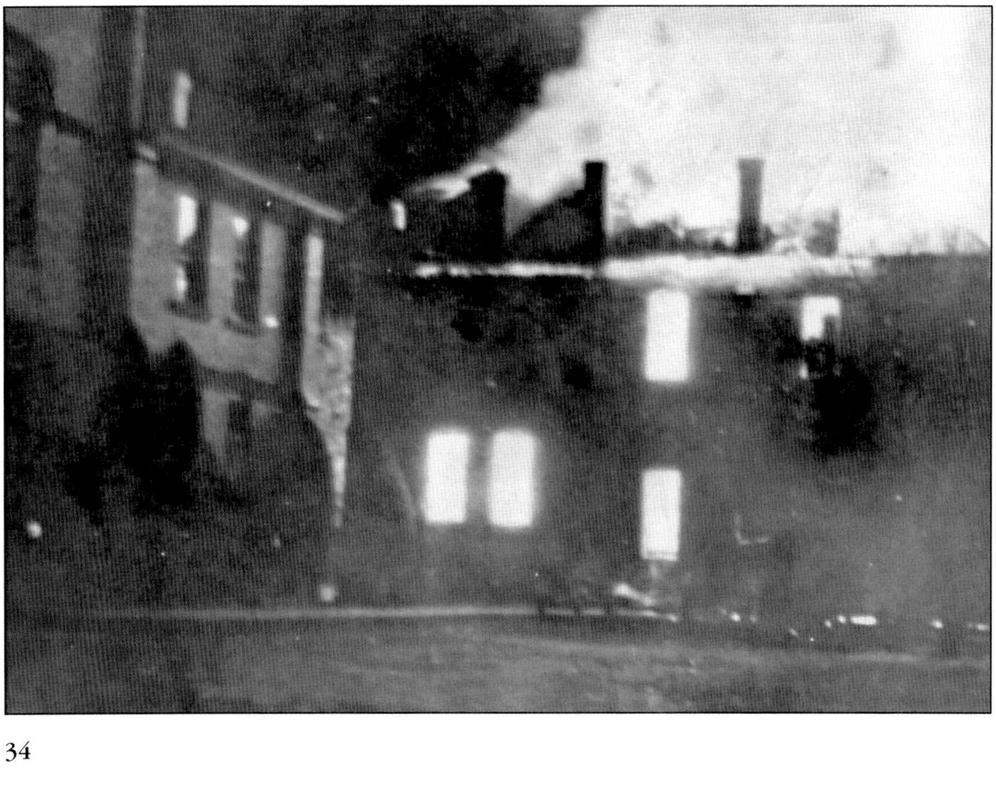

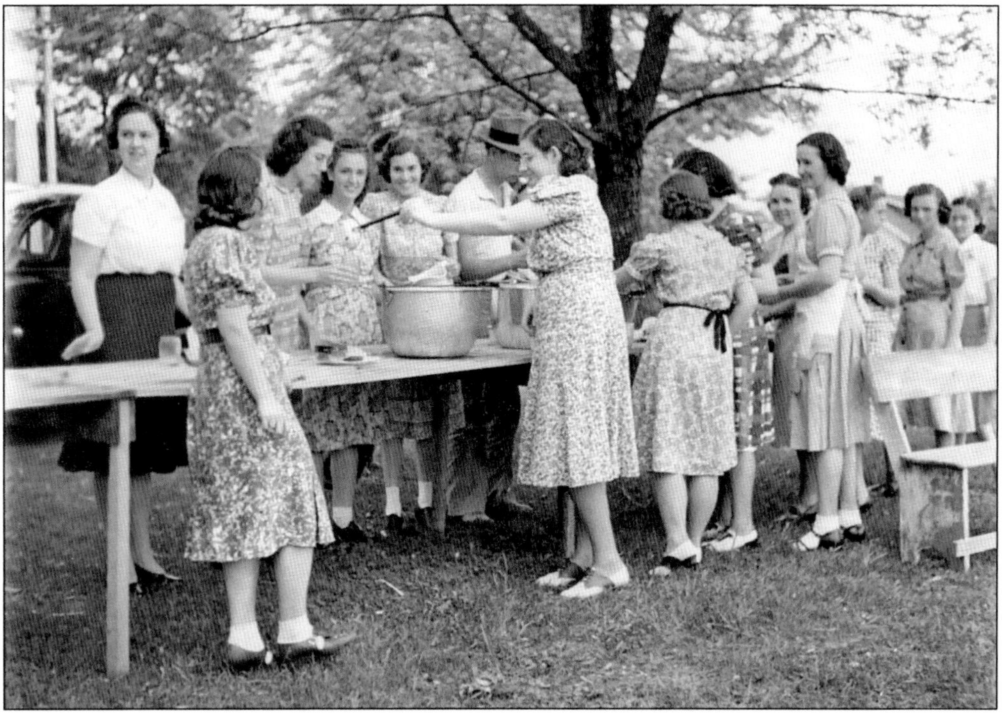

In the aftermath of the fire, food was prepared and served by the ladies on campus for the men who were assisting in the cleanup following the destruction of the Administration Building.

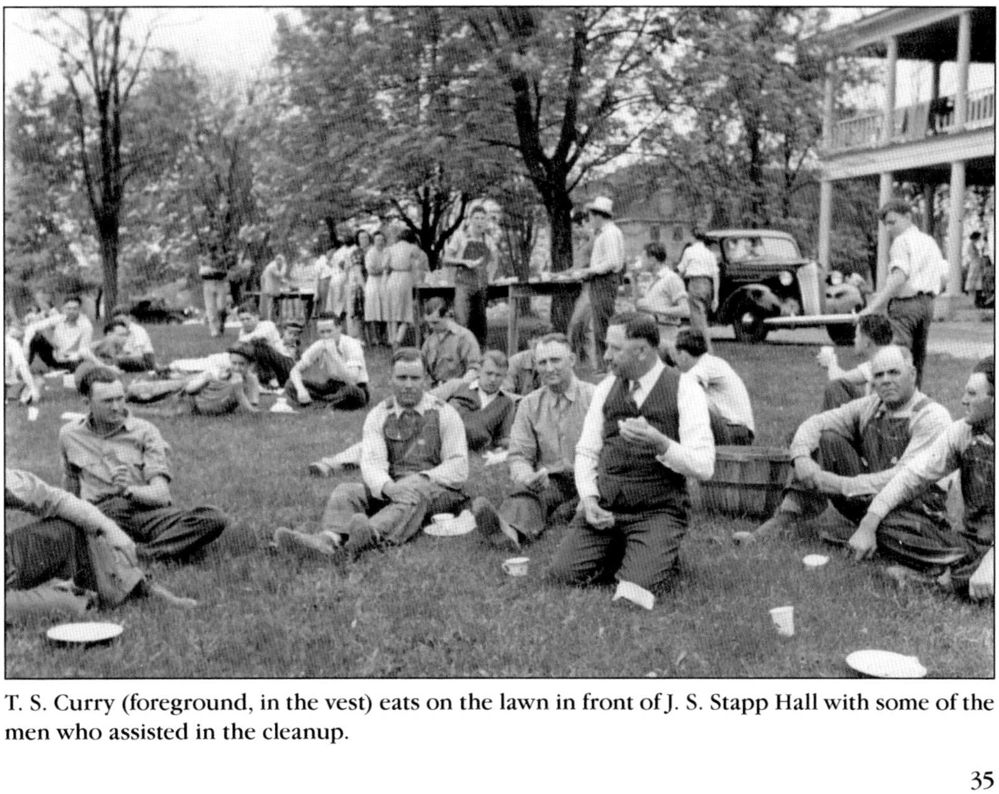

T. S. Curry (foreground, in the vest) eats on the lawn in front of J. S. Stapp Hall with some of the men who assisted in the cleanup.

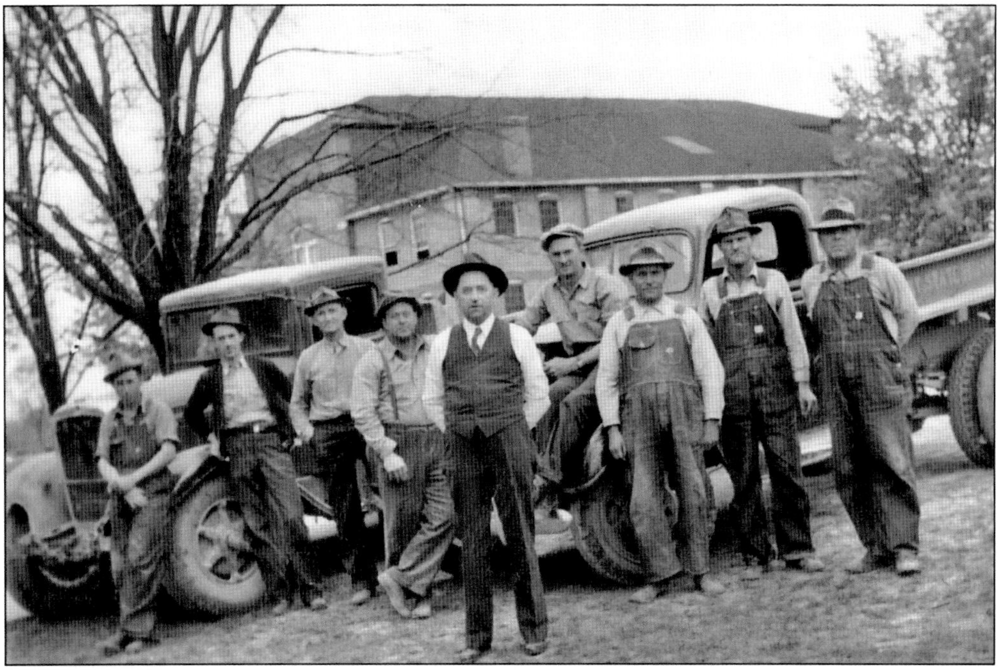

T. S. Curry (center foreground) stands with some of his fellow workers in front of the vehicles used to clear debris.

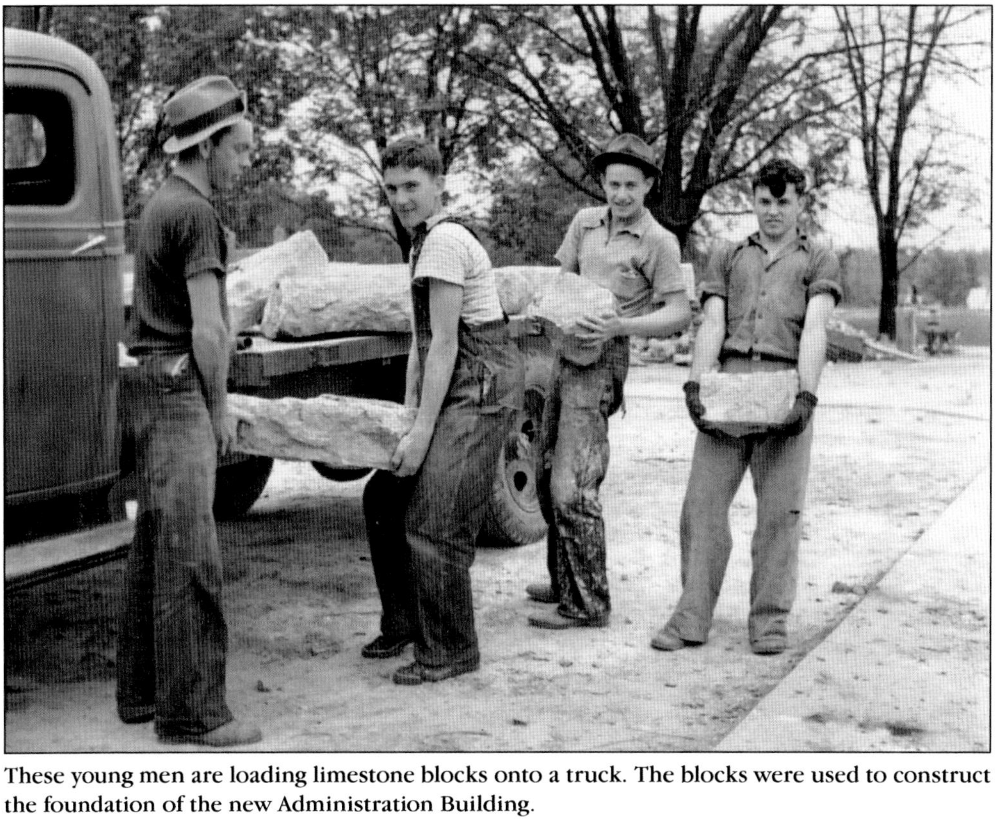

These young men are loading limestone blocks onto a truck. The blocks were used to construct the foundation of the new Administration Building.

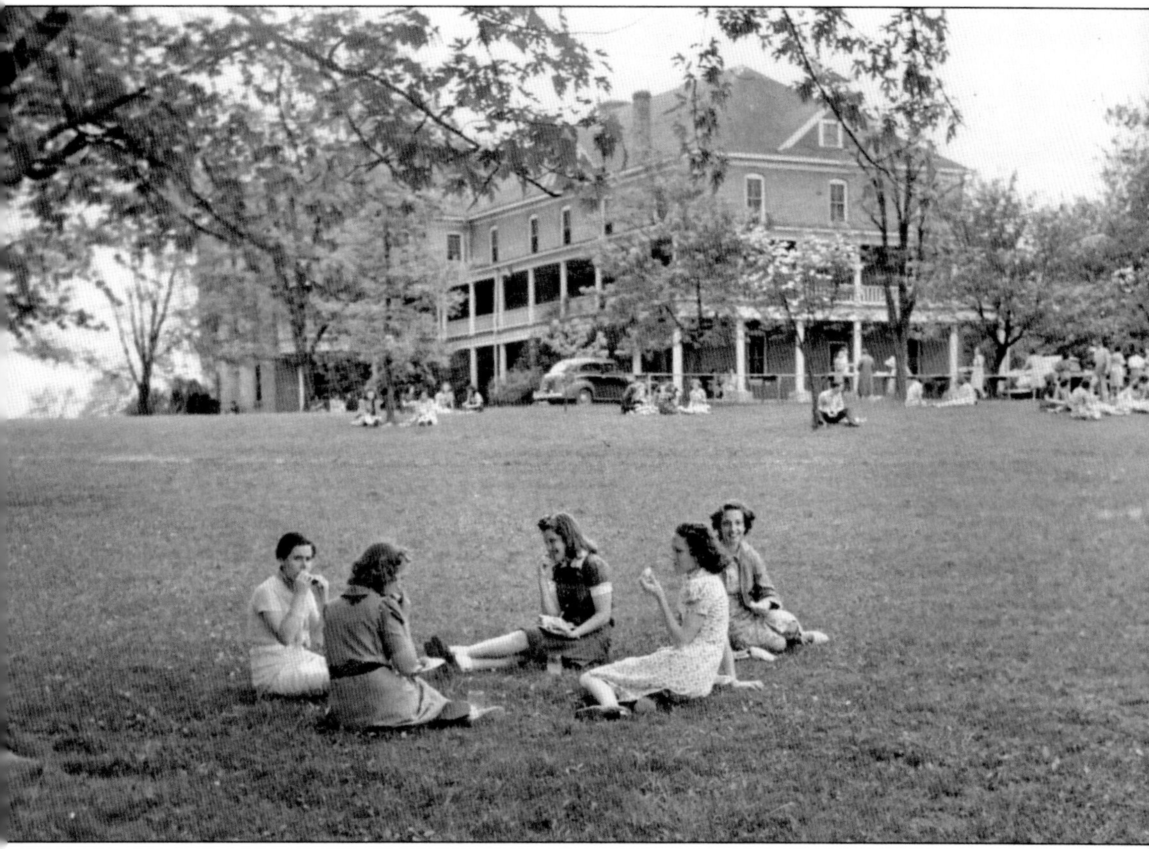

A group of female students enjoys a campus picnic on the lawn in front of J. S. Stapp Hall *c.* 1940. Picnics that bring together the entire campus community to eat and socialize are still an integral part of campus life at Campbellsville University, most notably during homecoming weekend in the fall and graduation in May.

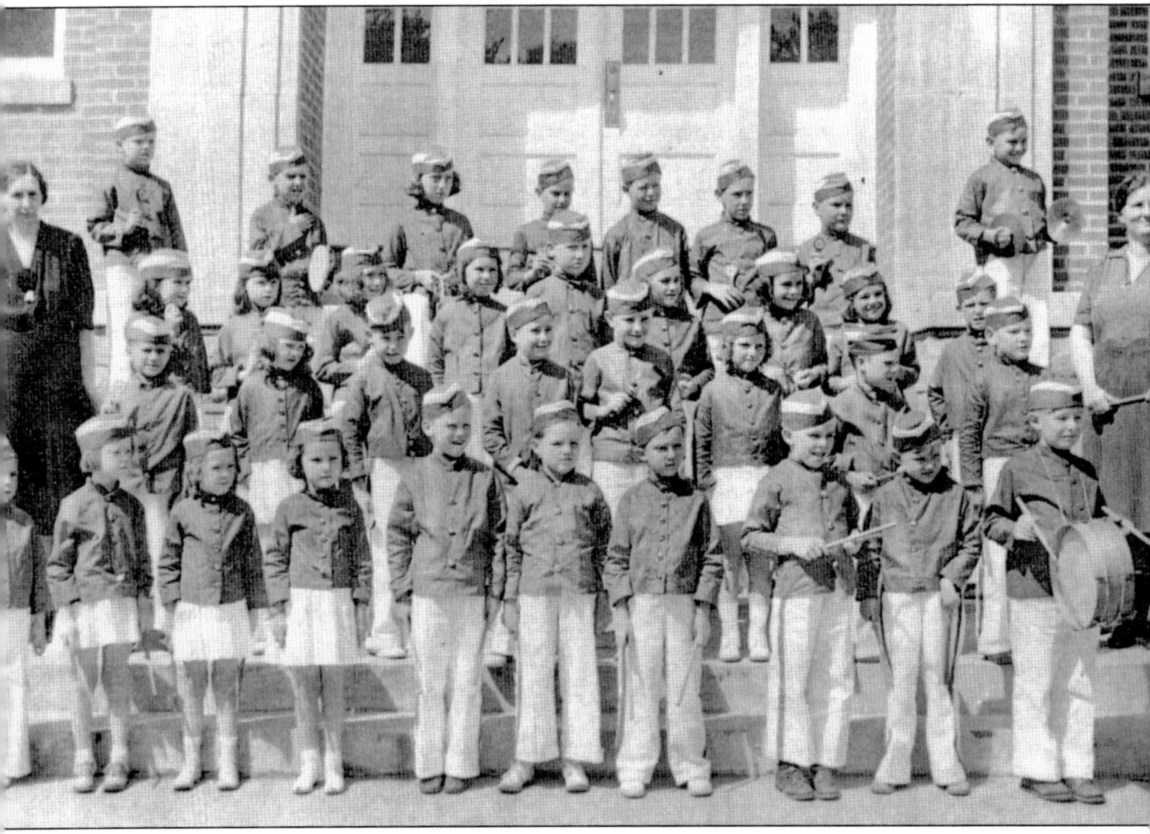

The members of the Campbellsville College Elementary School Rhythm Band, *c.* 1940, were among the last elementary school students to attend Campbellsville College. Both the elementary and secondary school programs were discontinued in 1941.

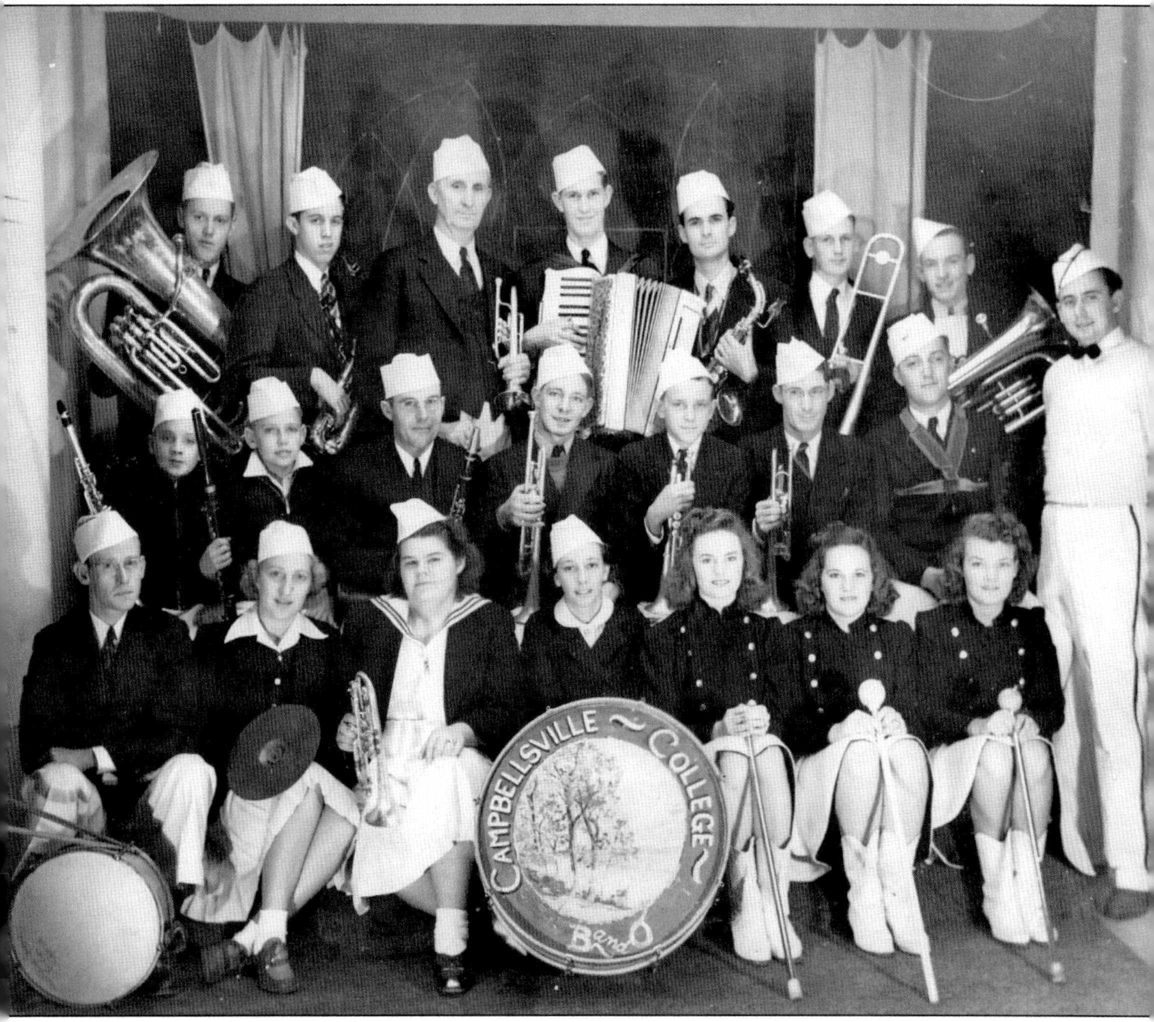

The Campbellsville College Band was directed by Prof. Homer Felts during the 1941–1942 academic year.

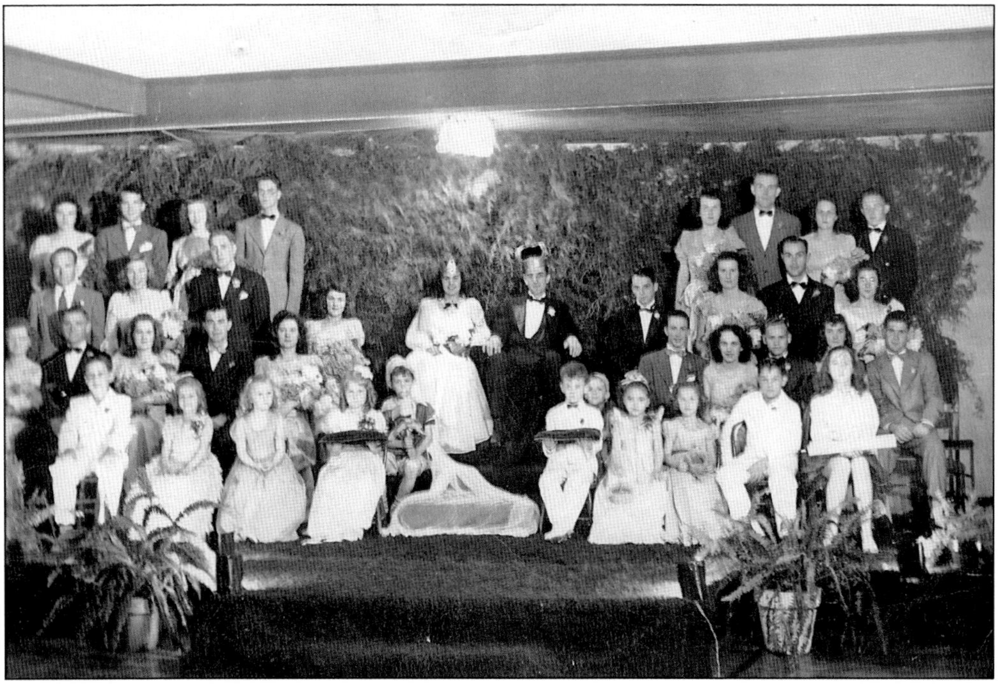

The May Day king, Abel T. Harding, and his queen, Dolly Bandy, hold court at the 1946 May Day celebration. Ellen Faulkner was selected to serve as the queen's maid of honor, and the king's escort was Kenneth W. Hadley.

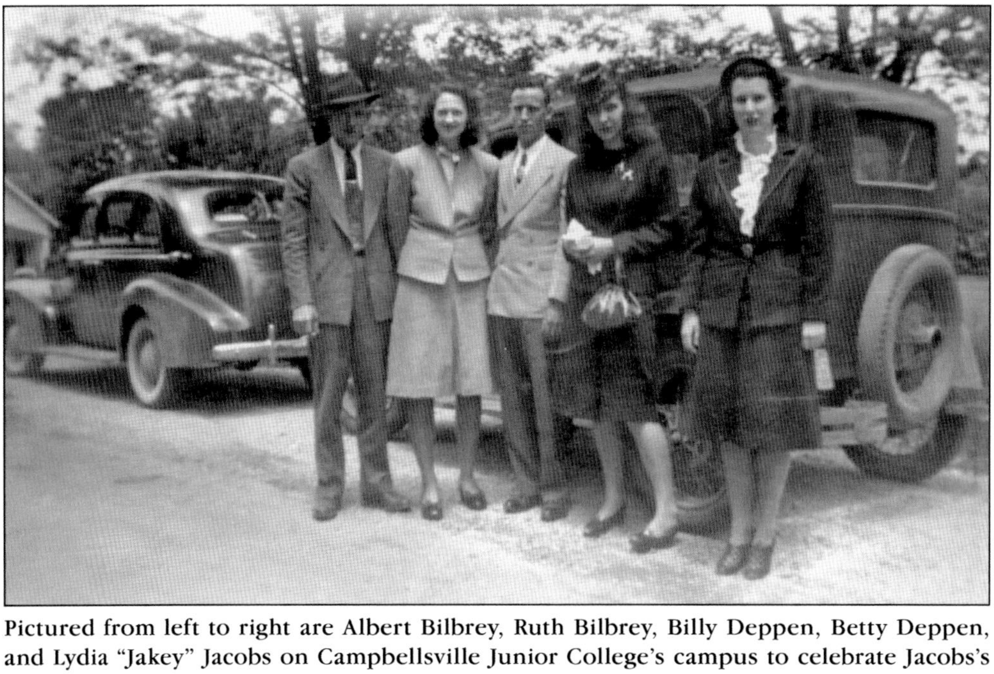

Pictured from left to right are Albert Bilbrey, Ruth Bilbrey, Billy Deppen, Betty Deppen, and Lydia "Jakey" Jacobs on Campbellsville Junior College's campus to celebrate Jacobs's 1946 graduation.

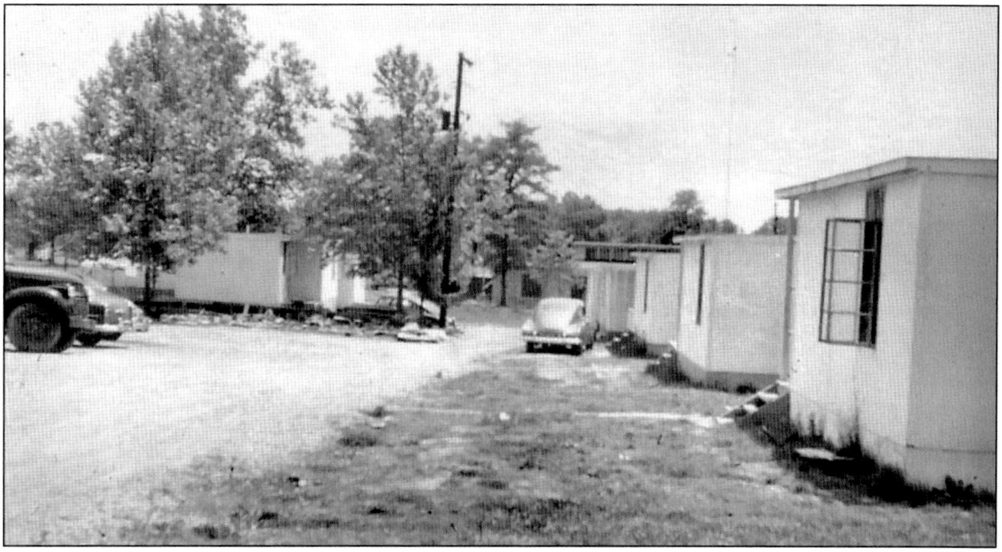

Following World War II, the federal government began selling surplus housing structures for the bargain price of $5. The administrators and trustees took advantage of the opportunity and purchased some of the buildings to house married students.

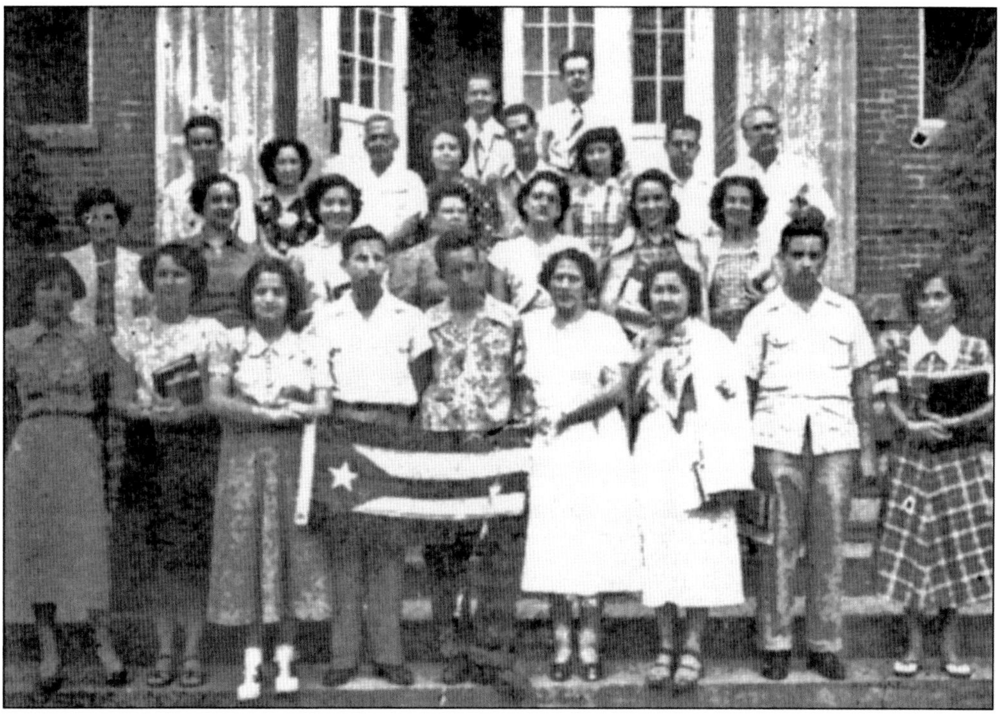

Twenty-five students from Cuba proudly display their country's flag in front of the Administration Building in 1951. Joining them in the photograph is Arch S. Lacefield, professor of Spanish, who stands on the far right in the back row.

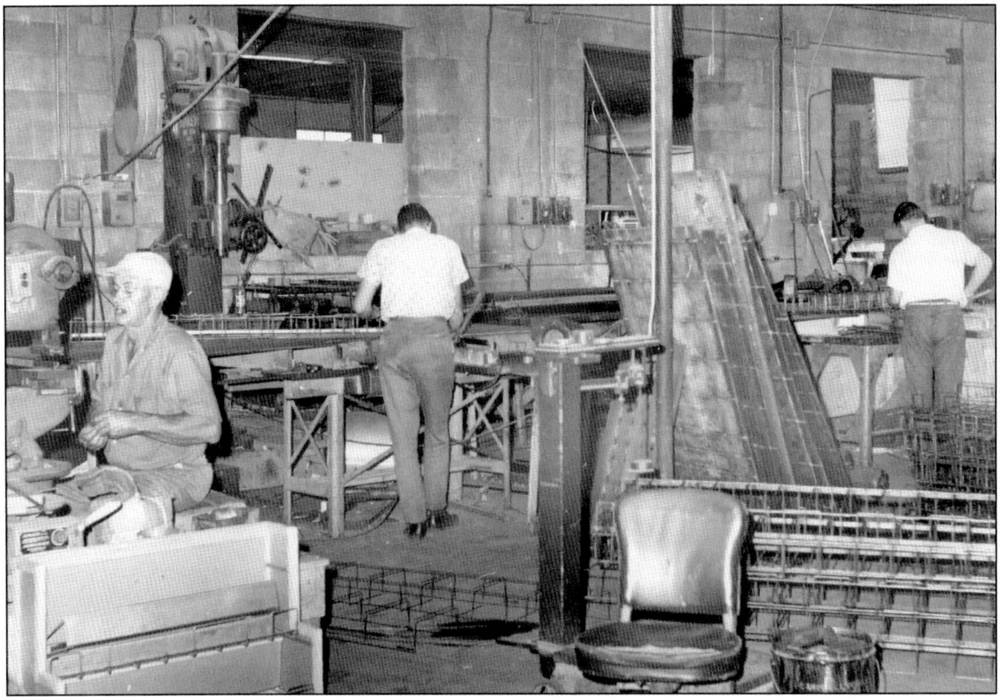

Using Berea College's student-labor program as his model, Dean John M. Carter inaugurated Campbellsville College's work-study program in August 1947 by opening a woodworking plant. Dr. Carter designed the program to provide an opportunity for students who could not afford to pay for their education. In the program, these students could earn the money required for expenses such as tuition, lodging, meals, and books.

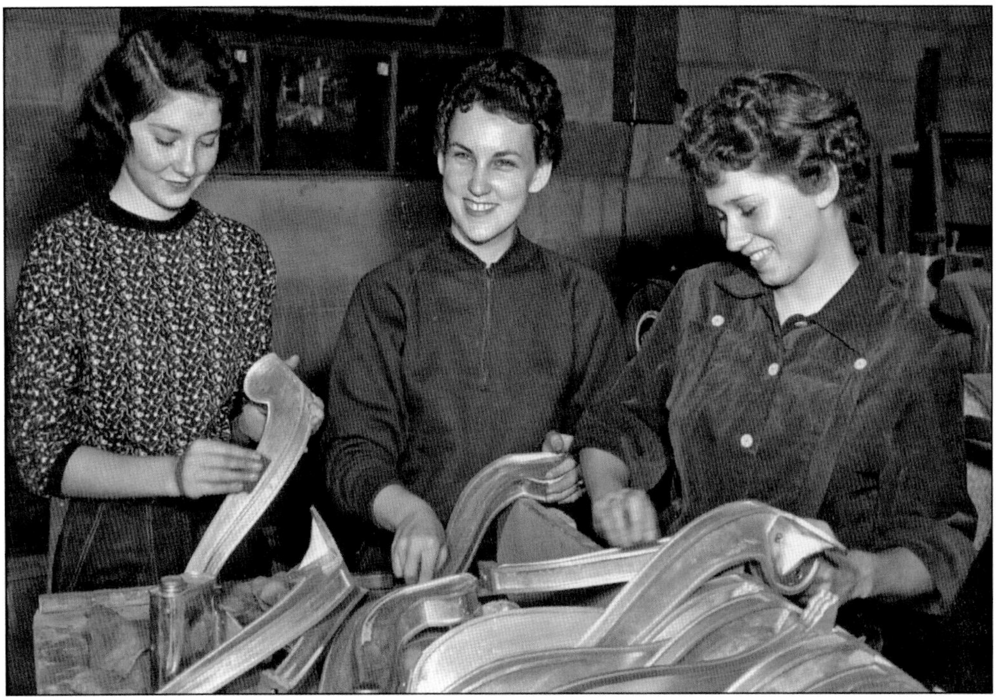

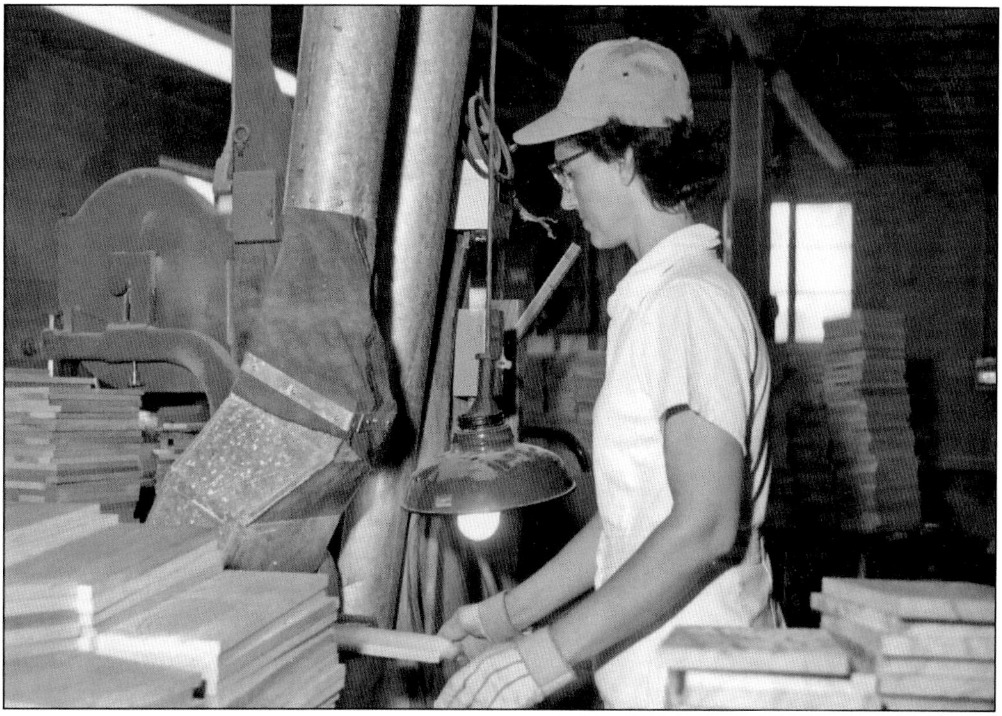

The work-study program was incorporated in 1956 as College Industries. By 1964, the trustees had determined that it was in the best interest of both Campbellsville College and College Industries to become separate entities. The trustees began the process on September 14, 1965, when they drew up the articles of incorporation for the newly dubbed Campbellsville Industries. Campbellsville Industries was sold to private interests in 1969.

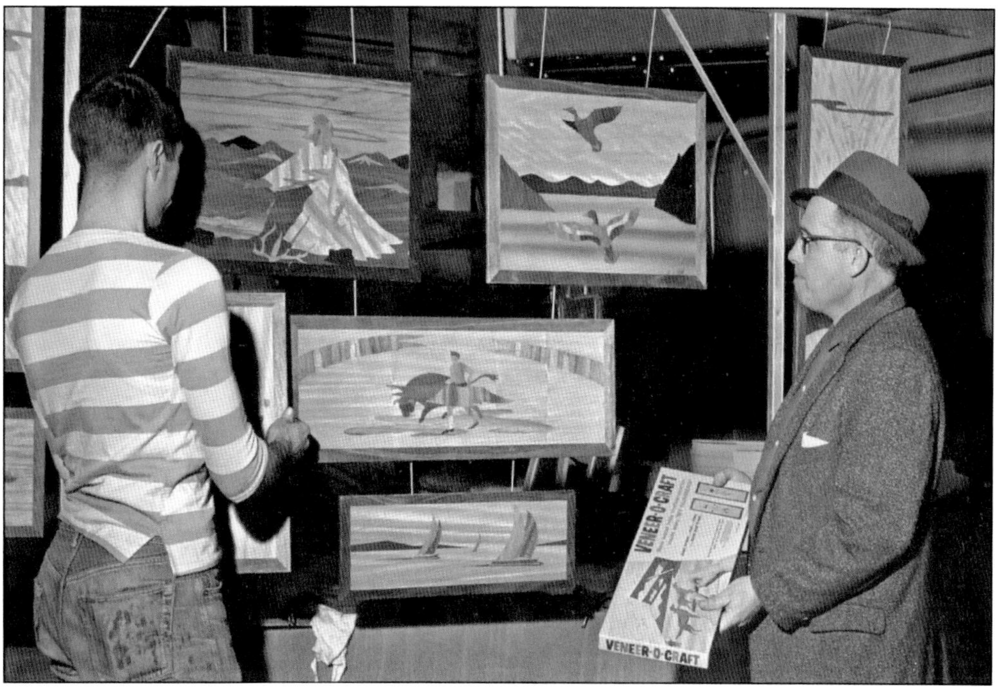

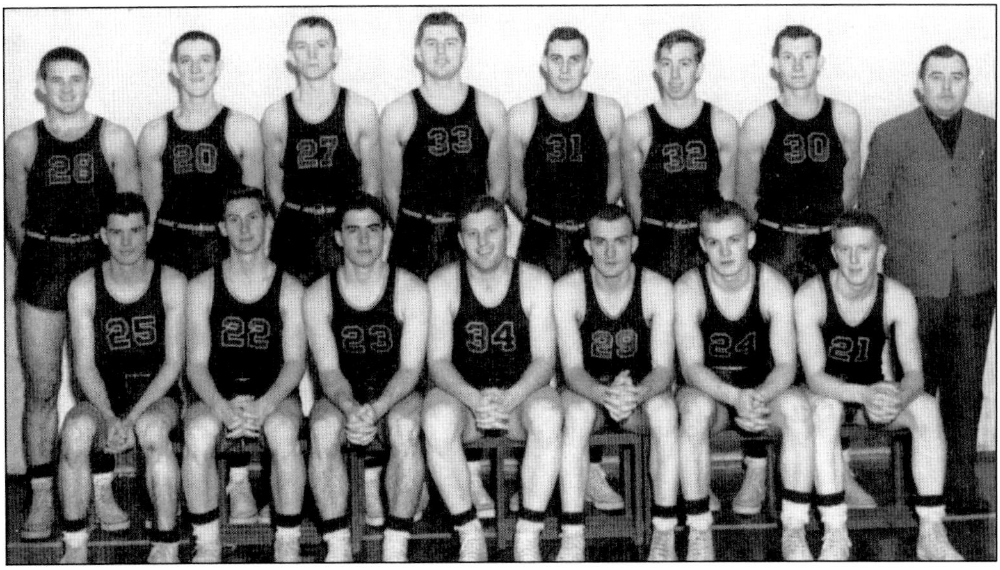

The 1949–1950 basketball team claimed the Kentucky Junior College Conference crown with a perfect record of 12-0.

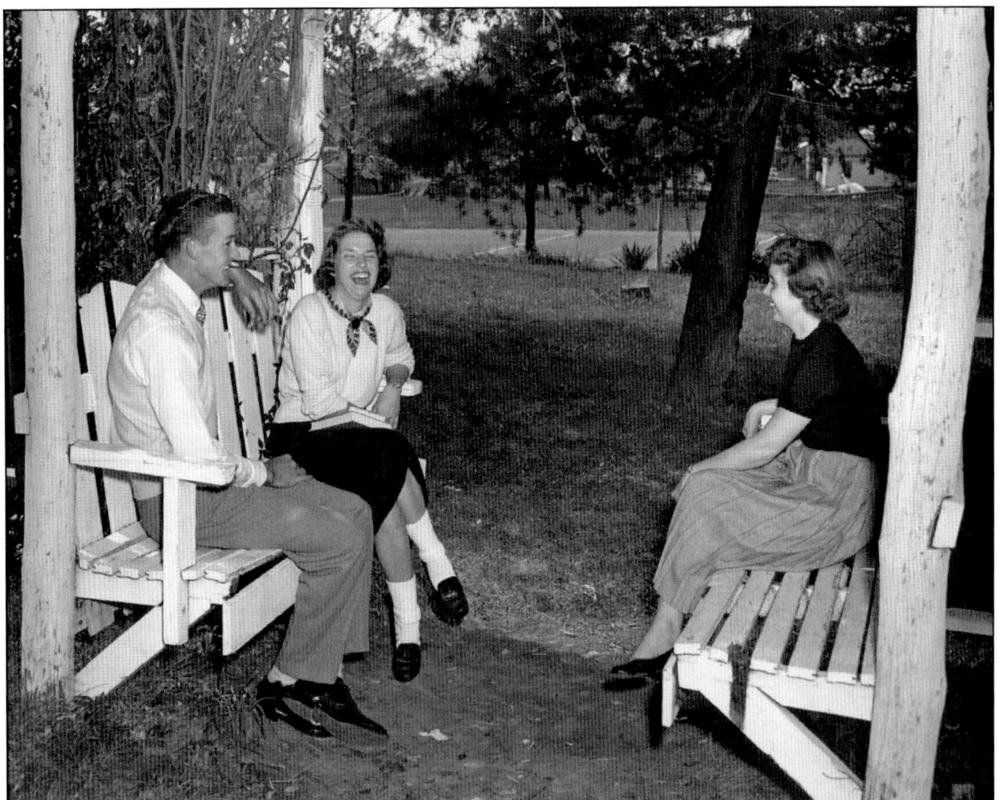

A group of students relaxes in the Rose Garden.

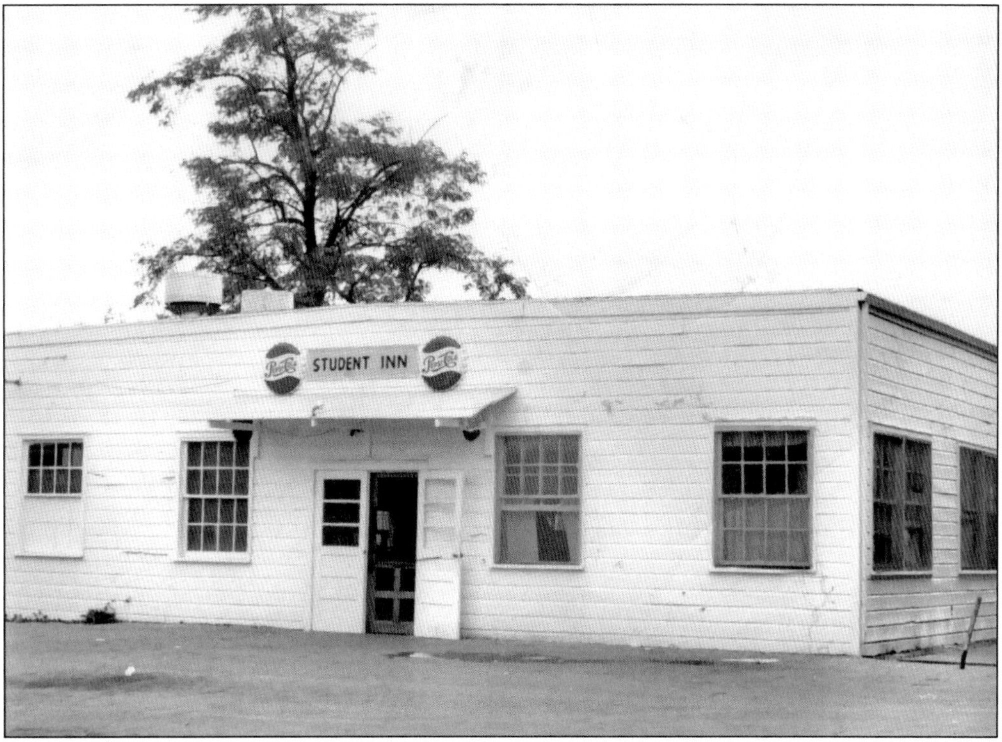

The Student Inn was a small building located to the left side of the Gymnasium. It was an extremely popular place for the students to congregate and socialize during the 1950s.

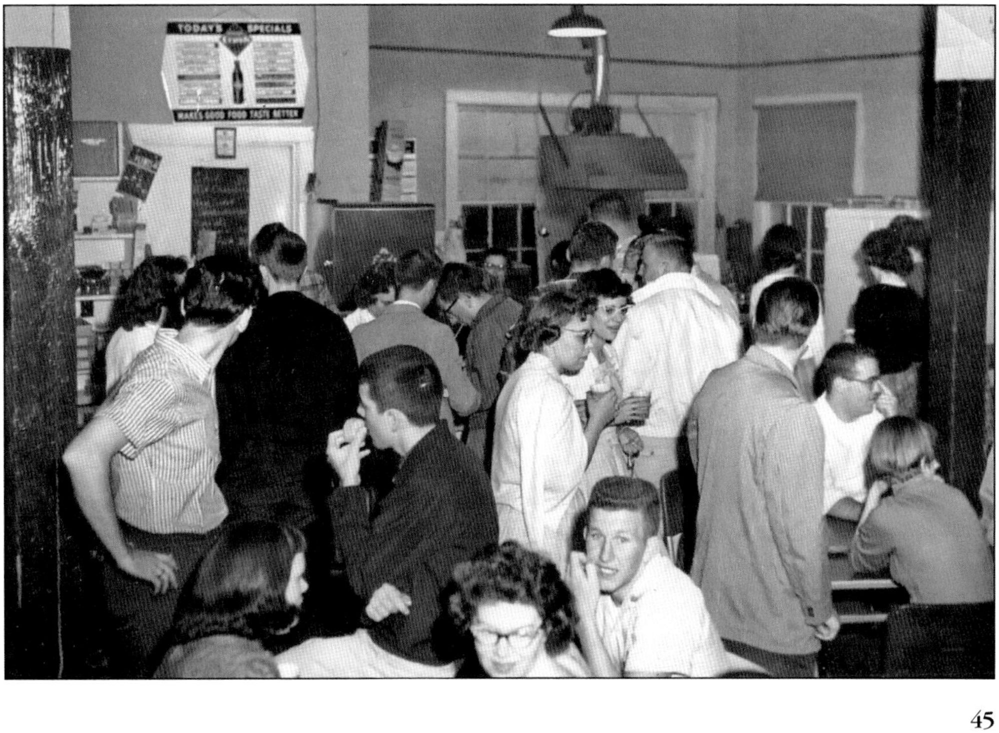

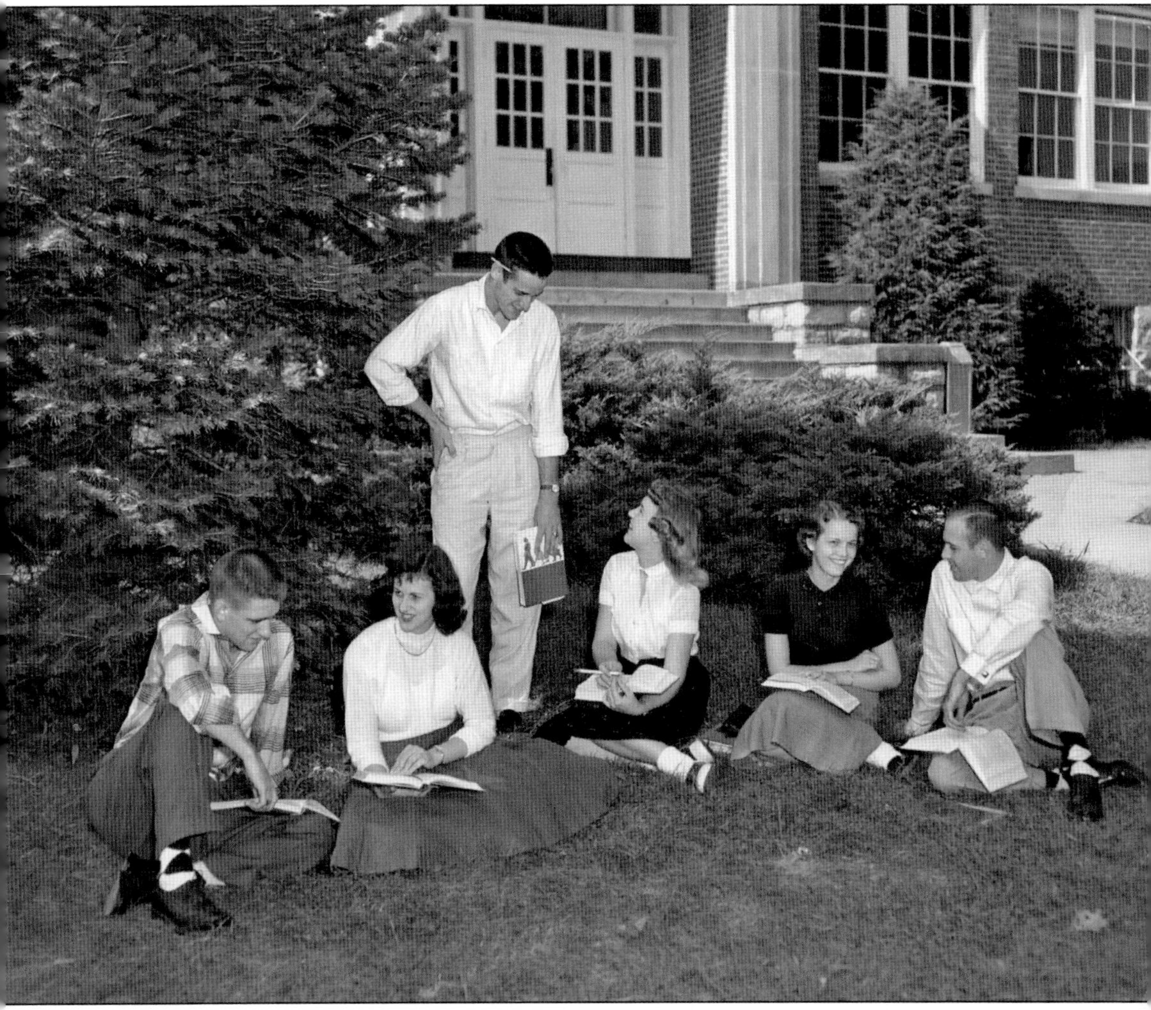

A faculty member holds class on the lawn in front of the Administration Building in 1950. It is not uncommon today to find classes conducted outside on beautiful spring days.

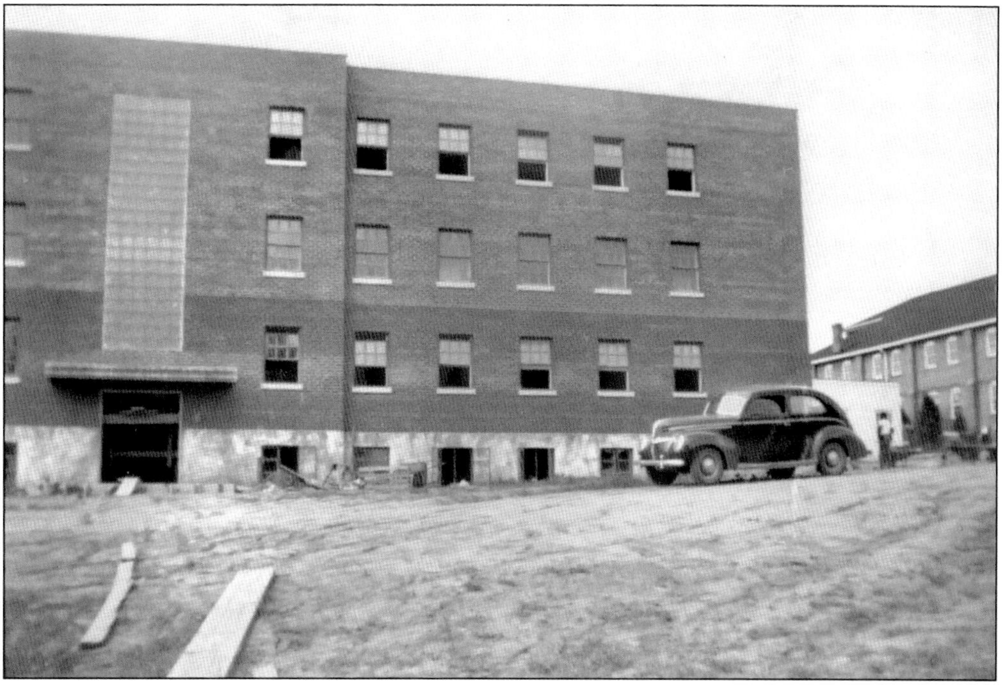

The Boys Dormitory was completed in 1950. The dormitory was later renamed Carter Hall, in honor of John M. Carter, a president of the college. The building was boarded up in 1979 in order to save Campbellsville College the expense of maintaining the structure.

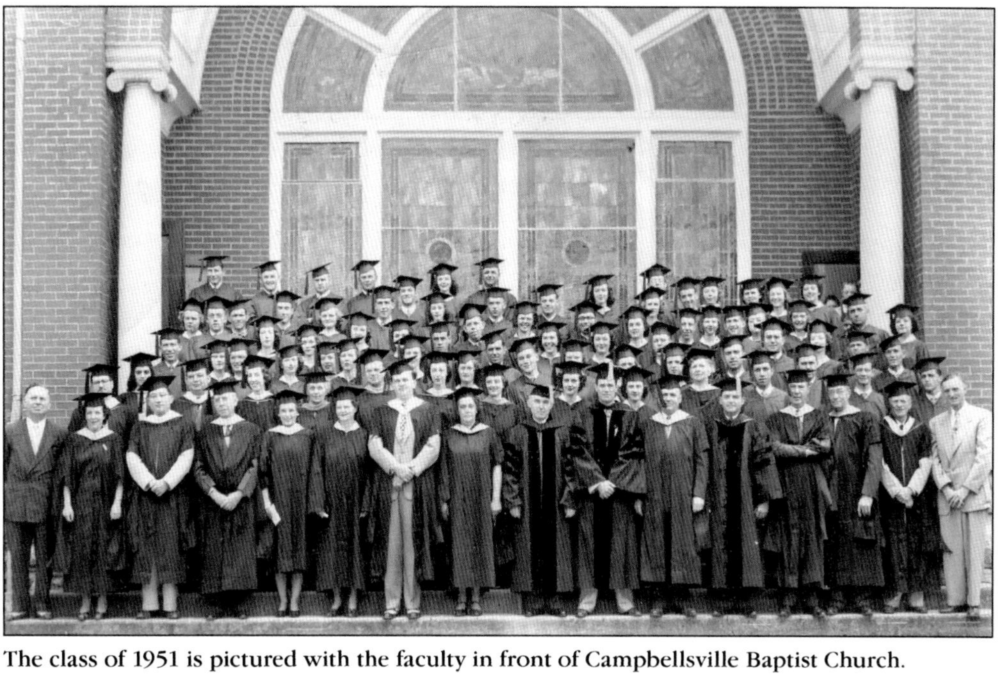

The class of 1951 is pictured with the faculty in front of Campbellsville Baptist Church.

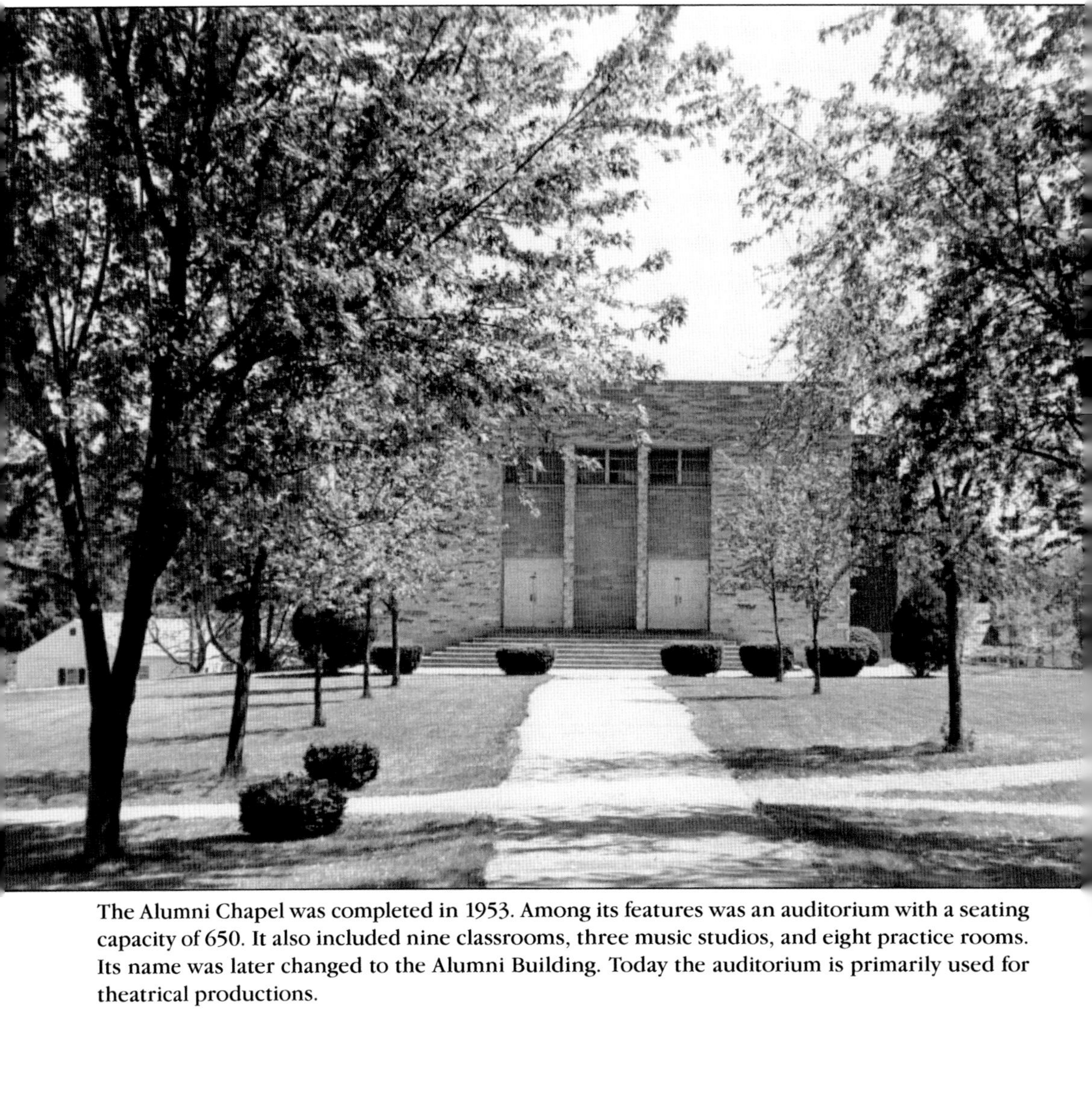

The Alumni Chapel was completed in 1953. Among its features was an auditorium with a seating capacity of 650. It also included nine classrooms, three music studios, and eight practice rooms. Its name was later changed to the Alumni Building. Today the auditorium is primarily used for theatrical productions.

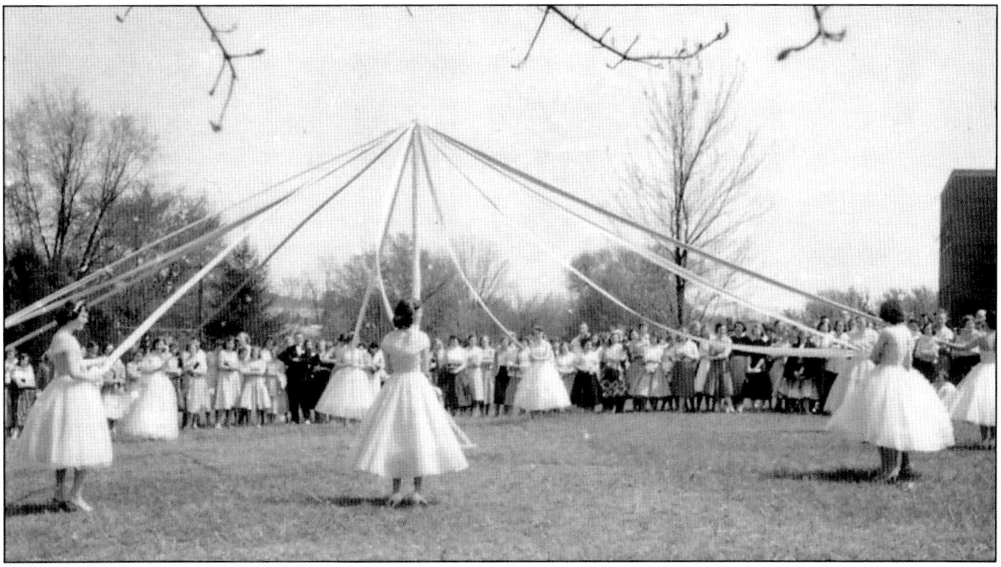

Young ladies dressed in formal gowns dance around the maypole. During the 1950s, Campbellsville College scheduled High School Senior Day to coincide with the May Day festivities in hopes of making the college more appealing to prospective students.

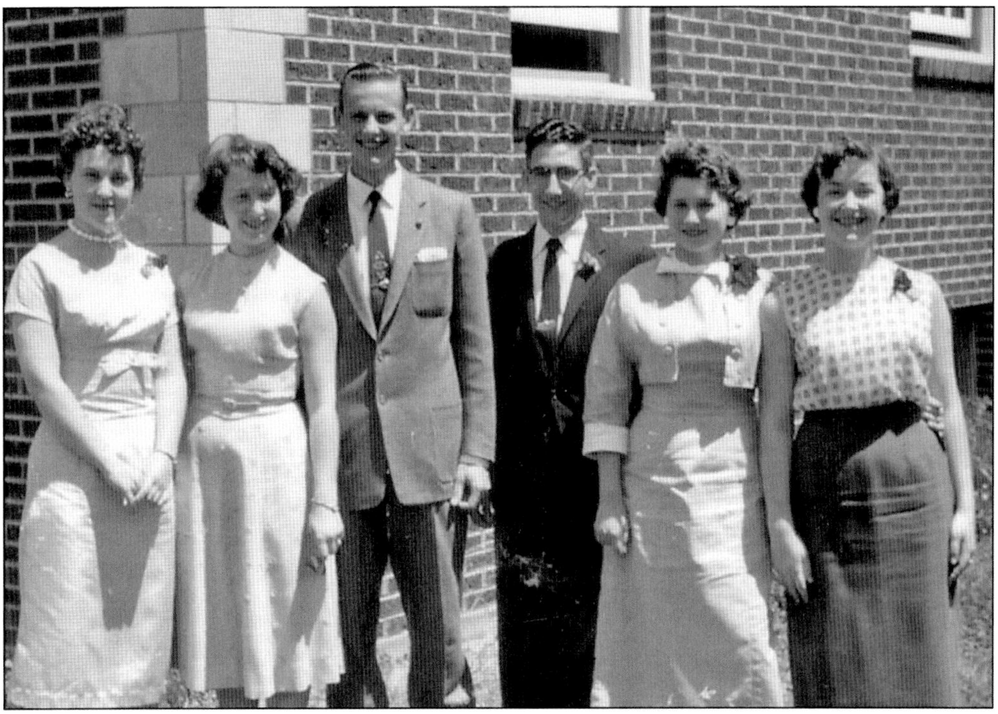

The members of the admission office's youth team in 1956 were, from left to right, Connie Street, Sylvia Richardson, Robert Richardson, J. Alvin Hardy, Karen Hendricks, and Valett White.

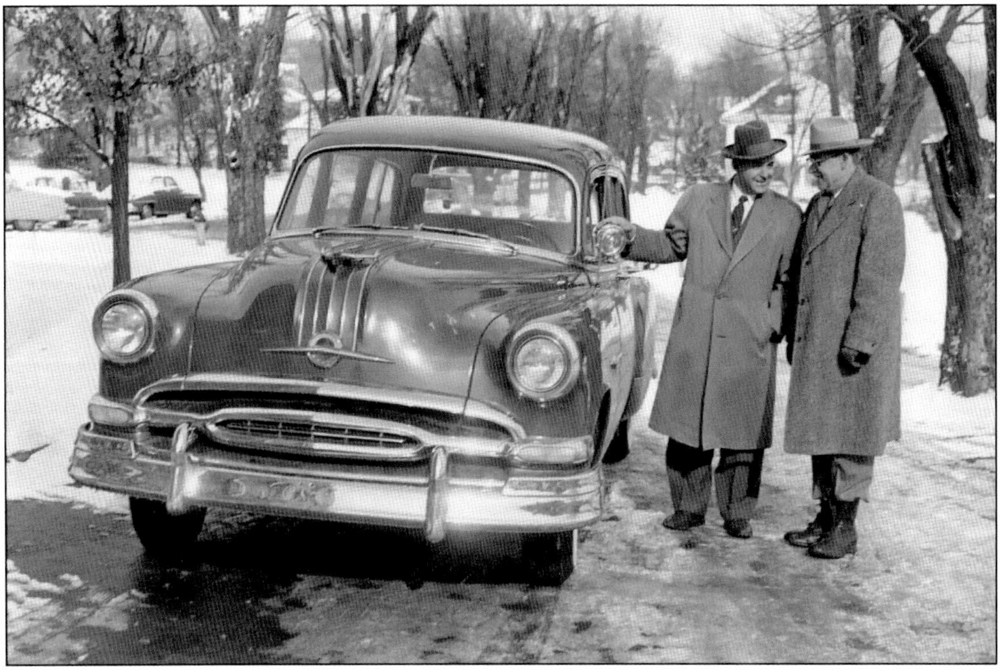

Pres. John M. Carter (left) and Dr. Paul Horner, director of development, are standing next to a station wagon that was donated to Campbellsville Junior College in 1957. The station wagon was gifted to the institution as part of the expansion of the college's woodworking business.

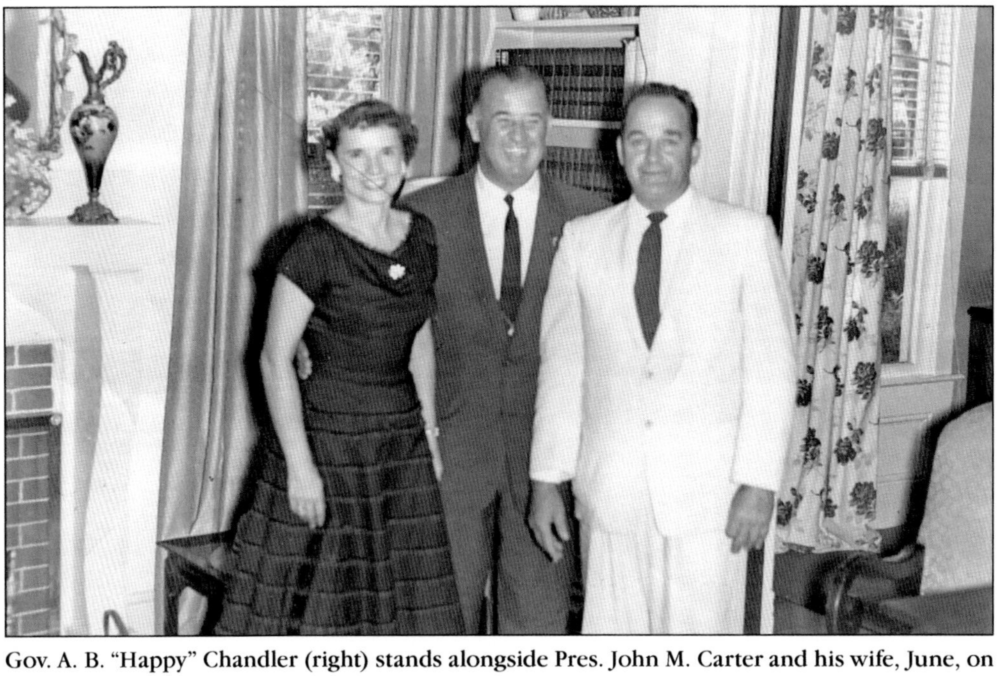

Gov. A. B. "Happy" Chandler (right) stands alongside Pres. John M. Carter and his wife, June, on May 17, 1957, which was designated by the institution as Governor's Day. Governor's Day marked the beginning of Campbellsville Junior College's 50th anniversary celebration. The celebration concluded at commencement on May 26, where U.S. senator John Sherman Cooper addressed the graduates.

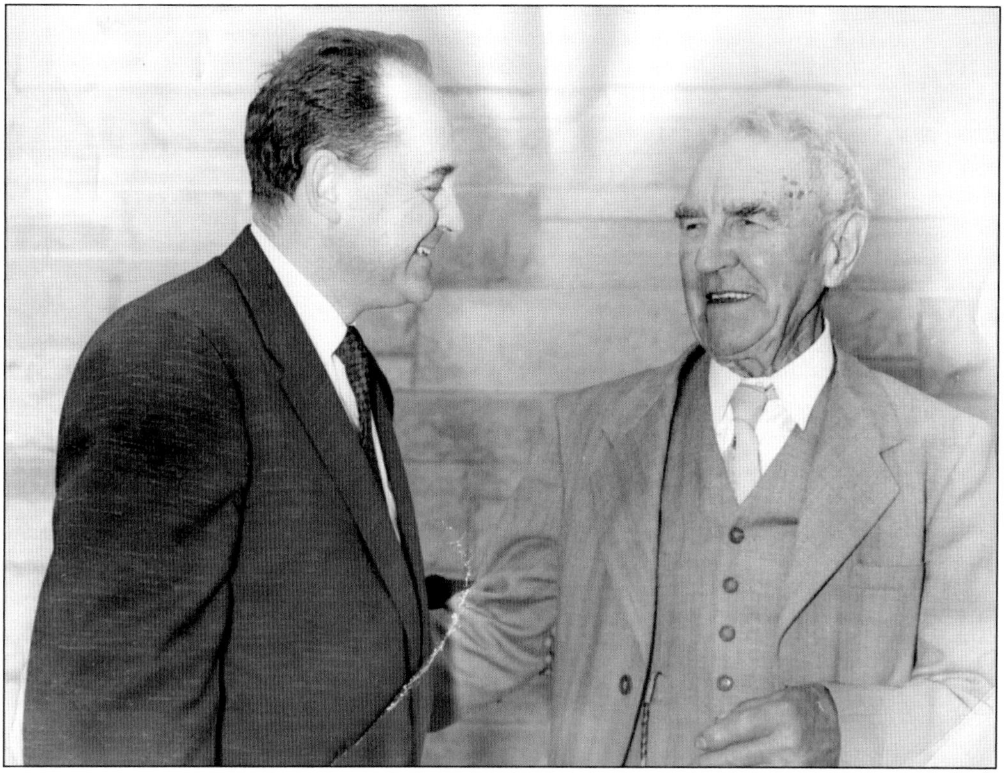

Pres. John M. Carter (left) and Prof. W. G. Welborn share a light moment at Campbellsville Junior College's 50th anniversary celebration. Welborn had served as the first principal of Russell Creek Academy.

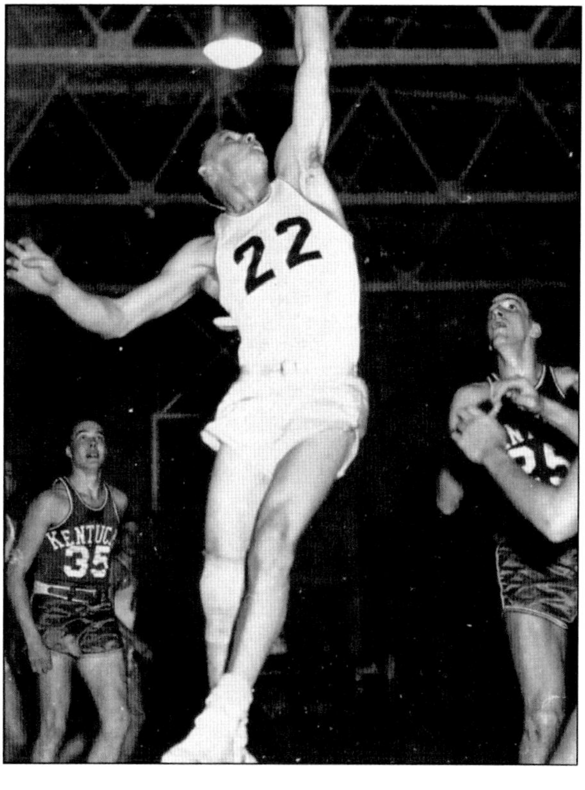

Campbellsville Tiger S. J. "Jughead" Irvin grabs a rebound against the University of Kentucky's freshman team in 1958.

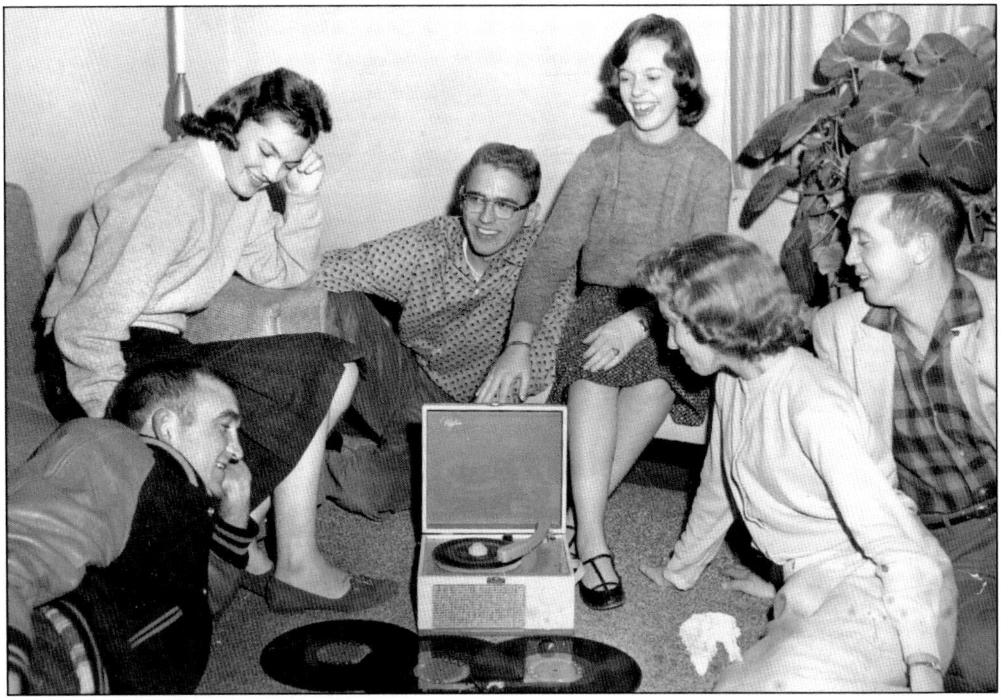

A group of students socializes around a record player.

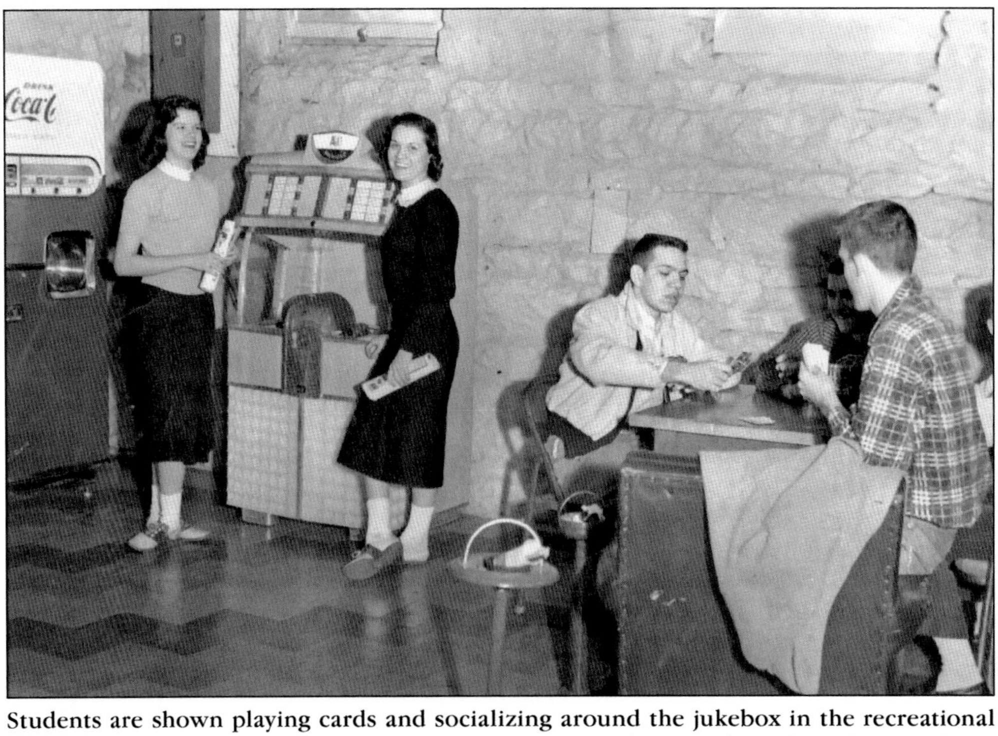

Students are shown playing cards and socializing around the jukebox in the recreational center during March 1958. The center, where students could gain a respite from their academic endeavors, was housed in the basement of the Gymnasium, which is now known as the Student Activities Center.

Three

Campbellsville College 1959–1996

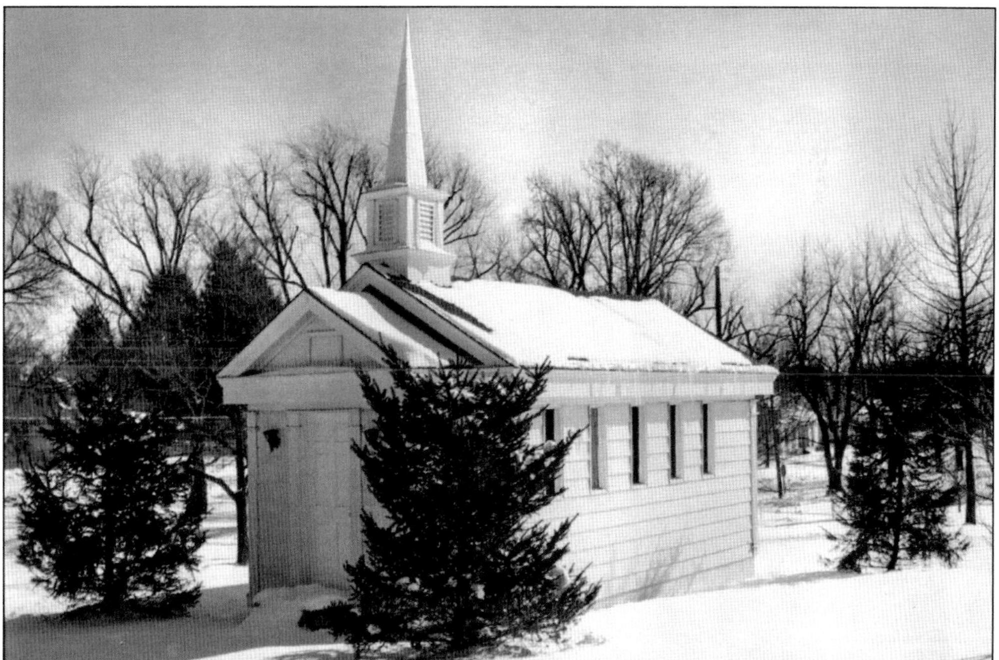

Dedicated on June 8, 1971, the Meditation Chapel was a gift to Campbellsville College from Campbellsville Industries. The donation provided an intimate setting for students, staff, and faculty to worship, thereby improving spiritual life on campus. (Photograph by Bogdan Ratiu.)

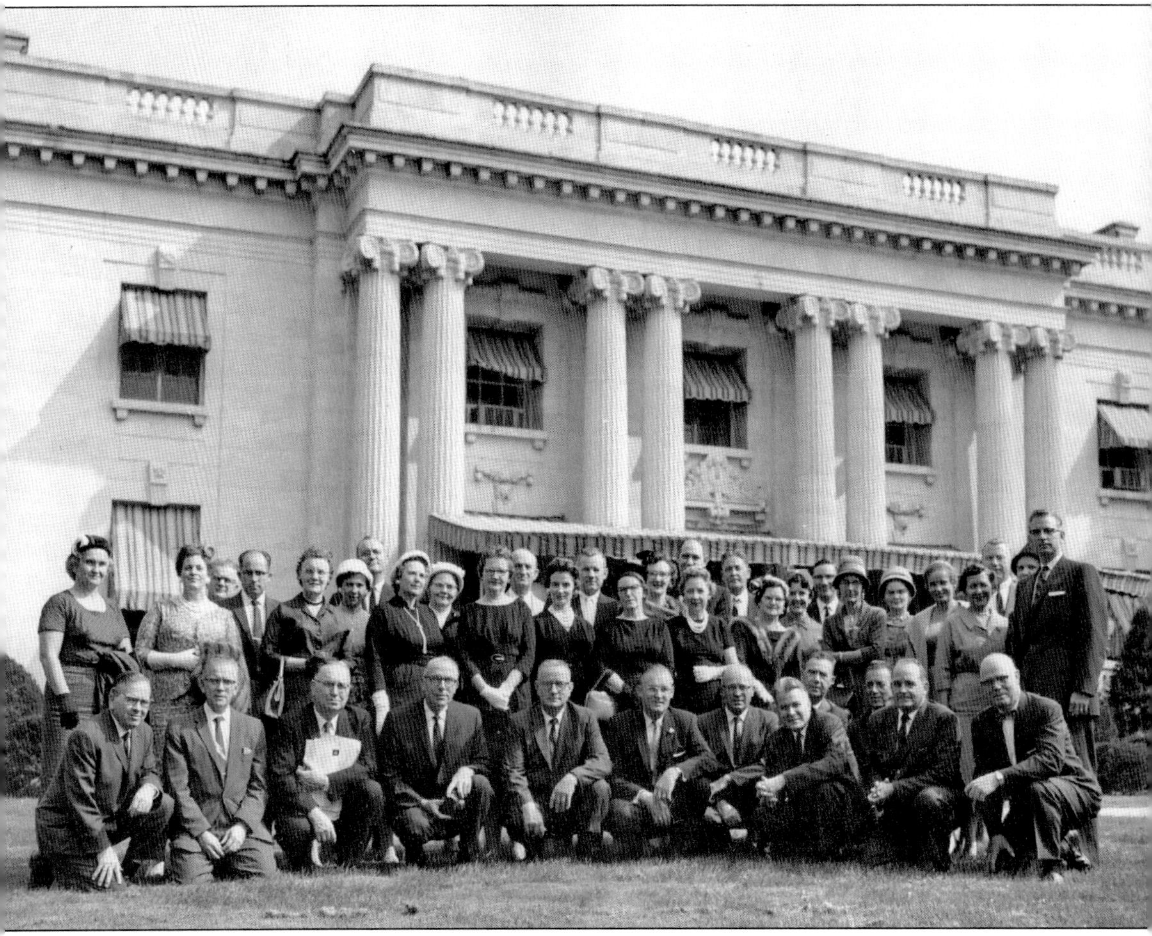

The board of trustees held one of its meetings at the Commonwealth of Kentucky's Governor's Mansion in 1960 at the invitation of Gov. Bert T. Combs. In addition to serving the commonwealth as governor from 1959–1963, Combs was also one of Campbellsville College's trustees.

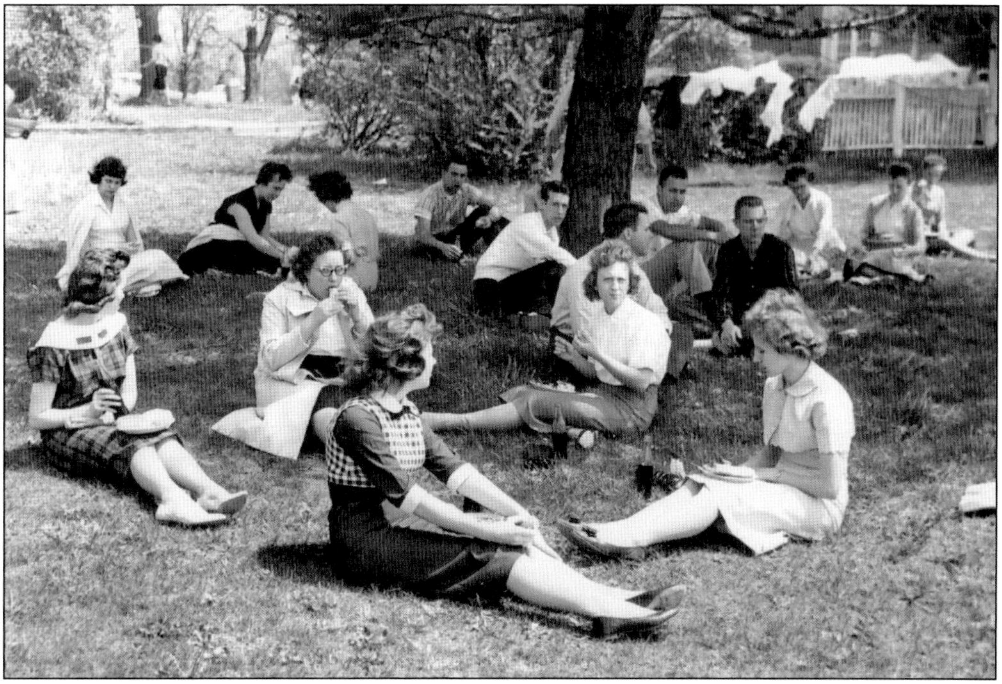

Students enjoy a brief respite from academic advising sessions.

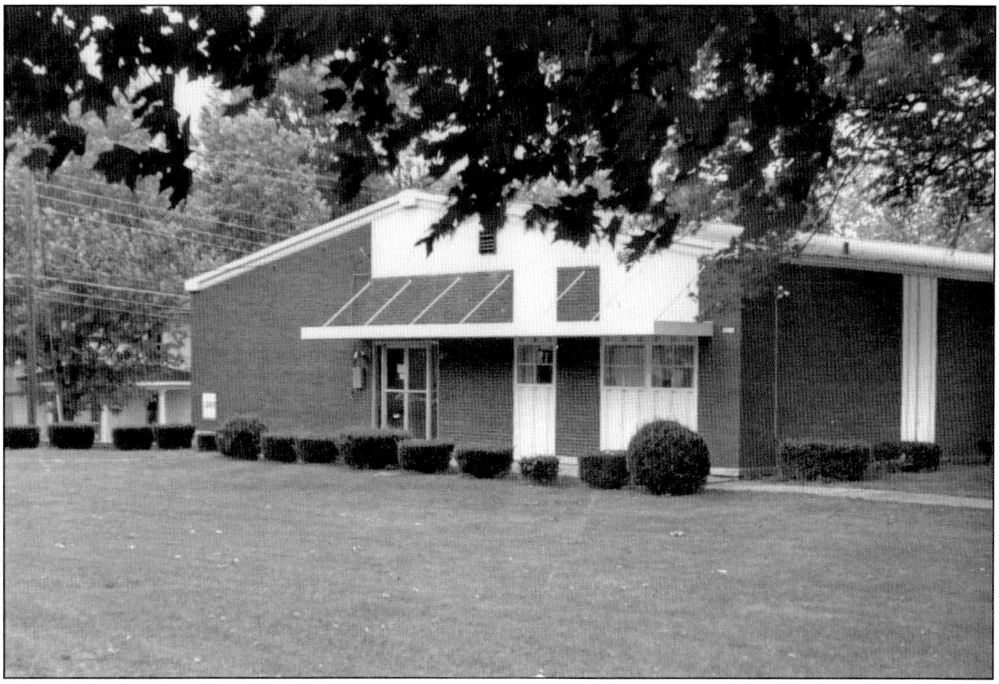

The Campbellsville College Library was constructed in 1961 and was a two-story building. This building is still part of present-day Montgomery Library. Its entire top floor is now the main stacks area and four adjoining rooms. The bottom floor of the library today would still be recognizable to alumni from the 1960s, with the exception of the elevator that was installed during the most recent renovation of the library.

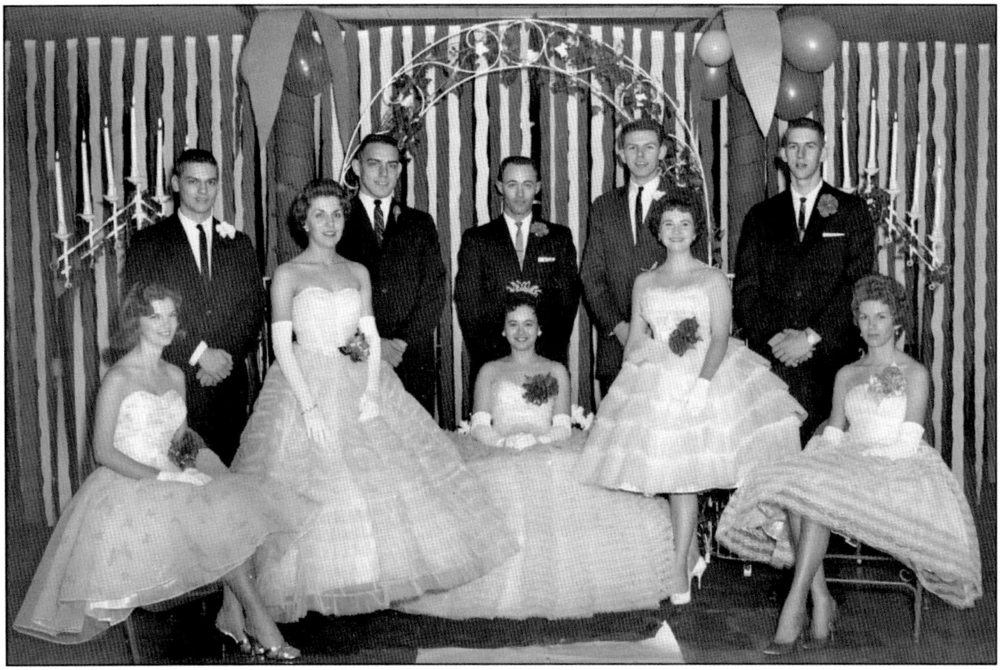

Phala DeVore (seated center) was selected Valentine Sweetheart in 1962. She is joined by the other candidates for the honor and their escorts.

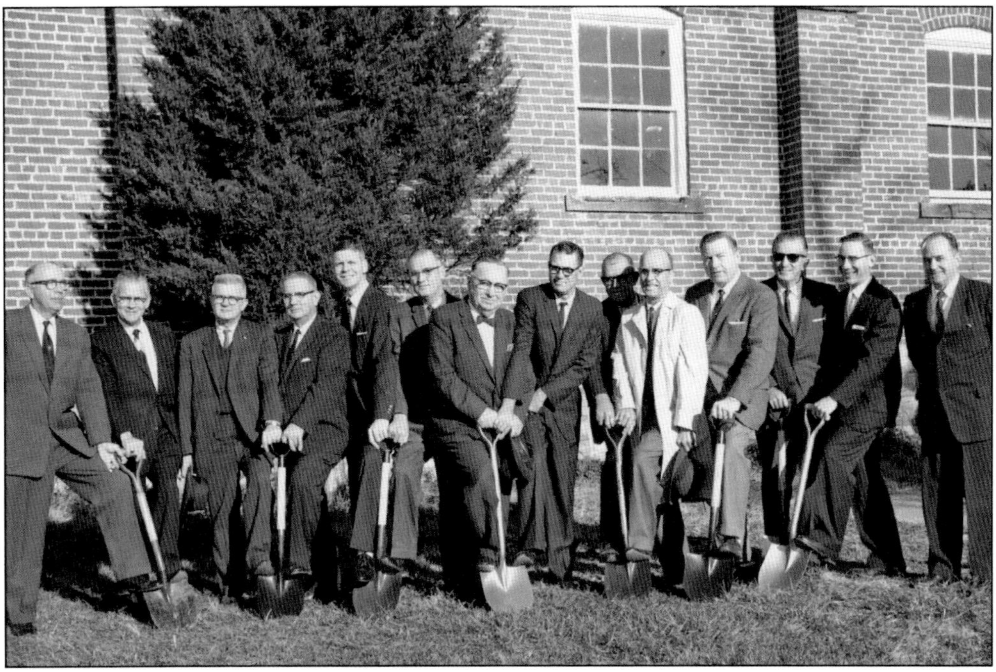

It is appropriate that members of the board of trustees in 1962 are carrying shovels because the change to senior-college status was accompanied by a building boom on Campbellsville College's campus.

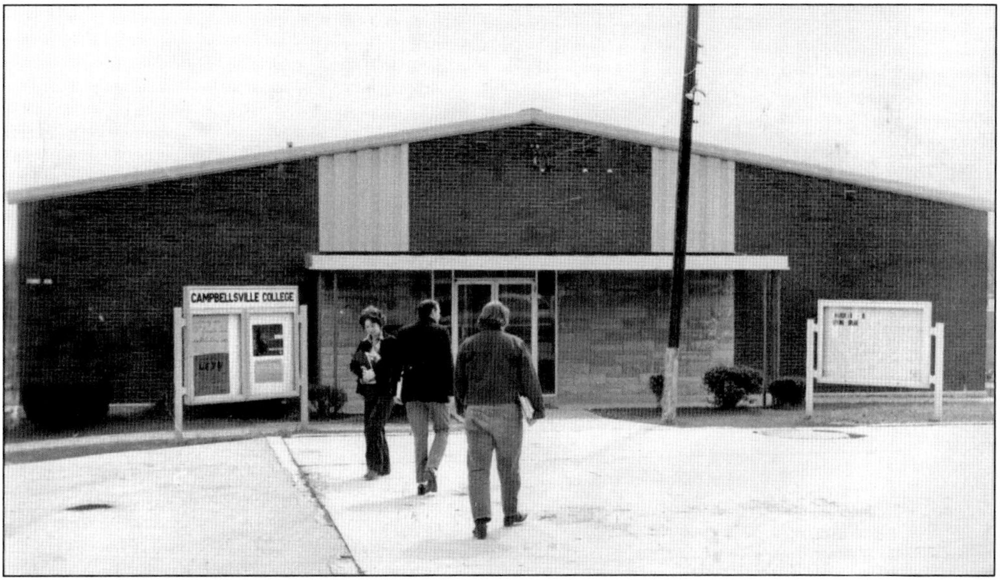

Following the completion of the library, it was determined that a Student Union Building should be constructed. It opened for use in 1963, although it was not completely finished until a year later.

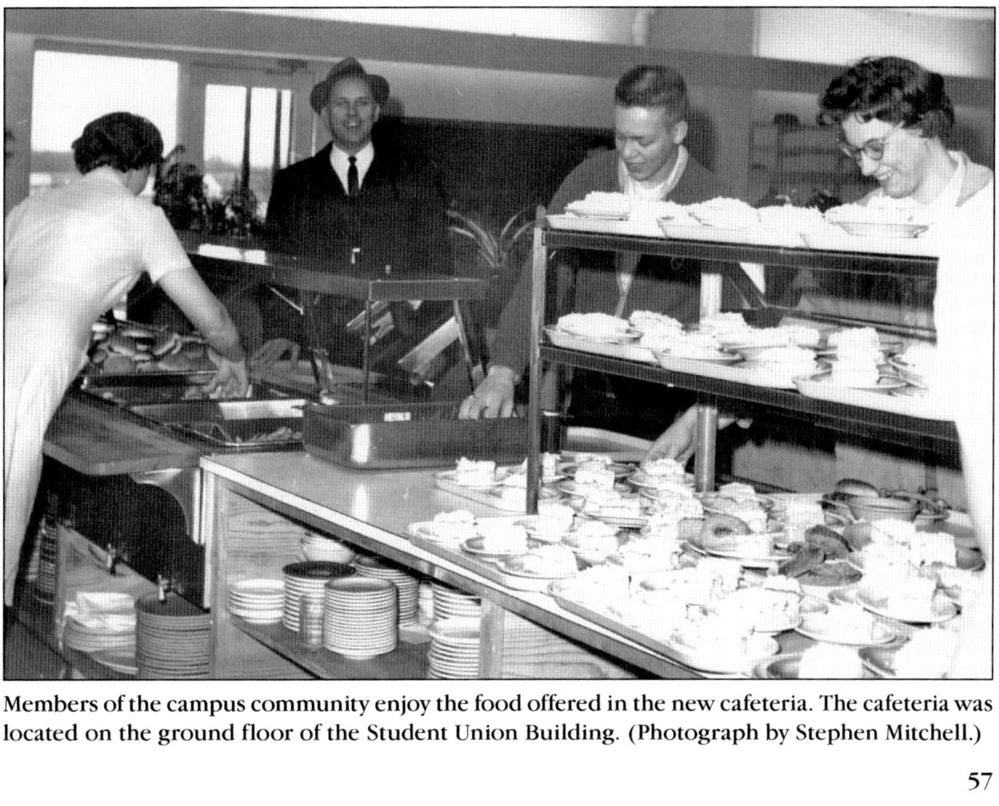

Members of the campus community enjoy the food offered in the new cafeteria. The cafeteria was located on the ground floor of the Student Union Building. (Photograph by Stephen Mitchell.)

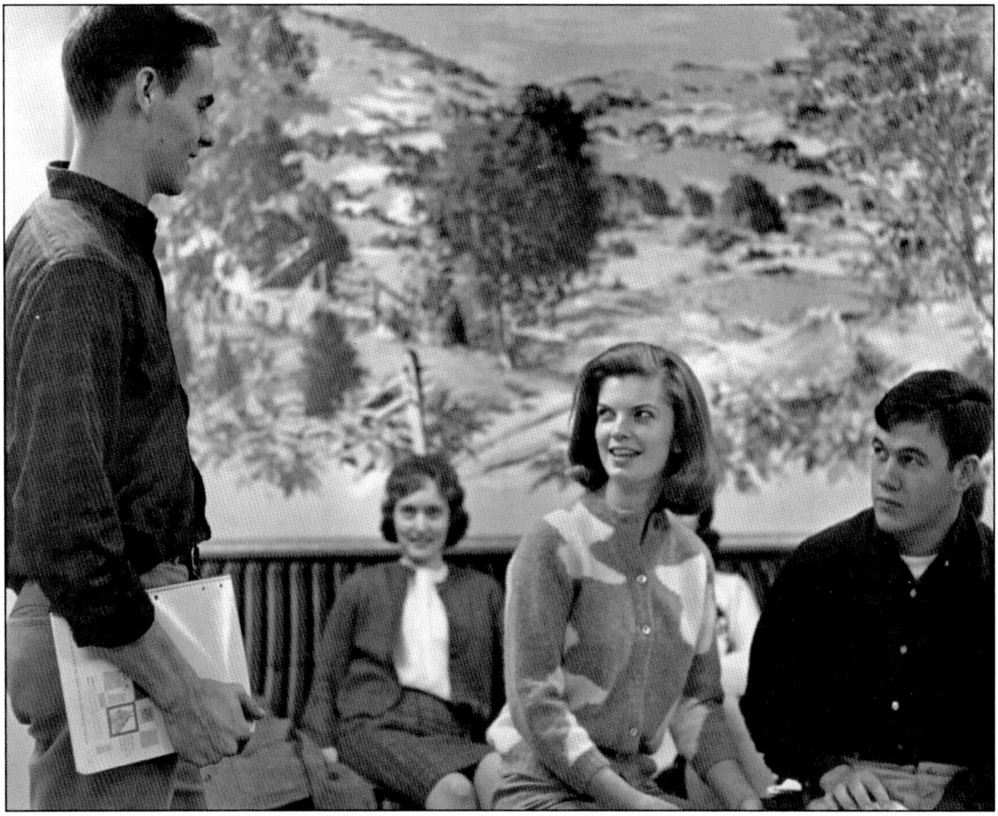

Students congregate in the Student Union Building.

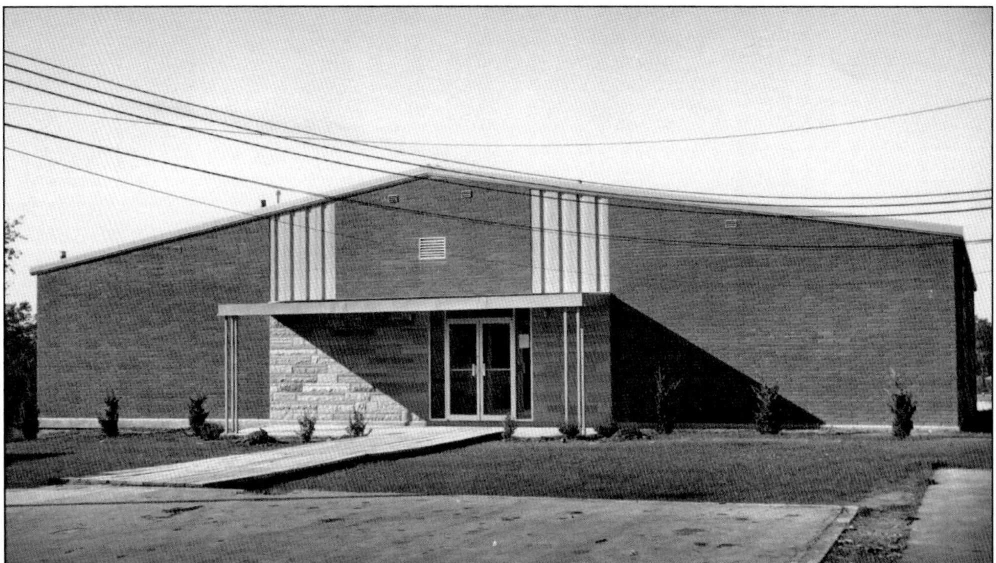

The Science Building, from the outside, looks remarkably similar to the Student Union Building. Like the neighboring Student Union Building, it was in use by 1963 despite not being completely finished until 1964.

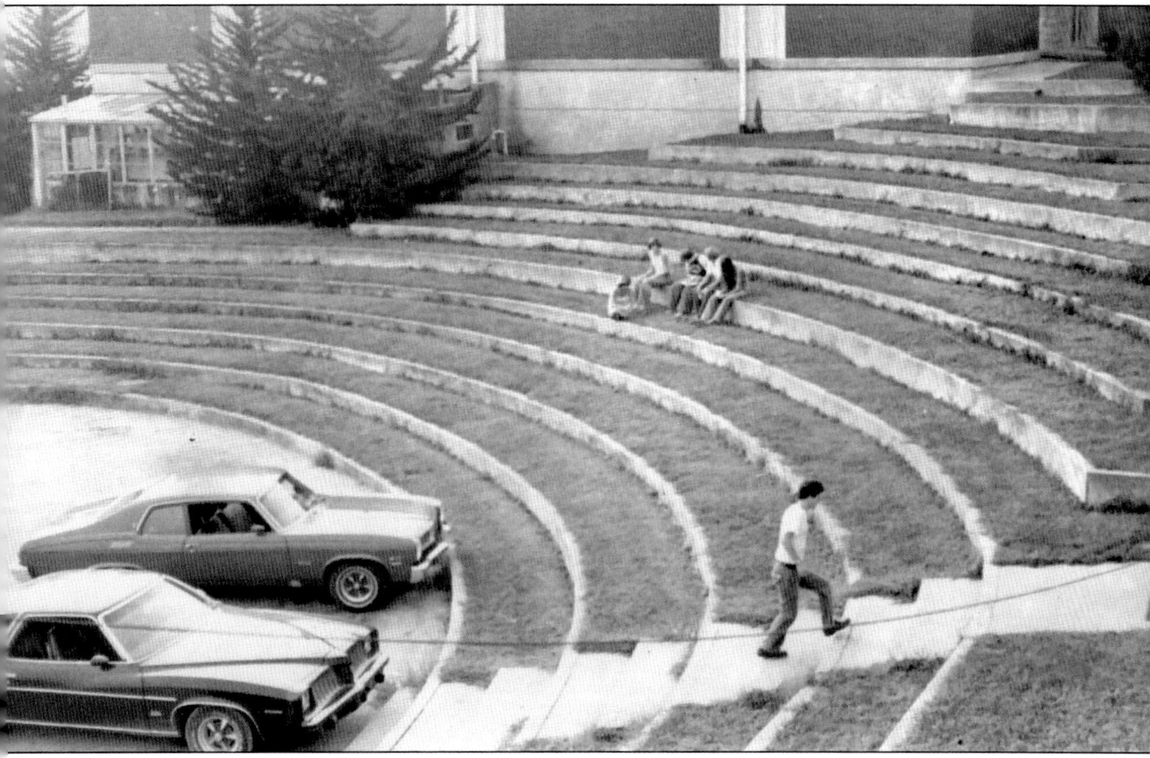

The outdoor amphitheater was constructed in 1964. It was located behind the Student Union Building.

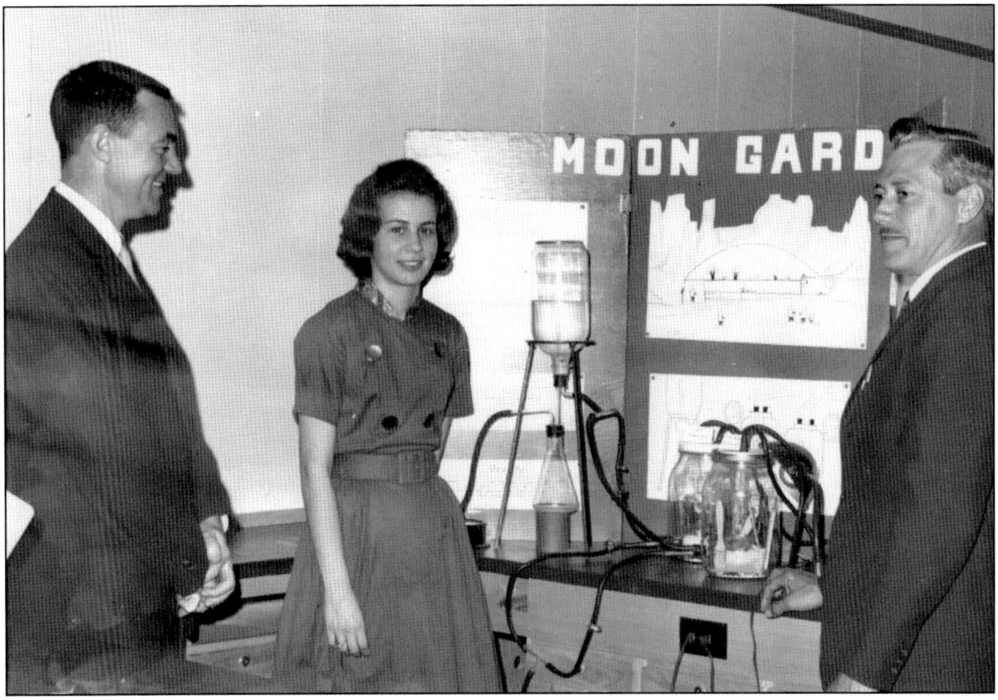

Dr. Clarence Chestnutt Jr. (left), chairman of the biology department, inspects a student's experiment in a scientific laboratory.

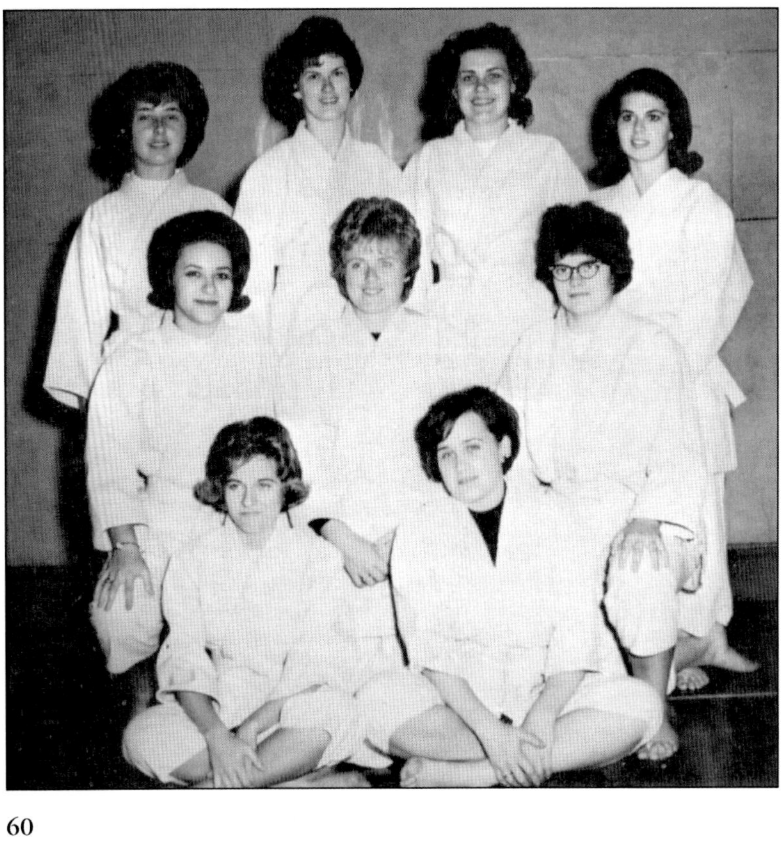

Judo was popular on campus during the 1960s, with teams established for both men and women. The members of the Women's Judo Club posed for this group picture in 1965.

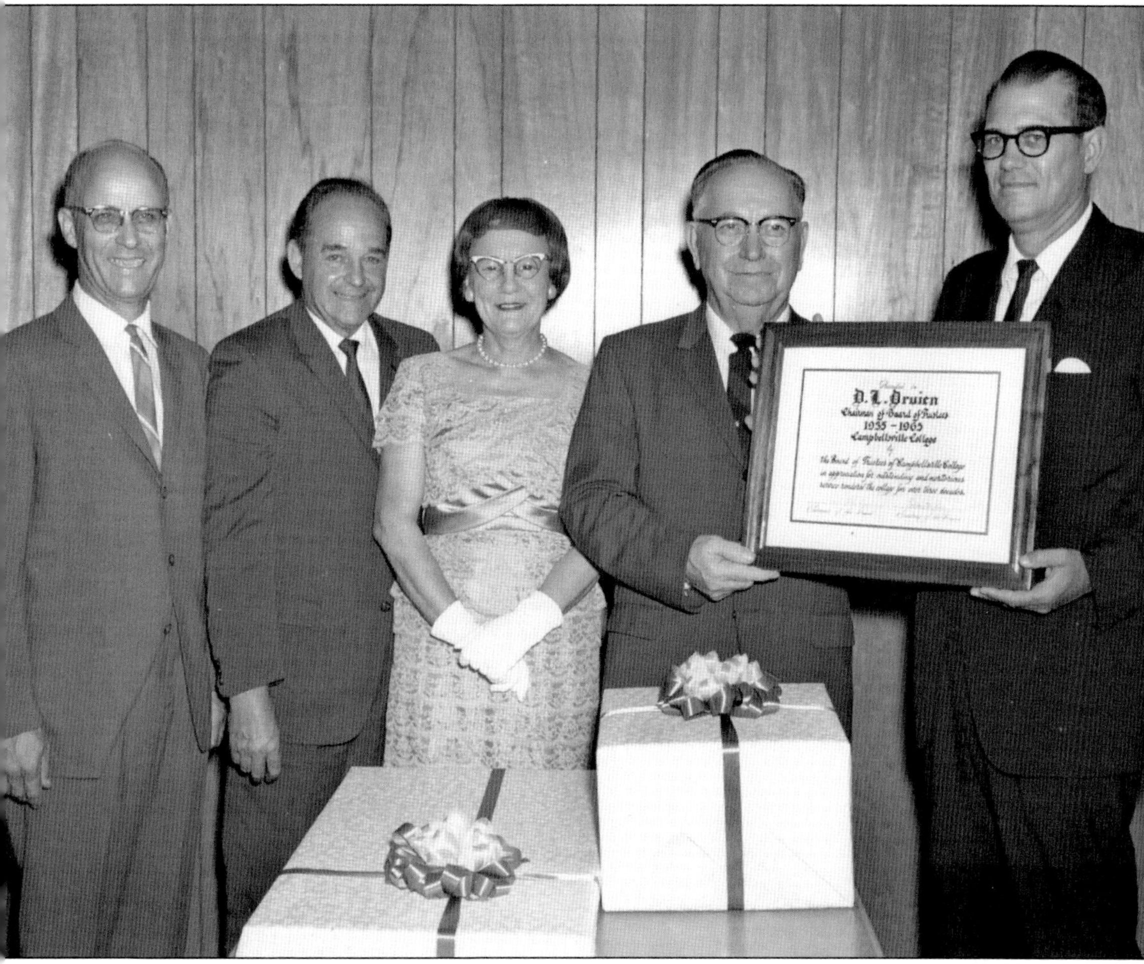

Dr. D. L. Druien is honored with a certificate commemorating his service as chairman of the board of trustees from 1935 to 1965. Dr. Druien was also the recipient of the first honorary Doctor of Divinity degree conferred by Campbellsville College. In 1976, he was named Trustee Emeritus.

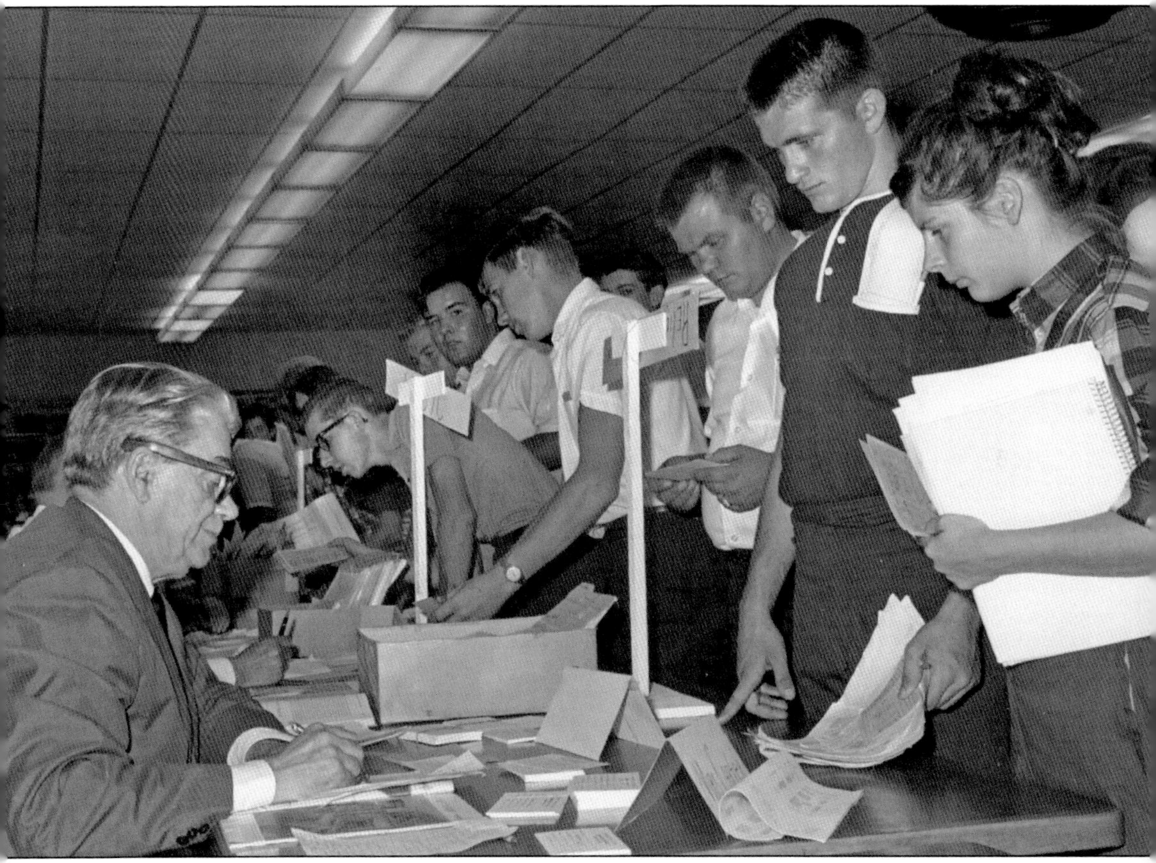

Dr. Paul Horner patiently helps students register for their fall 1965 classes.

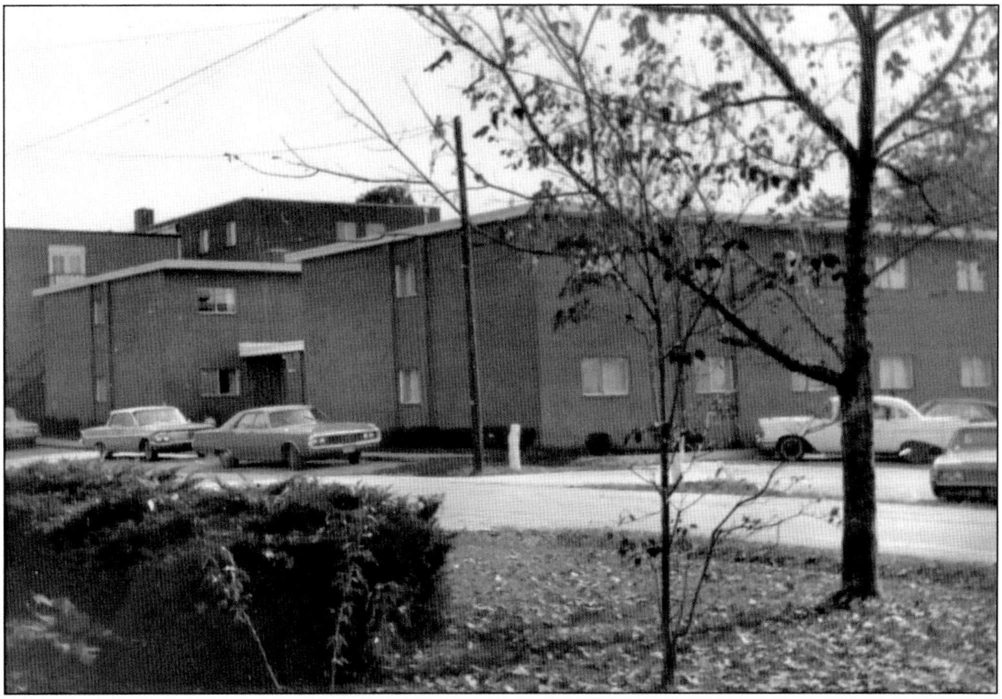

North Hall was constructed in 1965 as a women's dormitory designed to house 80 residents. Beginning in 1979, North Hall was only used as a residence facility when other dormitories were at full capacity. This decision was a cost-saving move that was needed to improve the financial stability of Campbellsville College.

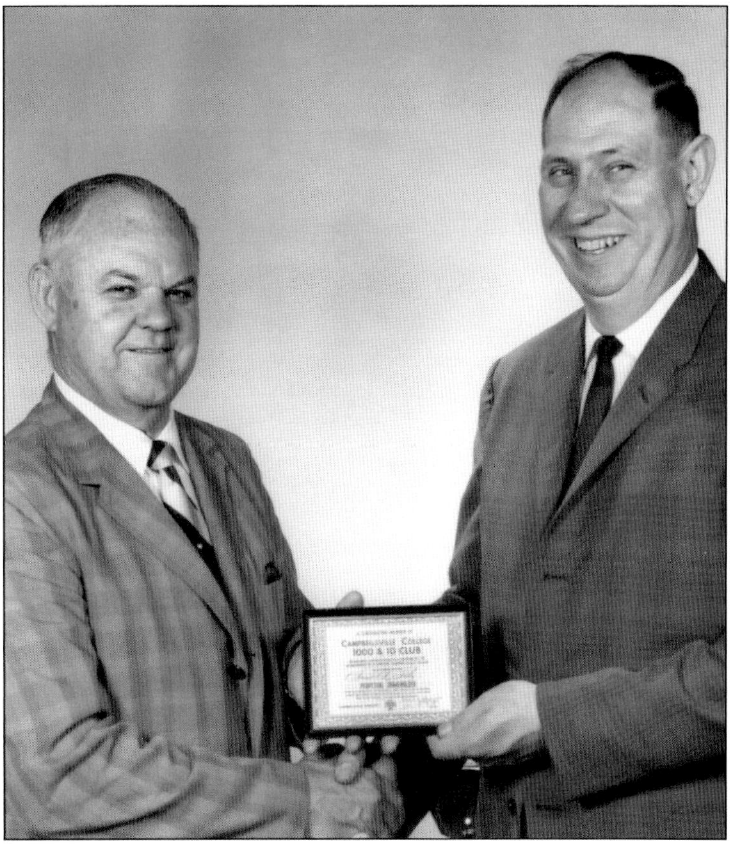

Kenton Cooper (left) welcomes Dr. Forest Shely to the Campbellsville College 1,000 and 10 Club.

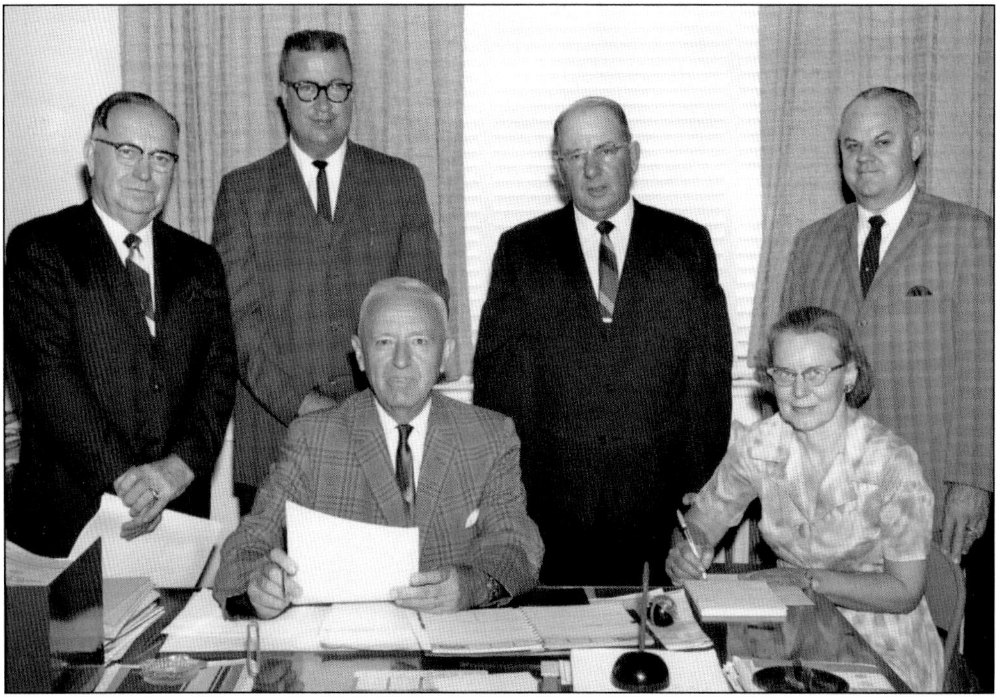

Campbellsville College's fund-raising team included Dr. Otis C. Amis, Dr. D. L. Druien, Col. ? Halsell, David McLellan, Kenton Cooper, and Mrs. ? Phillips.

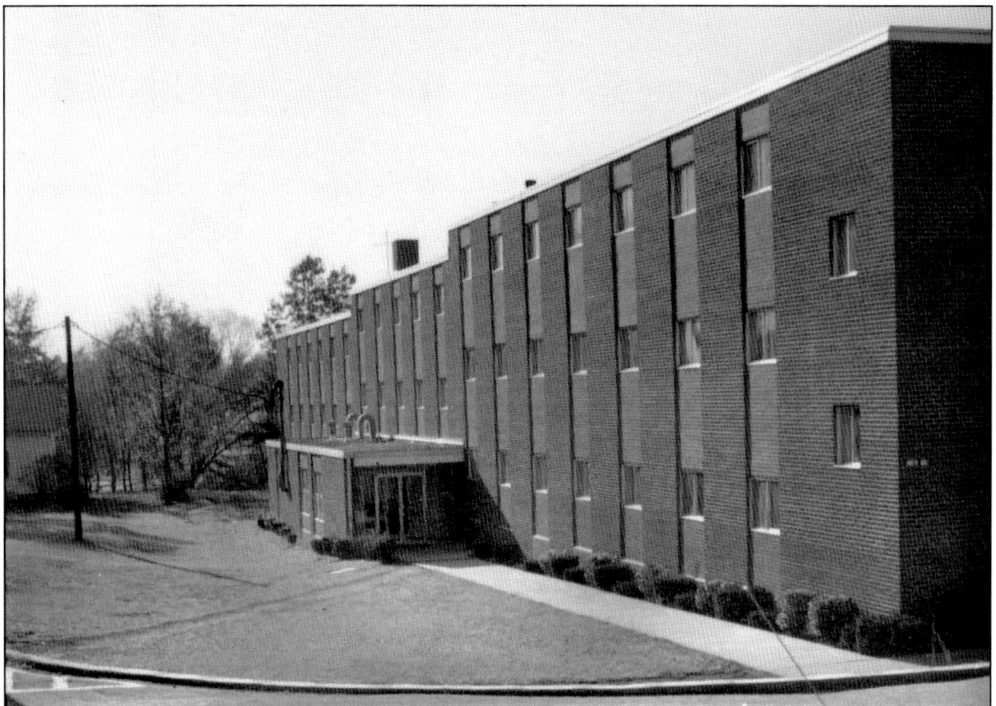

South Hall, a dormitory for men, was dedicated on April 7, 1967. One of the speakers at the ceremony was Alfred Tandy, whose company constructed the building.

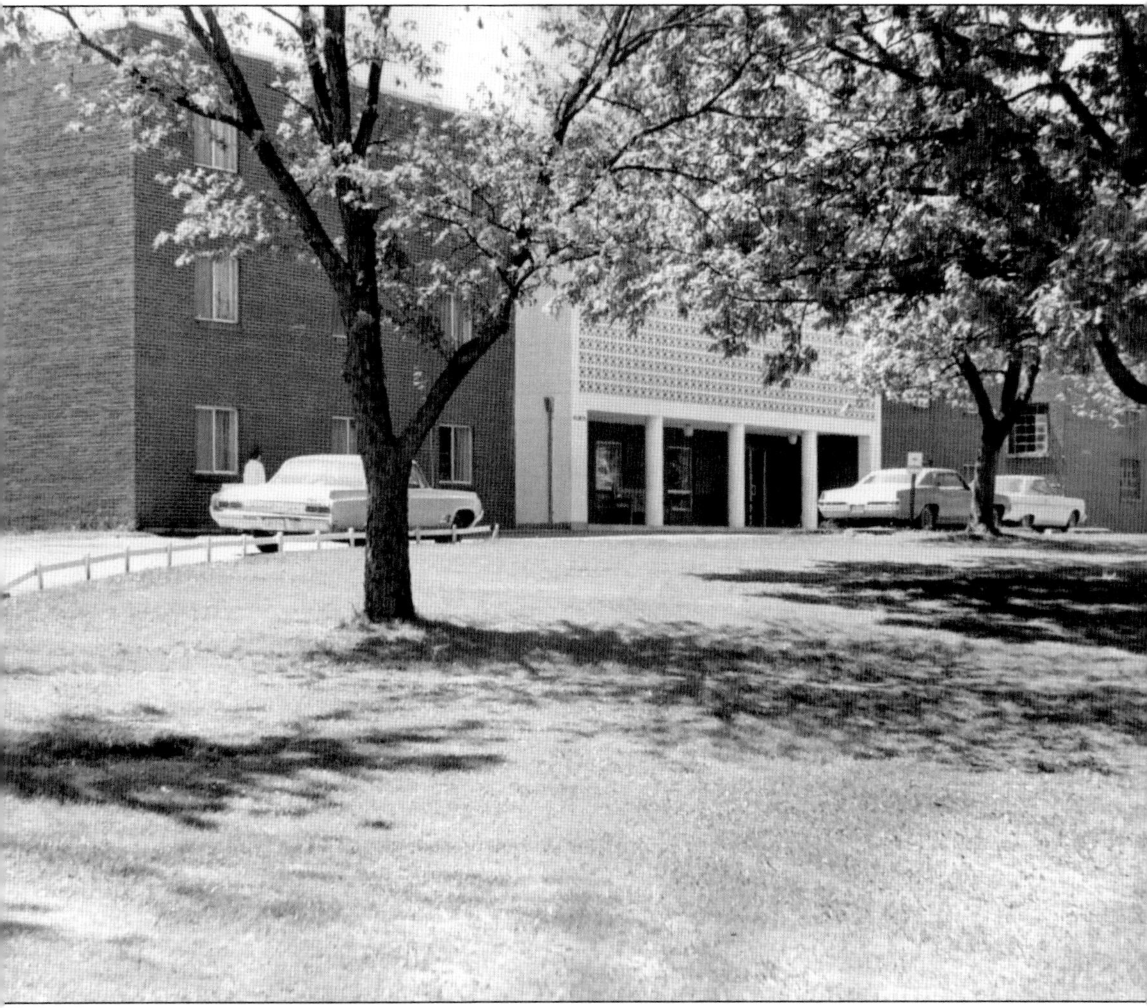

Since the original J. S. Stapp Hall could not be easily brought up to the 1966 fire-code standards mandated by the Commonwealth of Kentucky, the decision was made to completely raze the building. Thanks to the quick action of Pres. John M. Carter and the board of trustees, a new girls' dormitory bearing the J. S. Stapp Hall name was constructed in time for use during the fall 1967 semester.

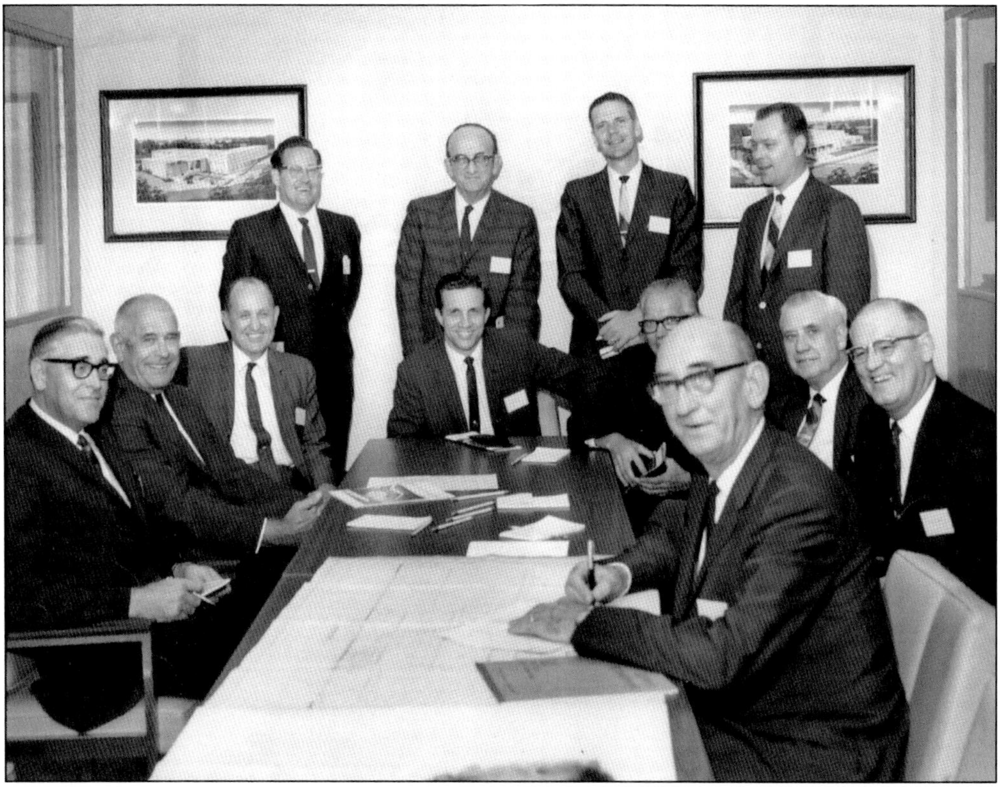

Julius Kemper Powell (right foreground), acting president, and 10 trustees traveled to Tulsa, Oklahoma, to sign a contract on August 14, 1967, with Tandy Industries to construct additional buildings on campus. Despite all of the initial smiles, the relationship with Tandy Industries soon soured. In 1969, Tandy Industries filed suit against Campbellsville College. The case was eventually settled amicably. Powell officially served as president of Campbellsville College from 1968 to 1969.

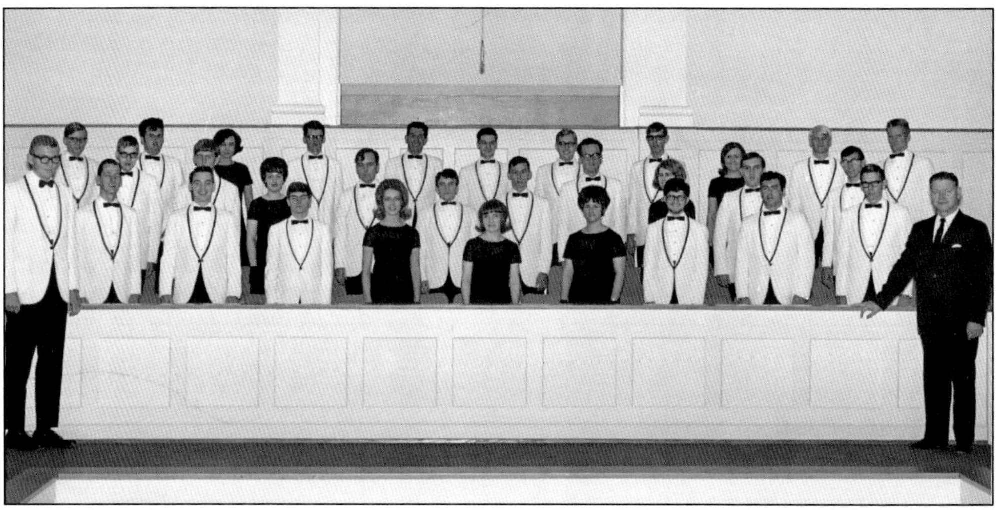

The Campbellaires Glee Club regularly performed in schools and churches around the region. Each spring, they undertook a tour of out-of-state venues.

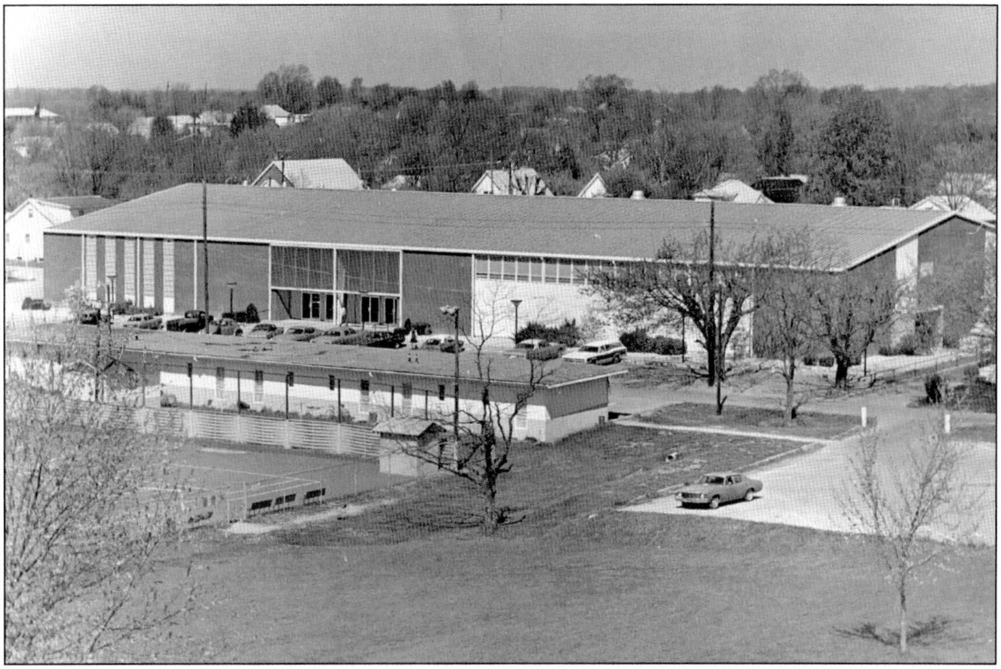

The J. K. Powell Athletic Center opened for use in 1969. The building located between the J. K. Powell Athletic Center and the tennis courts contained efficiency apartments that served as married-student housing.

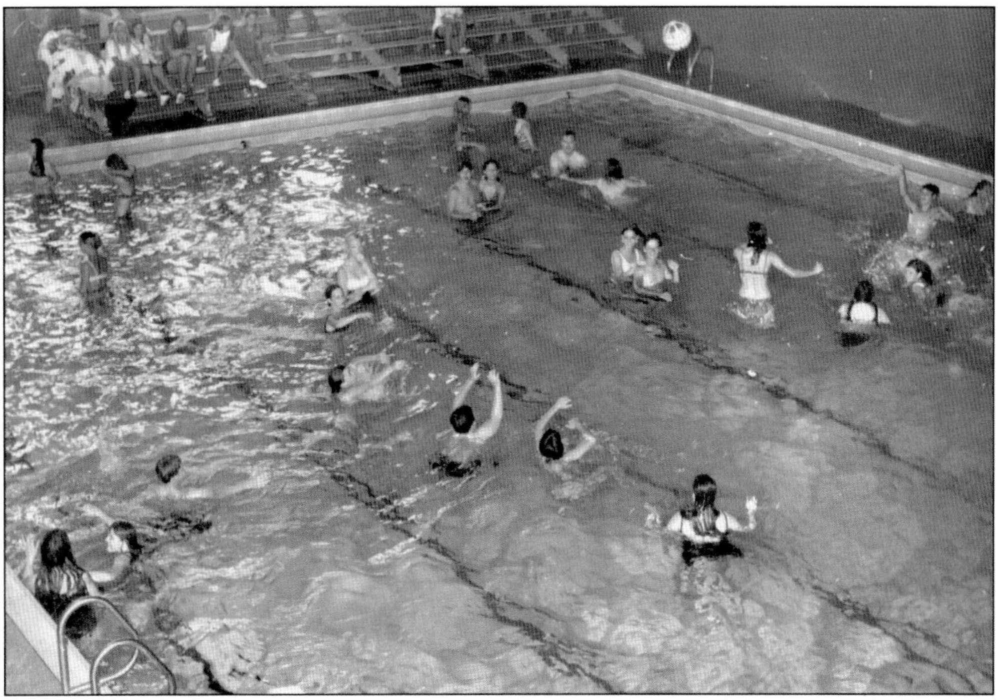

Members of the campus community are seen frolicking in the pool, which is located within the J. K. Powell Athletic Center. It served as the home of the Campbellsville College Tiger Sharks swimming and diving team.

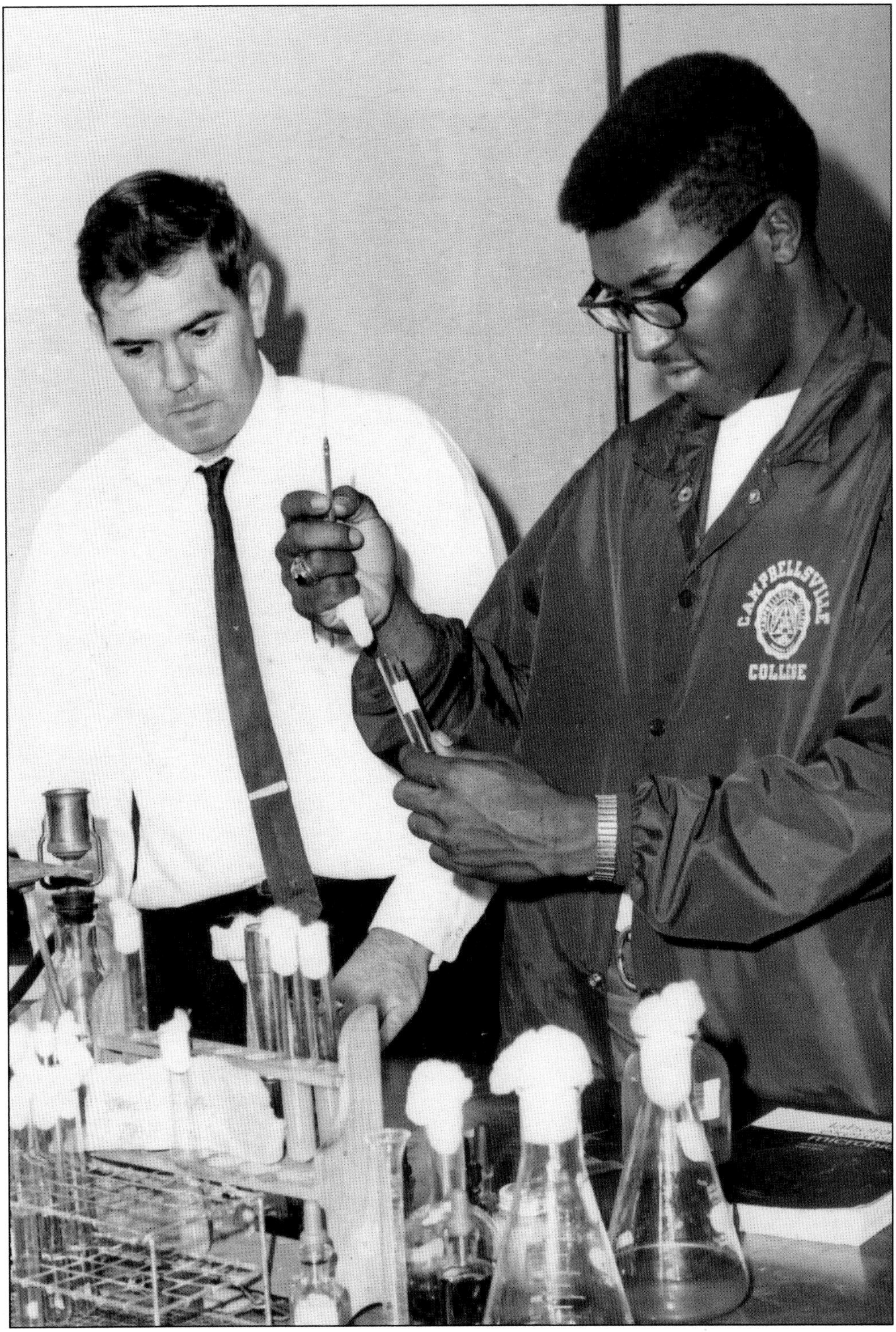

Dr. James A. Wolfe supervises a student conducting an experiment in his microbiology class. (Photograph by Don Elmore.)

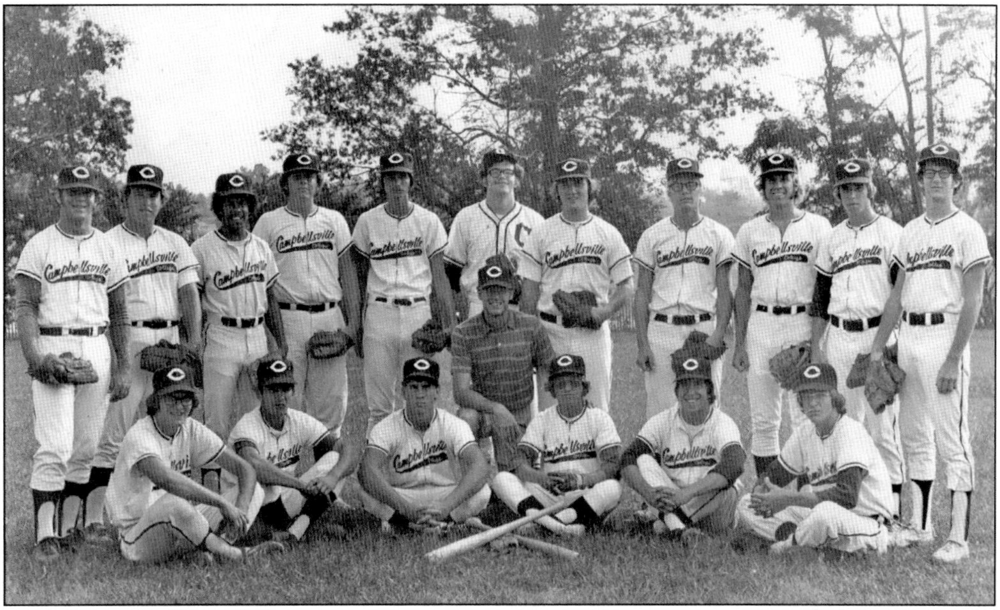

Pictured are the members of the 1972–1973 baseball team. Their uniforms are reminiscent of those worn by the Cincinnati Reds' Big Red Machine during the same time period.

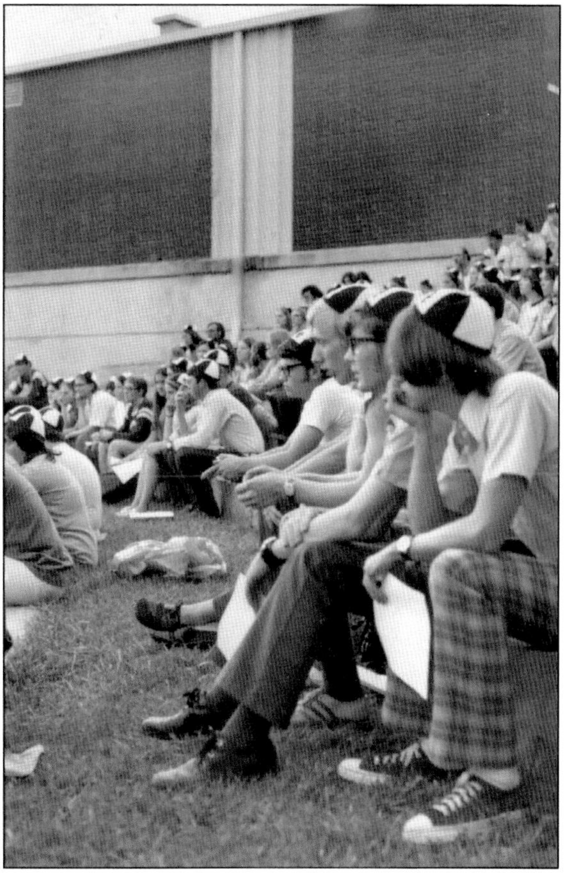

These freshmen are listening intently to an orientation session in the amphitheater. The sessions were designed to acquaint them to campus life. They are also making quite a fashion statement with their stylish freshmen beanies.

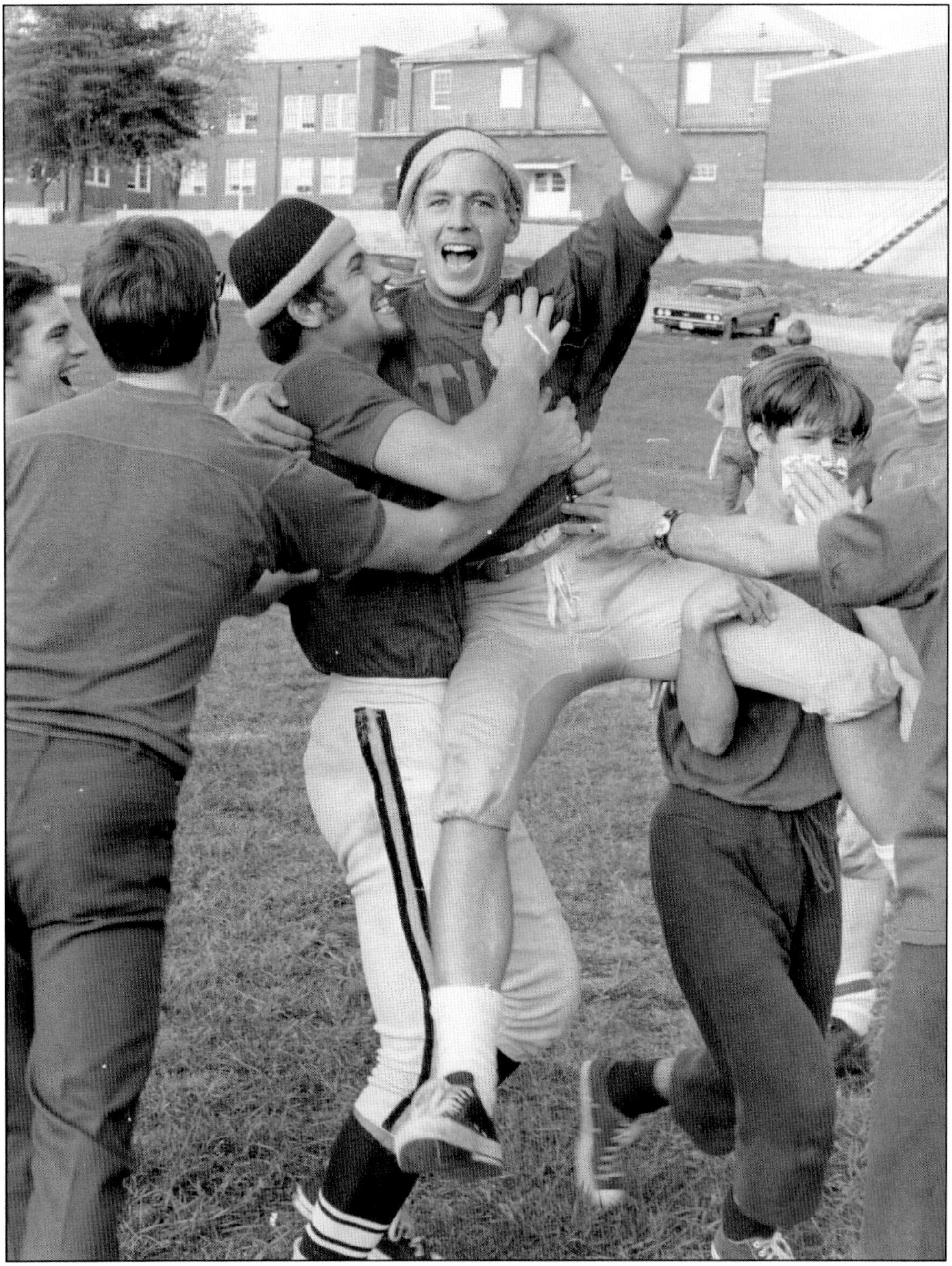

An intramural football team celebrates a victory on the gridiron. The present-day intramural program offers football, basketball, tennis, softball, dodgeball, soccer, and bowling as league sports. There are also assorted one-night intramural activities, such as a foosball tournament, that are offered during the course of the year. All intramural champions win what is purported to be the most coveted T-shirt on campus.

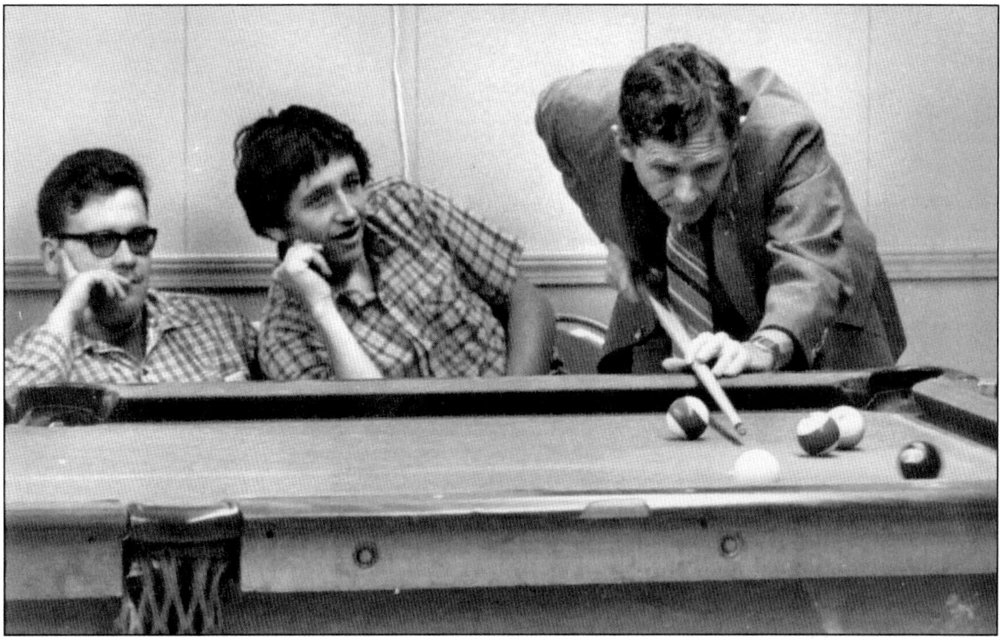

Pres. William Randolph "Randy" Davenport (right) enjoys a game of pool with several students.

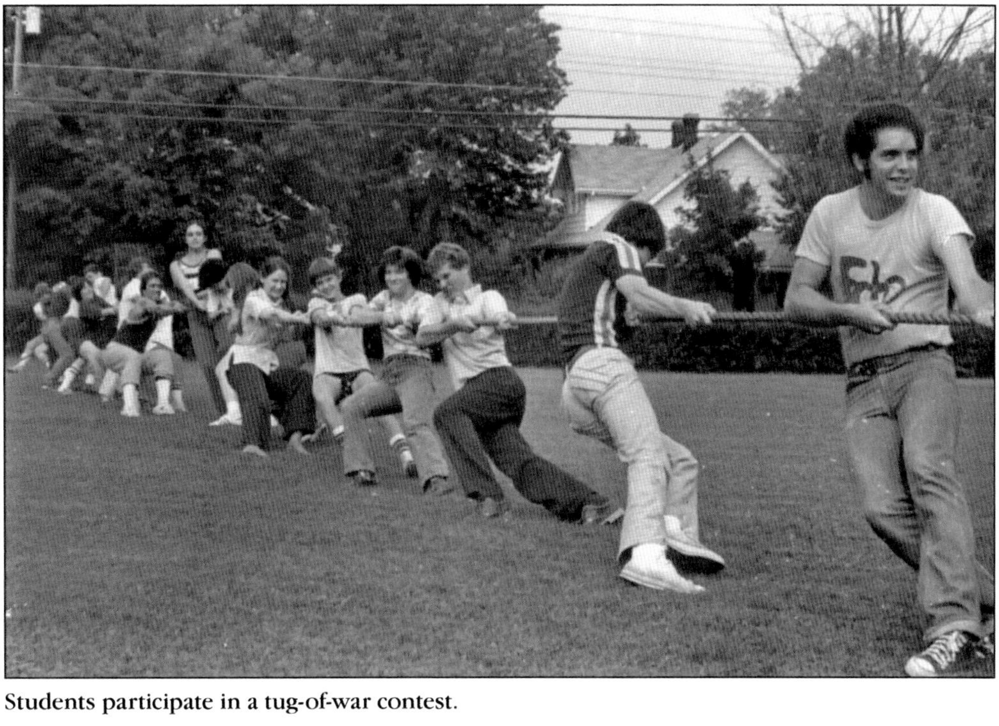

Students participate in a tug-of-war contest.

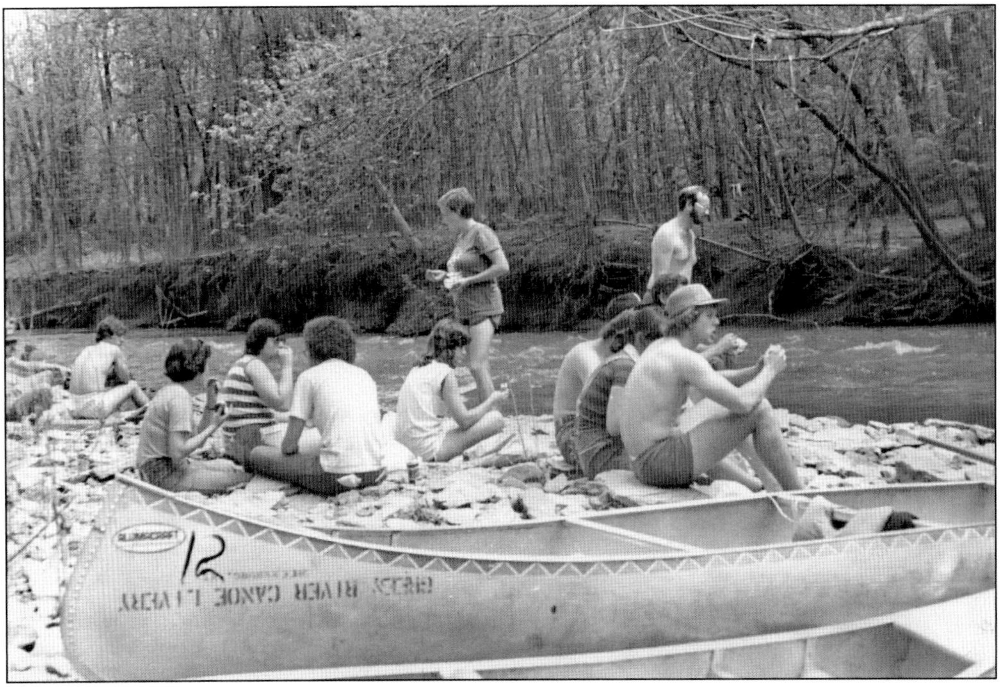

Members of the Baptist Student Union attend a retreat on the Green River in 1979.

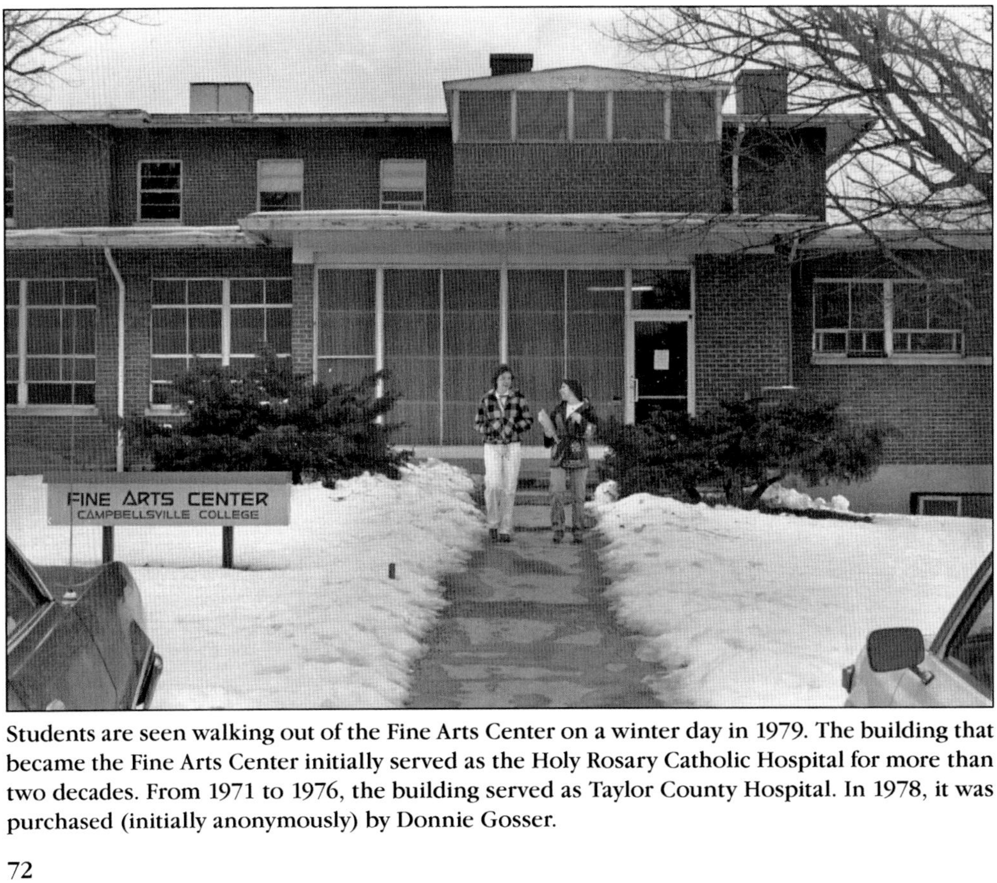

Students are seen walking out of the Fine Arts Center on a winter day in 1979. The building that became the Fine Arts Center initially served as the Holy Rosary Catholic Hospital for more than two decades. From 1971 to 1976, the building served as Taylor County Hospital. In 1978, it was purchased (initially anonymously) by Donnie Gosser.

Coach Ron Coleman stands at right alongside the members of the 1979–1980 golf team, which qualified for the national tournament. The athletes are, in no particular order, Barry Bonifield, Frank Moore, John Gupton, Mike Johns, John Whitaker, and Gary Allen.

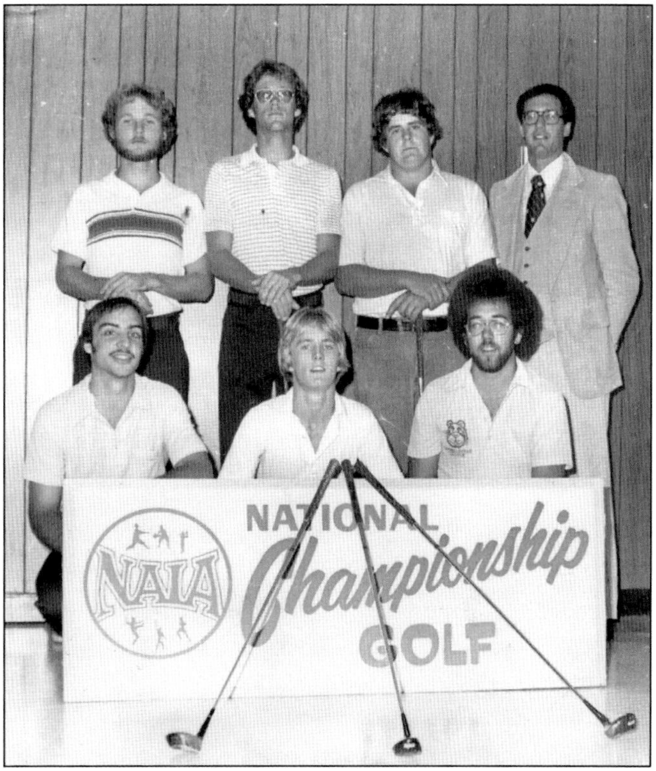

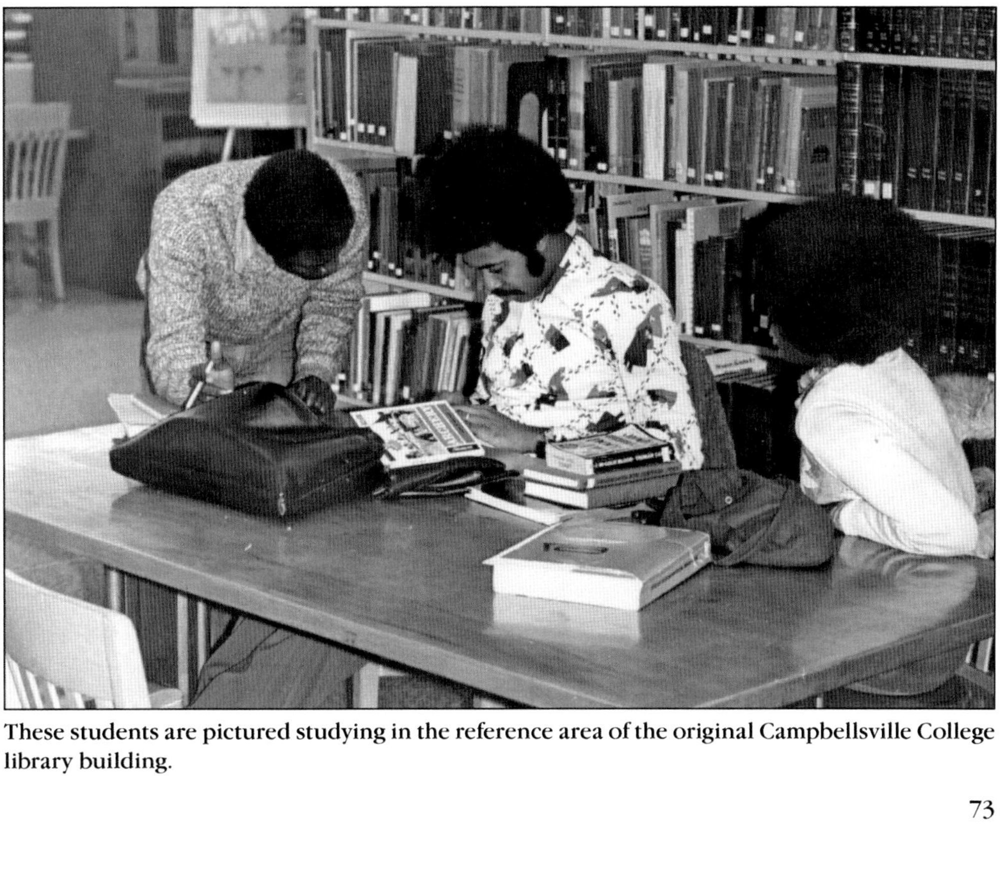

These students are pictured studying in the reference area of the original Campbellsville College library building.

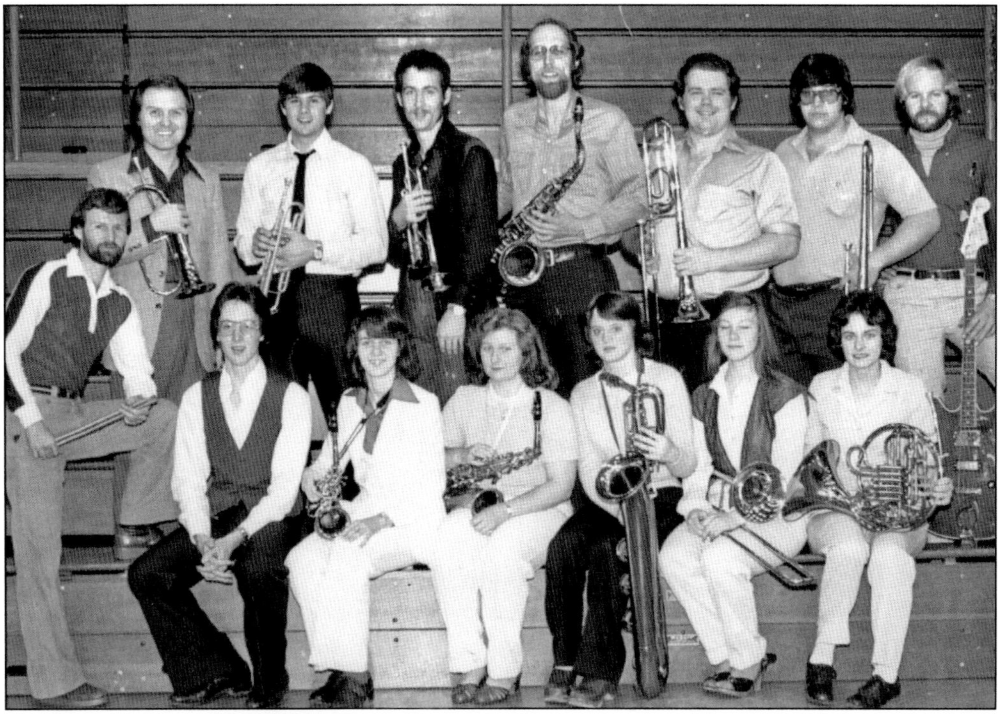

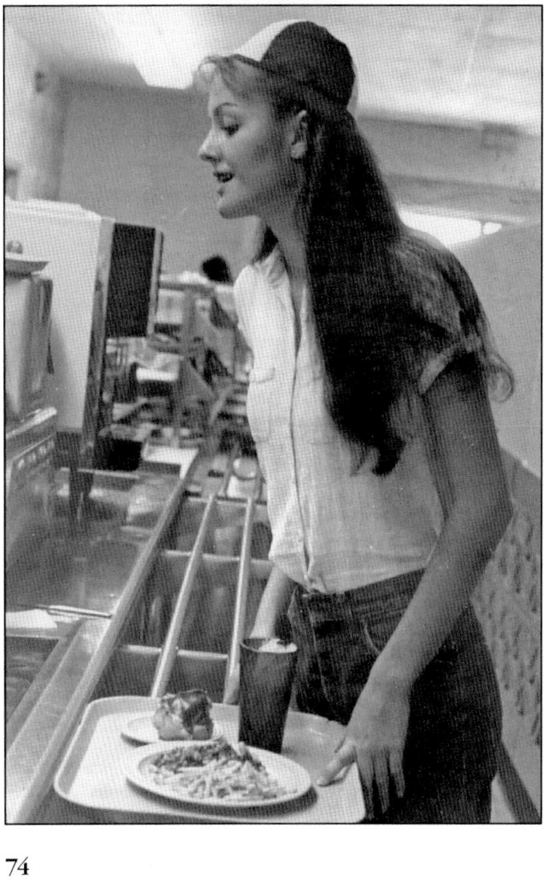

The members of the jazz ensemble in 1981 were Michael Austin, Deborah Walters, Donna Godbey, Mindy Dakin, Ramona Pendley, Diana Walters, Mark Hughes, Dallas Blair, James Hatcher, Don Nichols, Jim Moore, David Martin, Mark Shelton, and Gary Vidito. The jazz band performs each year at convocation, which is always well attended by students, faculty, and staff.

Miss Freshman 1981, Jeanette Jacobs, looks over the offerings at the cafeteria.

Dr. Robert Clark (left) and J. Alvin Hardy break ground on the library addition in 1982. The L-shaped addition was completed in 1984. (Photograph by Khamsing Norady.)

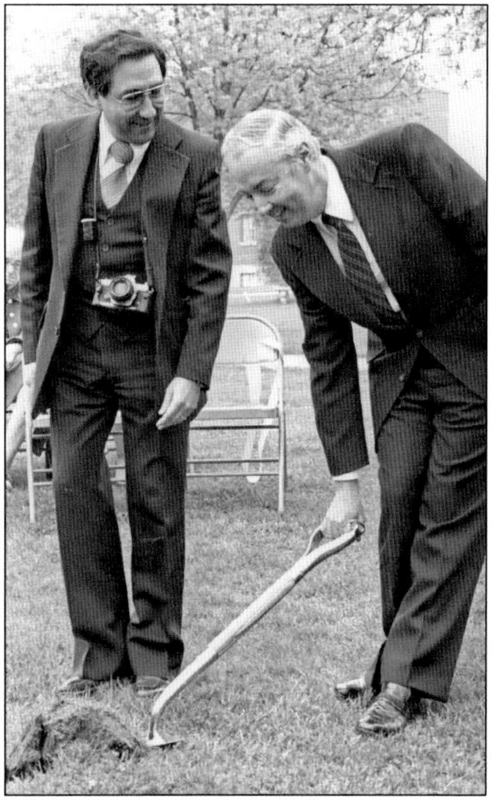

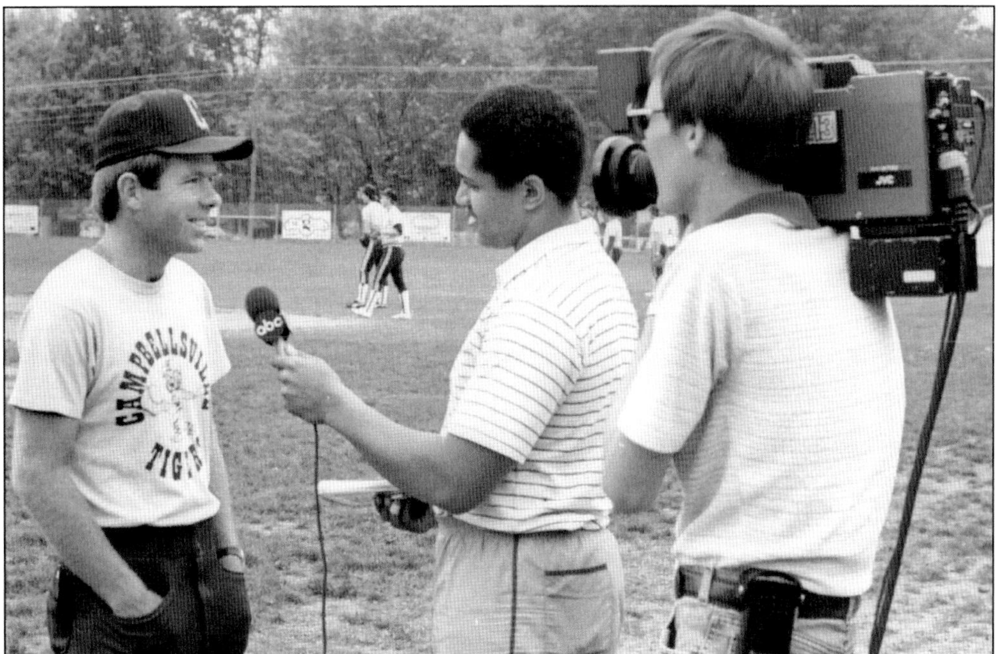

Baseball coach Danny Davis shares his perspective on the baseball team's season with a reporter prior to a game.

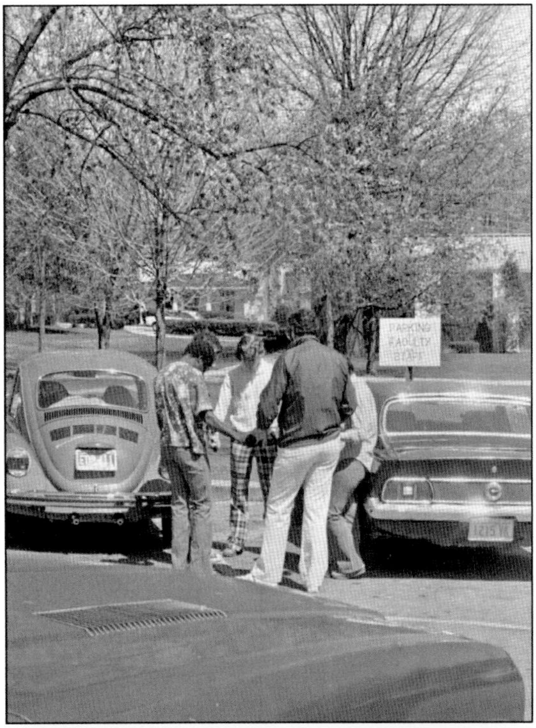

A group of students prays together in the parking lot in front of the library. Present-day faculty and staff might want to note that designated faculty-and-staff parking did exist at one time.

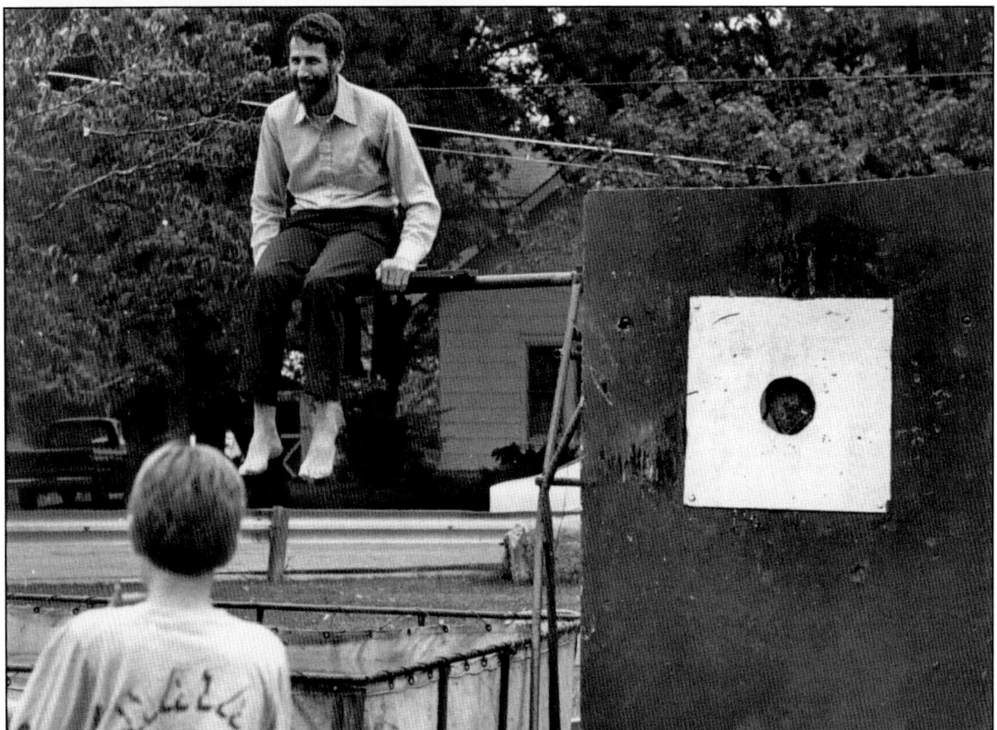

Dr. Robert Doty awaits his fate at the hands of vengeful students while sitting in the dunking booth during the 1984 Fall Festival. (Photograph by Tim Leonard.)

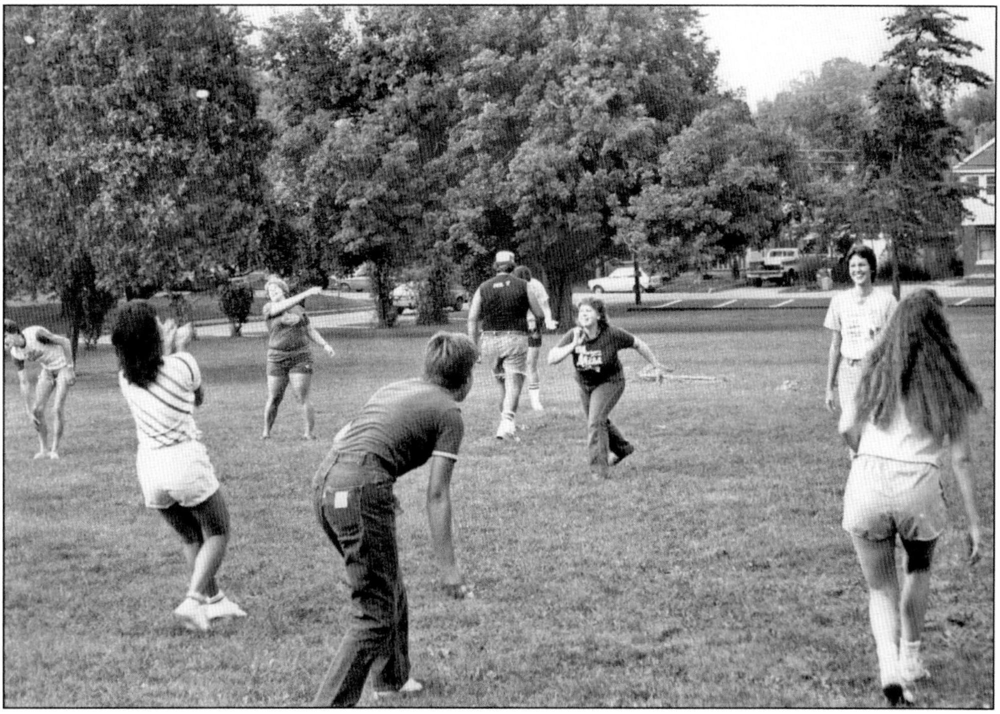

Students happily participate in an egg-toss contest during the 1984 Fall Festival. (Photograph by Tim Leonard.)

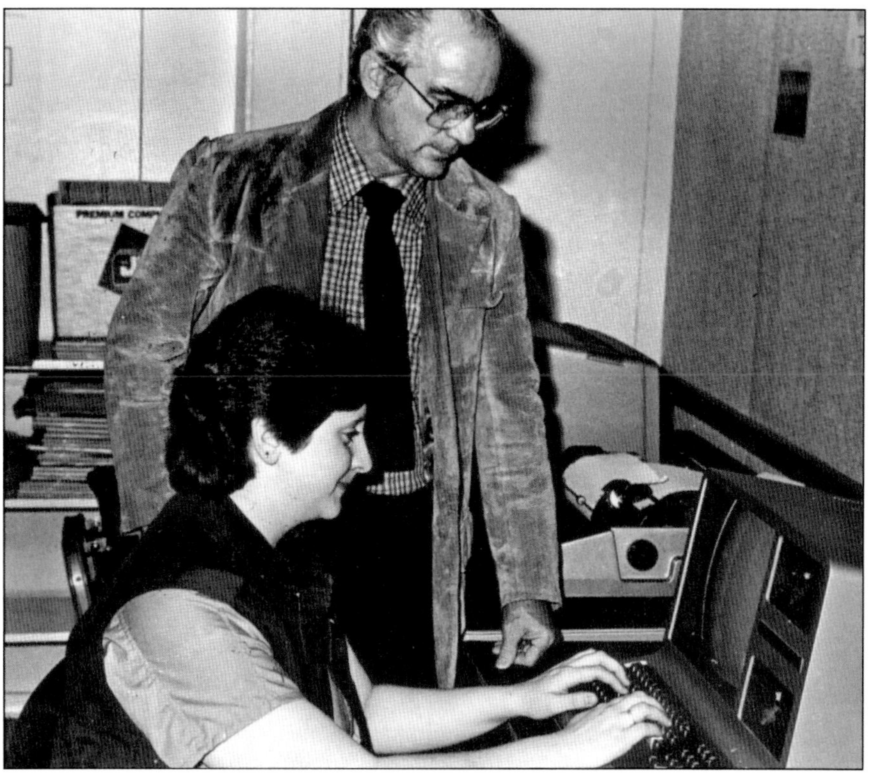

Harlie White helps a student with a computer program.

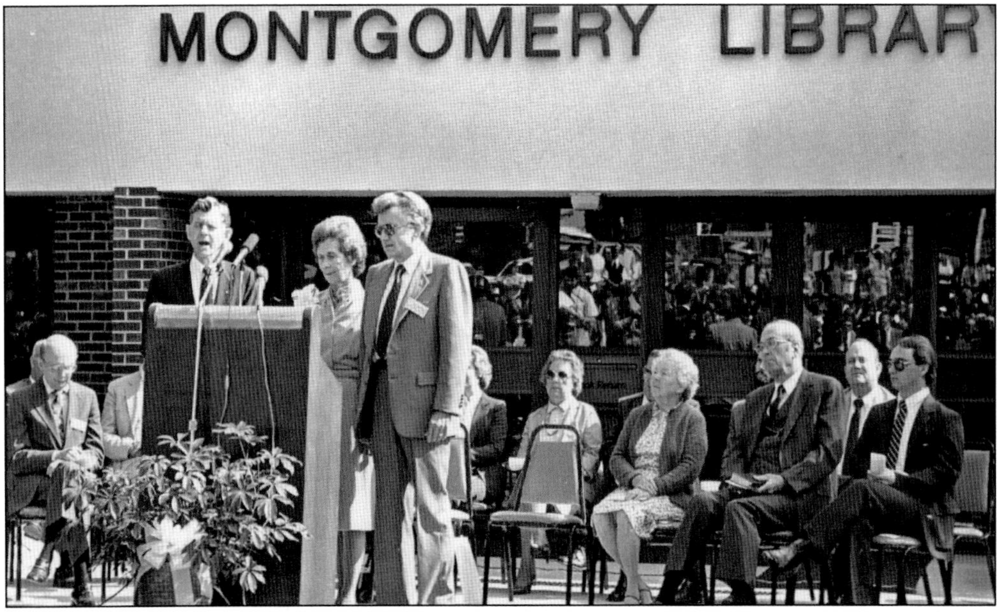

In 1982, Campbellsville College began an expansion of the original library building. After work had begun, it became evident that the cash-strapped institution did not have the money required to complete the project. Edwin and Ovaleta Montgomery stepped forward and donated some land for the institution to sell in order to gain the needed funds. (Photograph by Richard Robards.)

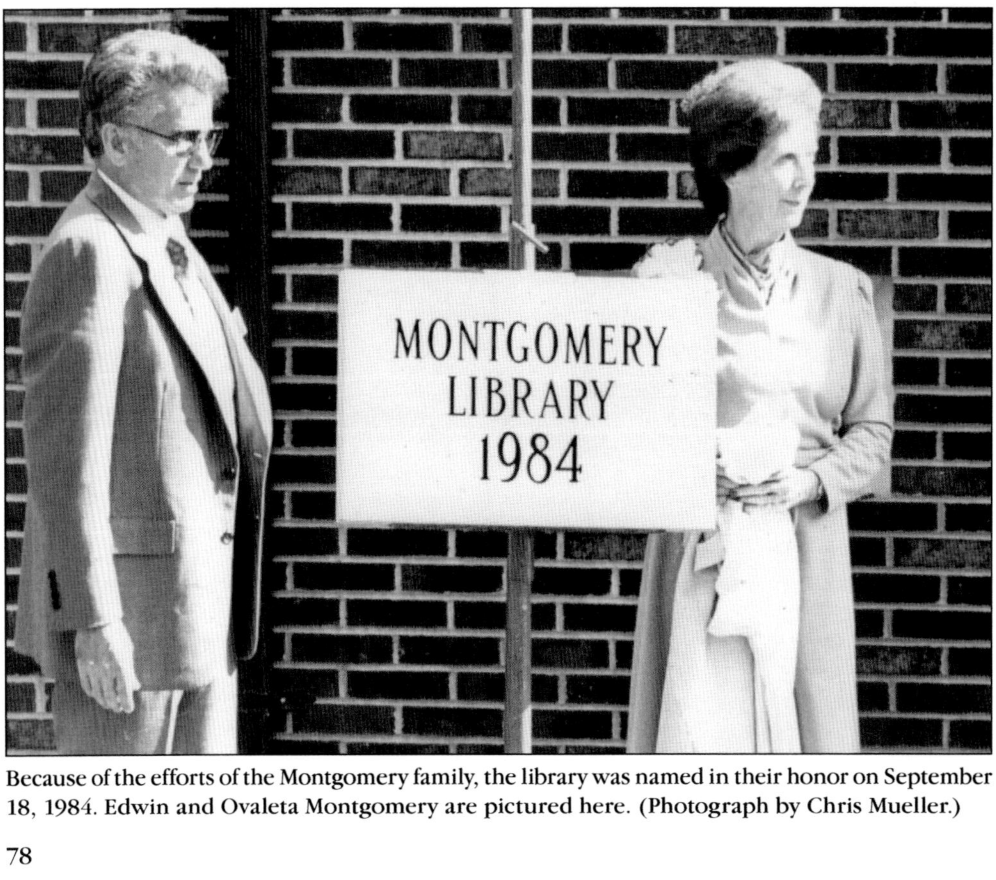

Because of the efforts of the Montgomery family, the library was named in their honor on September 18, 1984. Edwin and Ovaleta Montgomery are pictured here. (Photograph by Chris Mueller.)

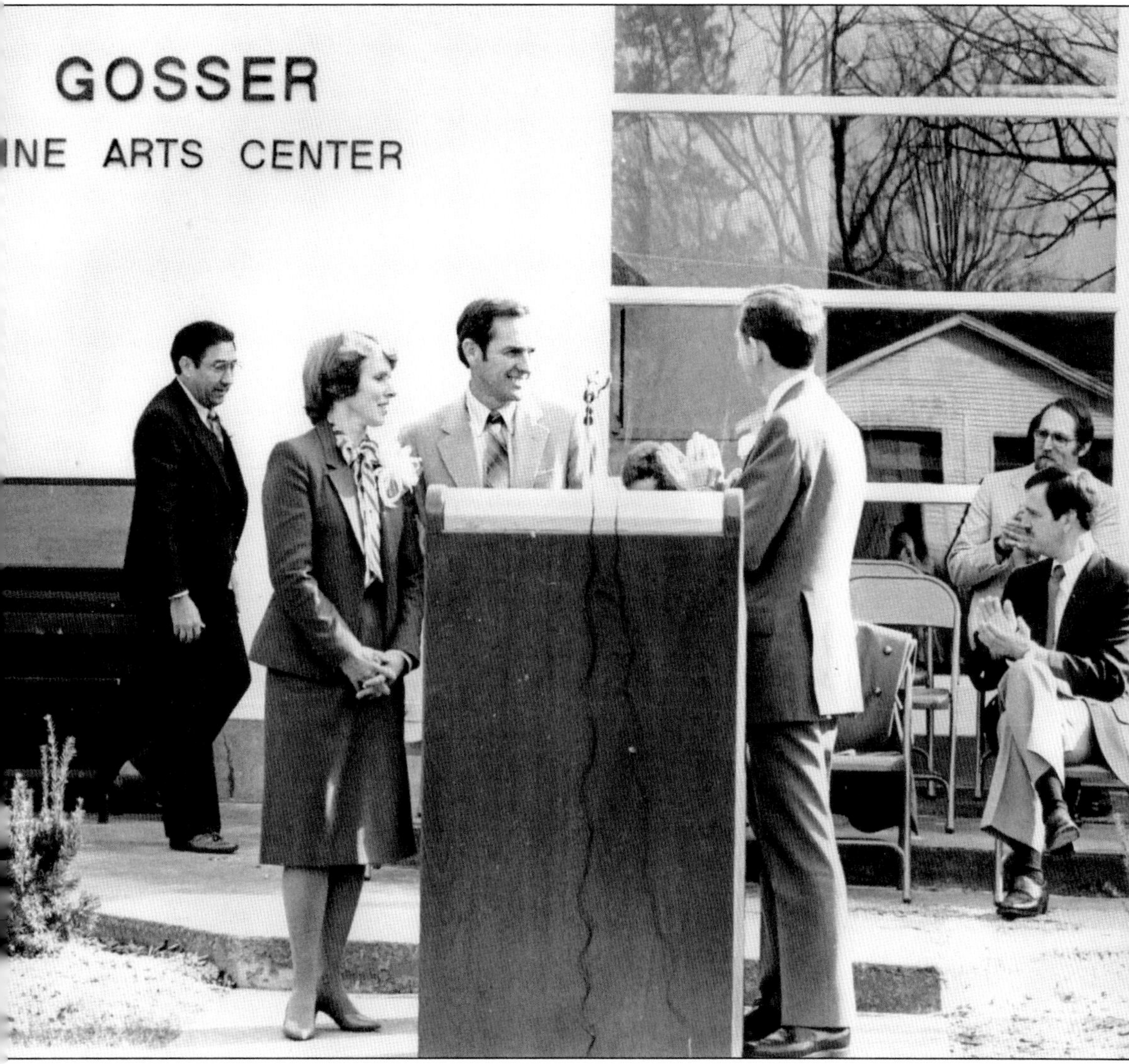

Donnie Gosser and his wife, Anna, donated the Fine Arts Center to Campbellsville College on November 17, 1984. It was subsequently renamed the Gosser Fine Arts Center.

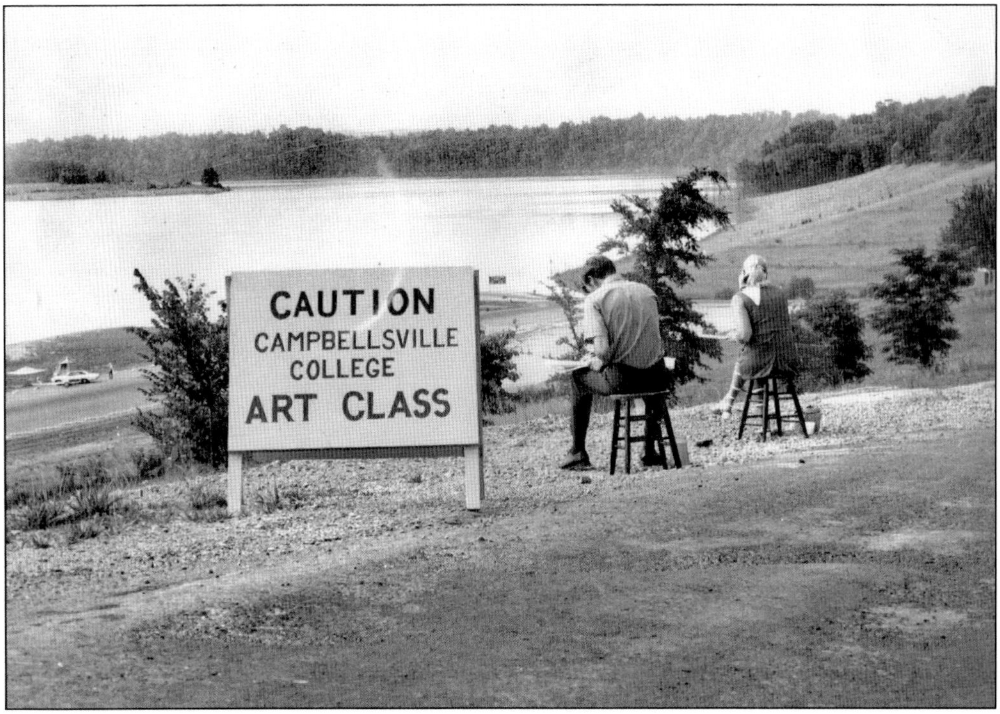

Campbellsville College students are pictured drawing at Green River Lake. (Photograph by Don Elmore.)

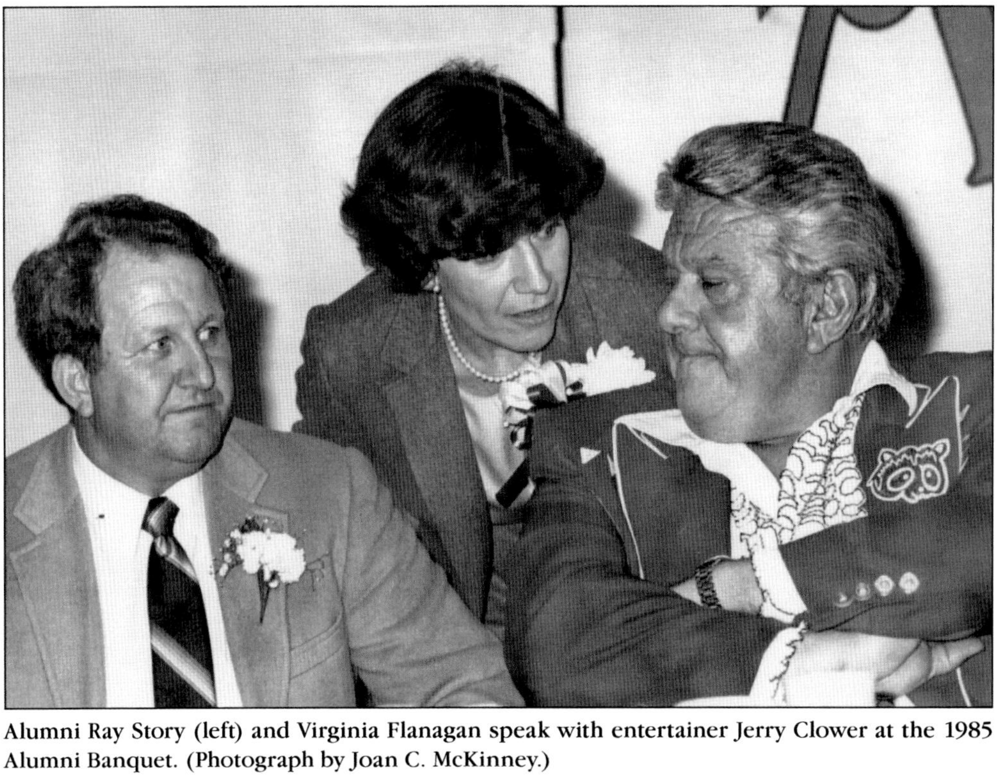

Alumni Ray Story (left) and Virginia Flanagan speak with entertainer Jerry Clower at the 1985 Alumni Banquet. (Photograph by Joan C. McKinney.)

Here is definitive proof that everyone had way too much fun at the 1985 homecoming celebration. (Photograph by Chris Mueller.)

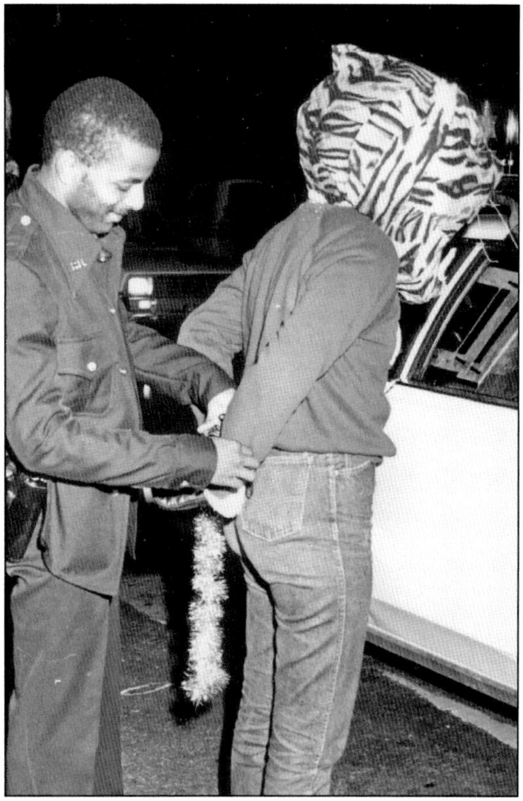

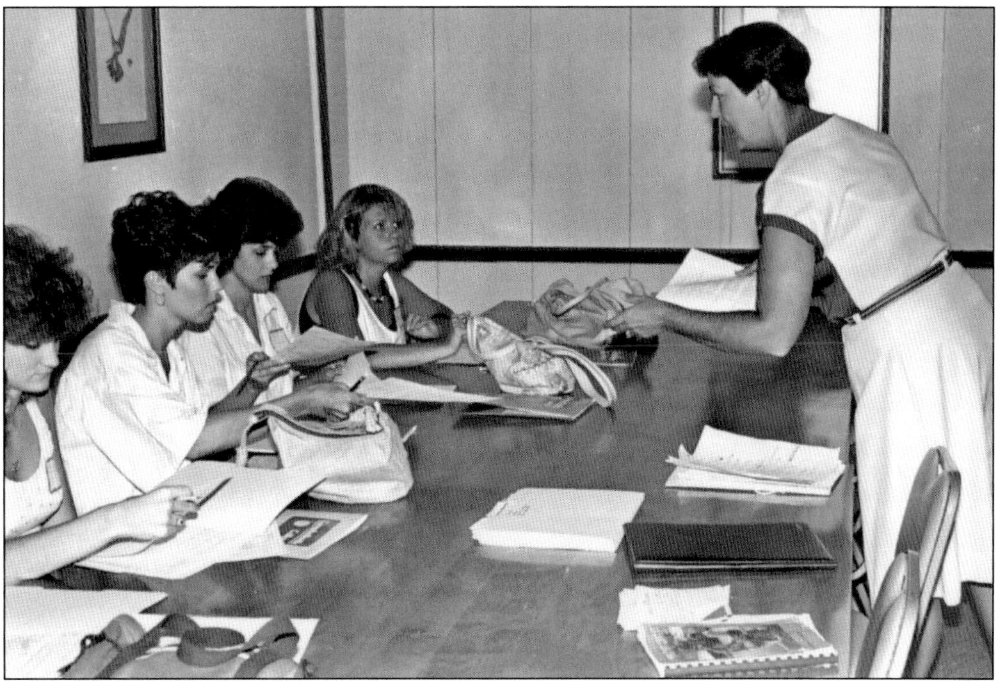

Pat Cowherd presents an orientation session attended by, from left to right, Penny Graham, Michelle Lee Bagby, Laura Thompson, and Lynn Canada. (Photograph by Joan McKinney.)

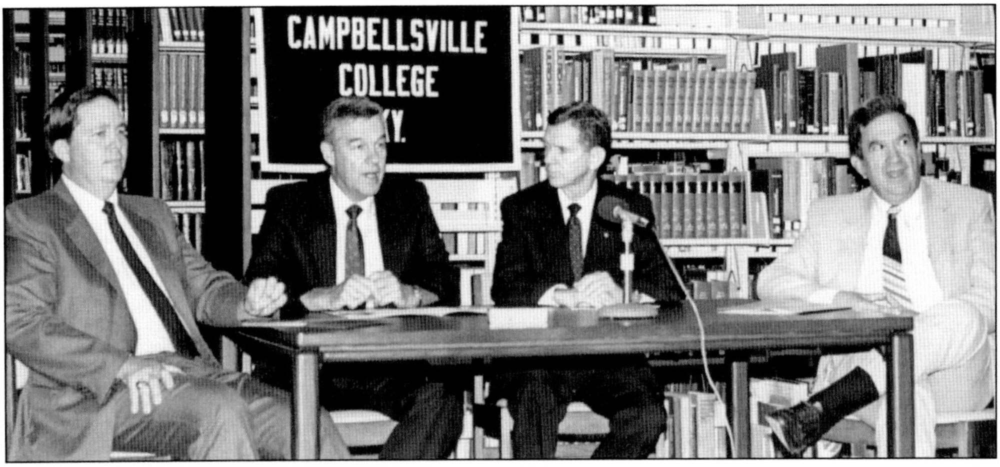

On April 24, 1987, Pres. William Randolph "Randy" Davenport announced that Campbellsville College would field its first football team since the 1930s in the fall of 1987. Pictured from left to right are David Fryrear, athletic director Don Bishop, President Davenport, and coach Ron Finley.

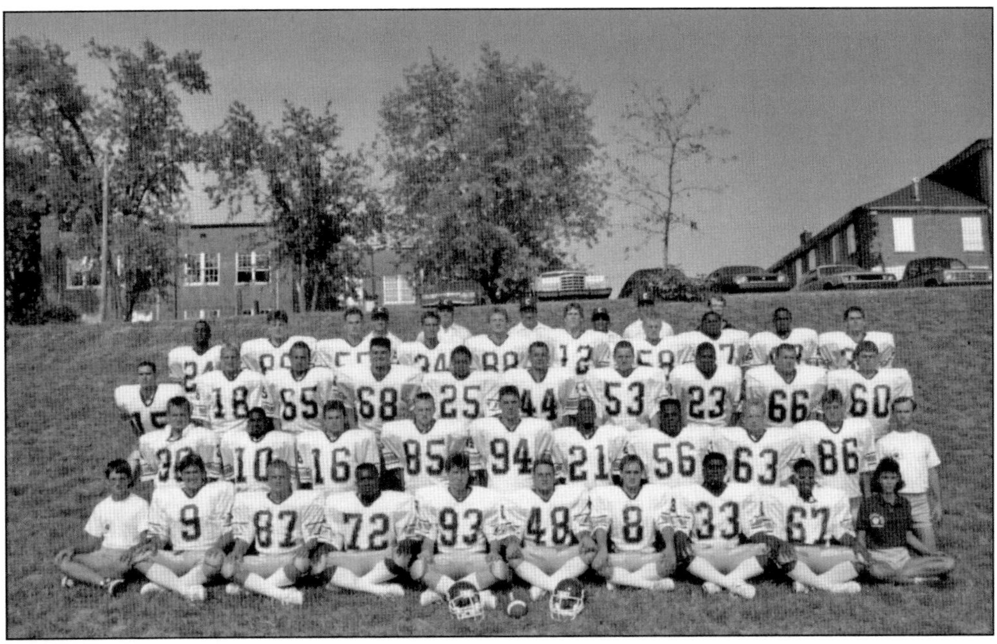

The 1987 Tiger football team played a six-game junior varsity schedule, which included a 30-20 victory over Cumberland College. Campbellsville College played its first varsity season during the 1988–1989 academic year.

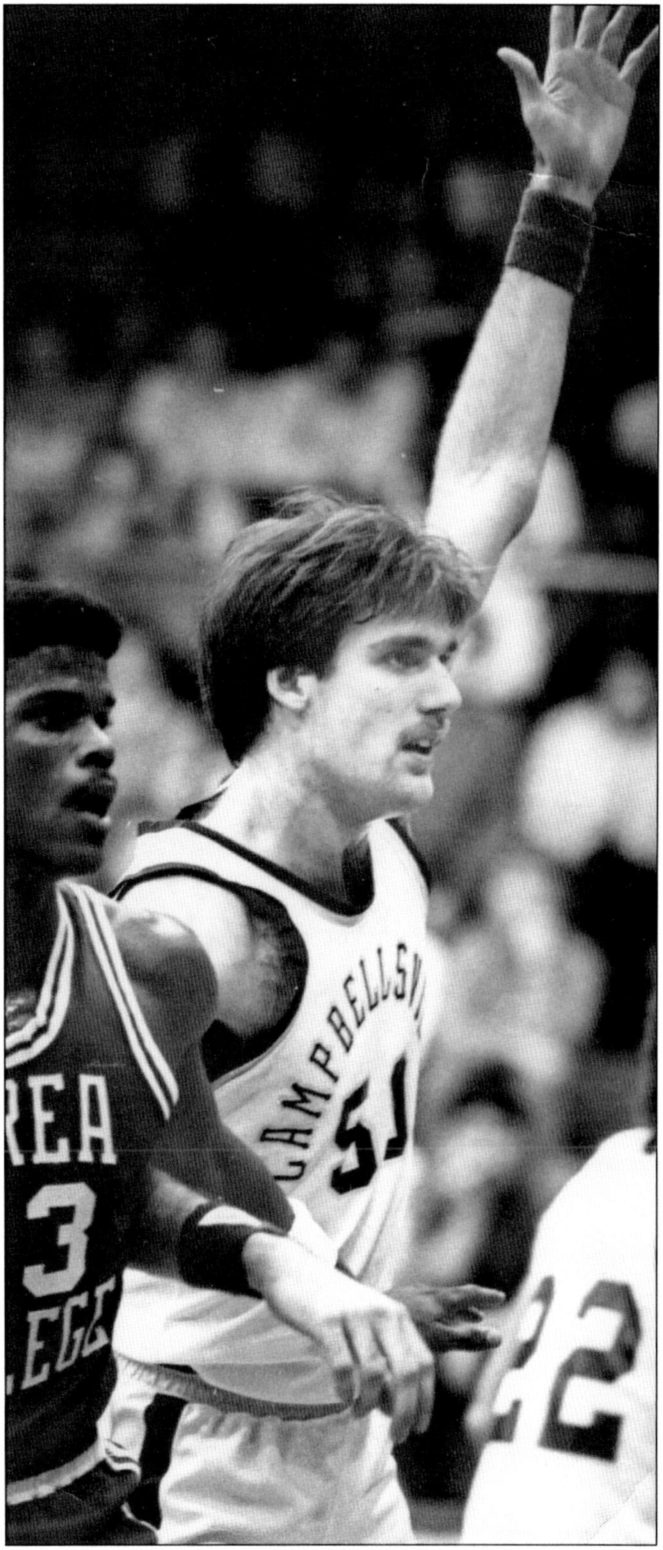

Campbellsville Tiger
Allen Bell posts up Berea
College's Willie Hill.

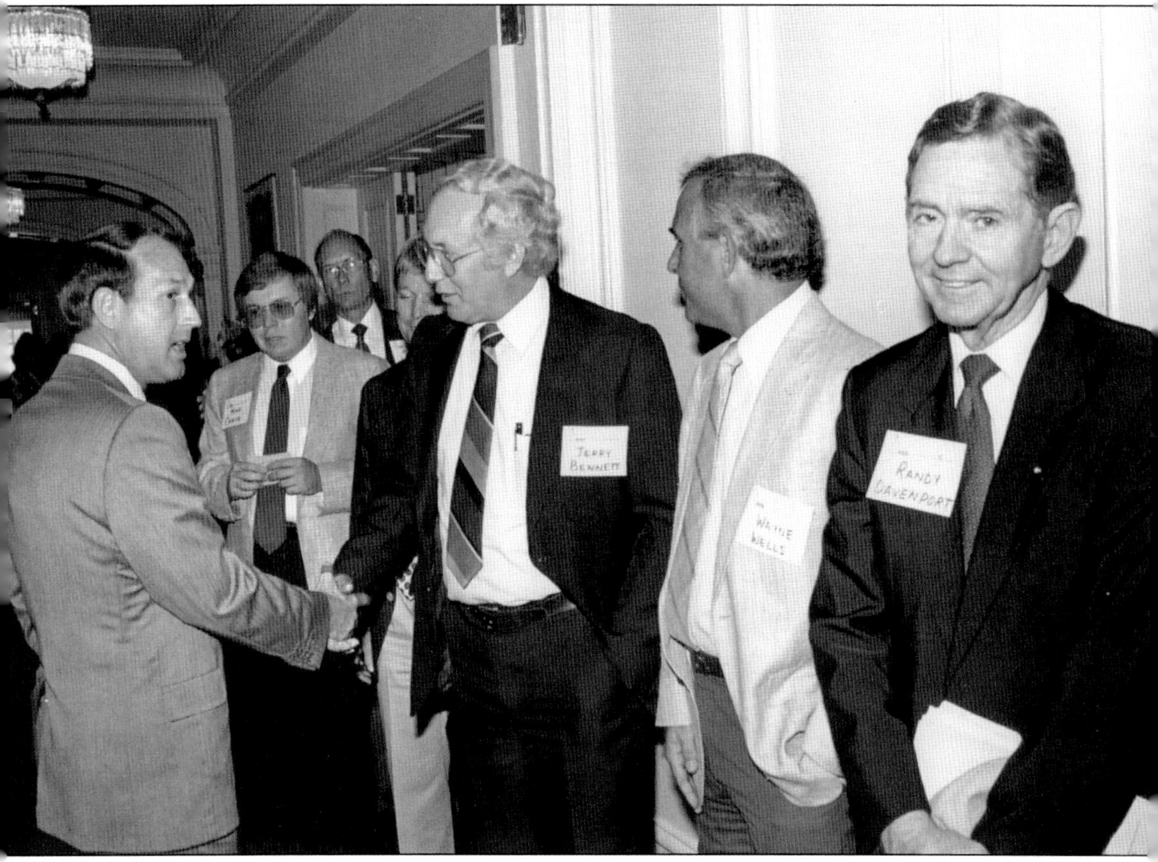

Gov. Wallace Wilkinson (left) shakes hands with Dr. Jerry Bennett at the June 1988 planning luncheon for a proposed alumni-giving campaign. Governor Wilkinson, a Campbellsville College alumnus, served as governor of the Commonwealth of Kentucky from 1987 to 1991. (Photograph by Steve Mitchell.)

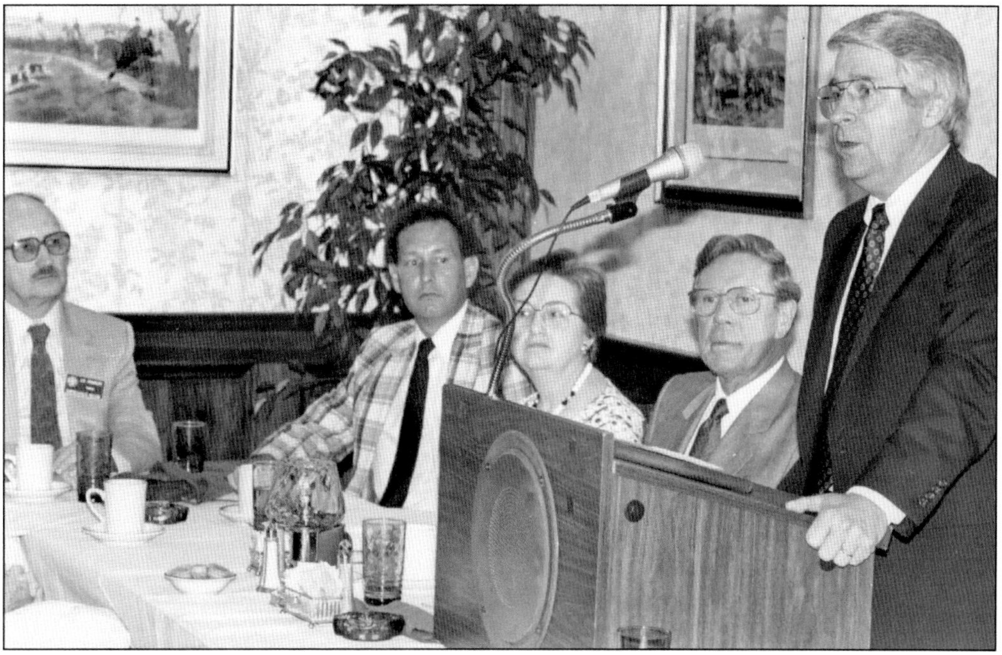

From left to right, unidentified, Dr. Franklin Cheatham, Dr. Marilyn Sanders, and Dr. George Ransdell listen to Dr. Kenneth Winters speak after he is introduced as Campbellsville College's ninth president.

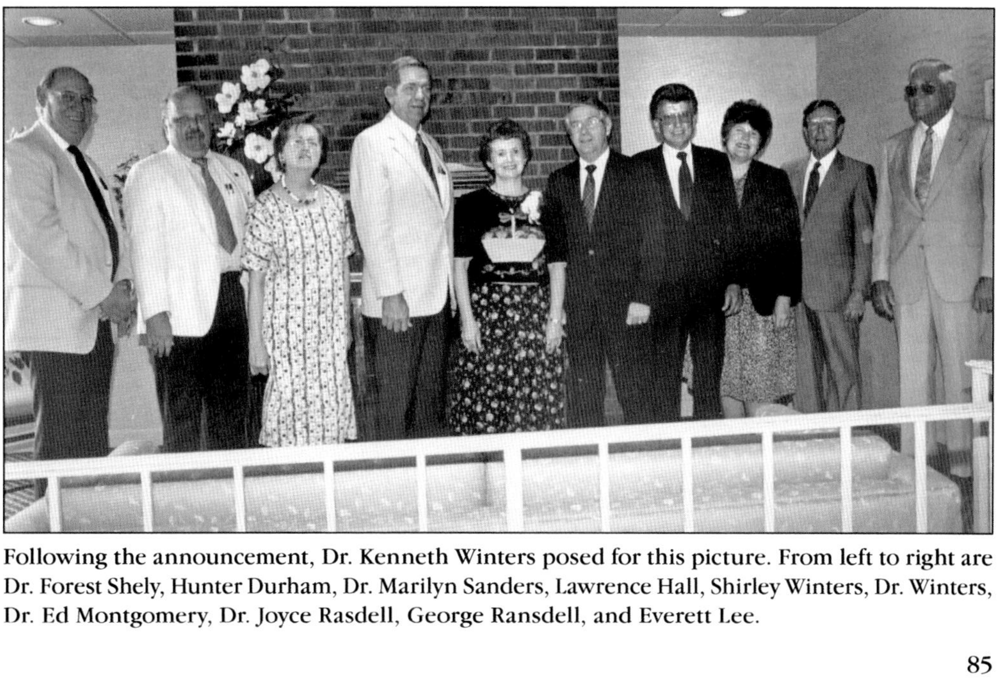

Following the announcement, Dr. Kenneth Winters posed for this picture. From left to right are Dr. Forest Shely, Hunter Durham, Dr. Marilyn Sanders, Lawrence Hall, Shirley Winters, Dr. Winters, Dr. Ed Montgomery, Dr. Joyce Rasdell, George Ransdell, and Everett Lee.

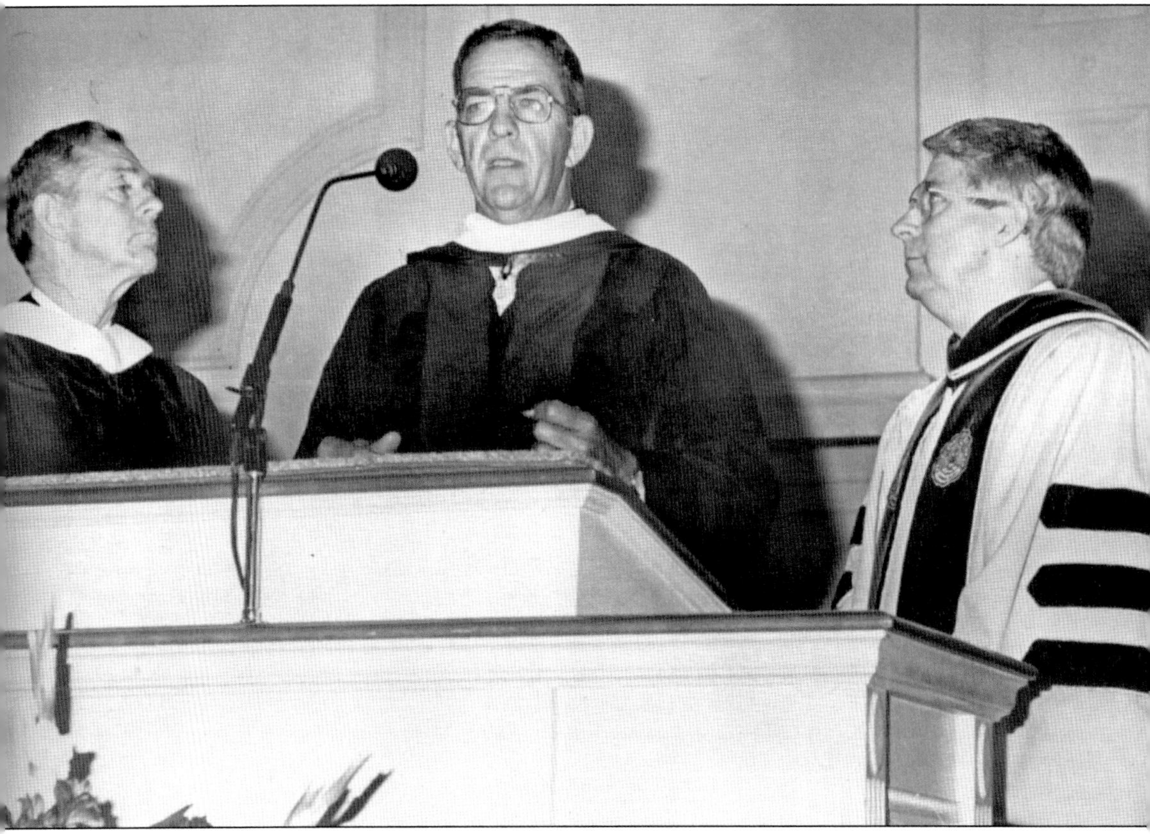

Lawrence Hall speaks during Dr. Kenneth Winters's inauguration as president of Campbellsville College. The installation of a new president is one of the landmark events in the history of every academic institution. Dr. Winters's predecessor, Dr. Randy Davenport, is at left.

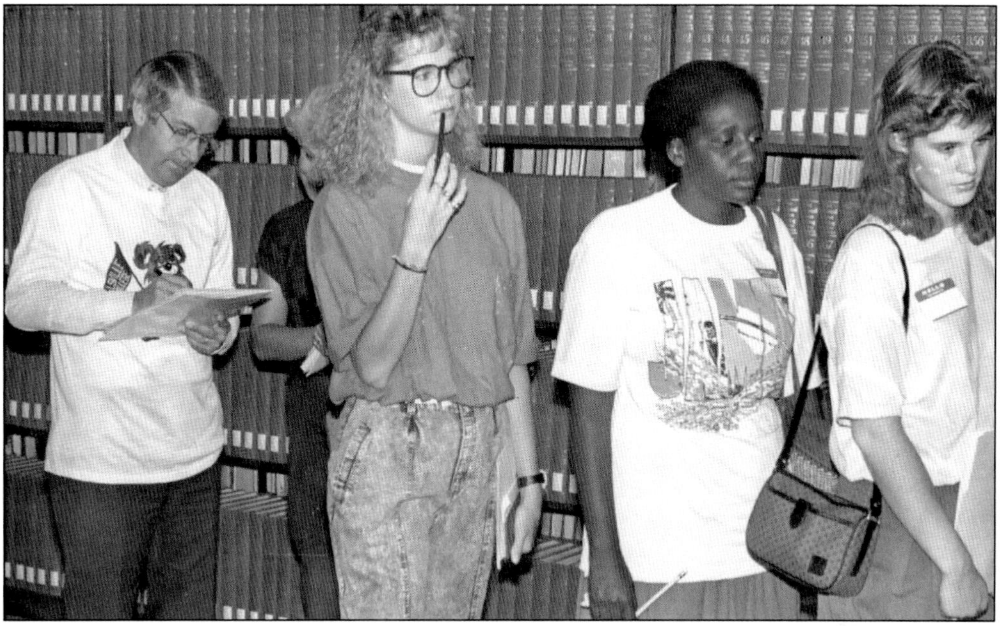

Since the school had a tradition for a while where a student got the opportunity to be president for a day, Dr. Kenneth Winters had the opportunity to be a student for a day. Here he waits in the back of the line to register for classes.

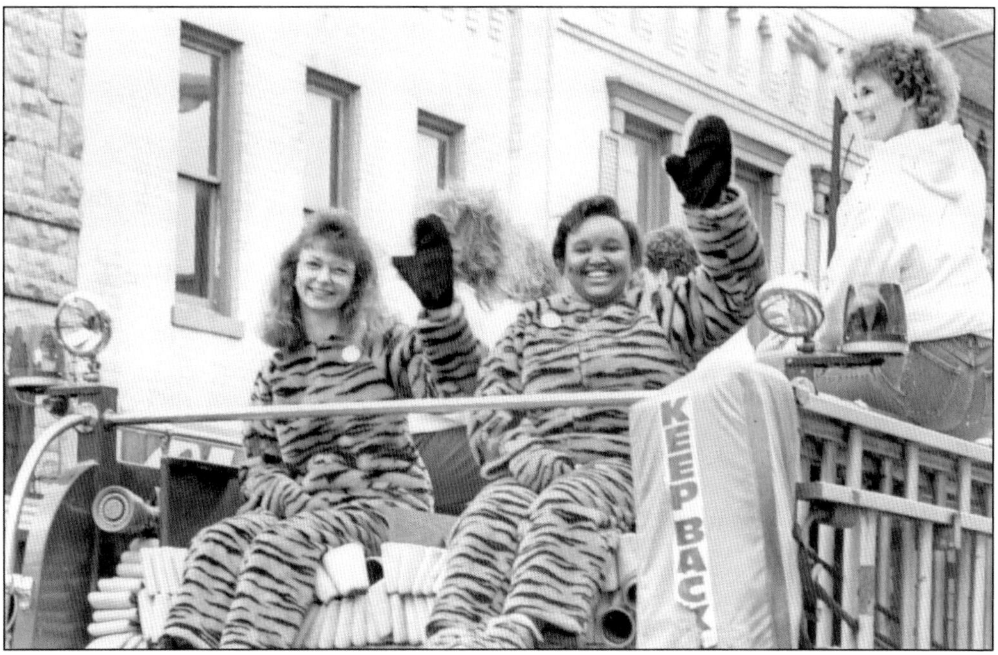

Melissa Sprowls (left) and Stacy Terry wave to the crowd from atop a fire truck during the 1988 Homecoming Parade. The parade is one of the highlights of the annual homecoming celebration. (Photograph by Ayo Olanyian.)

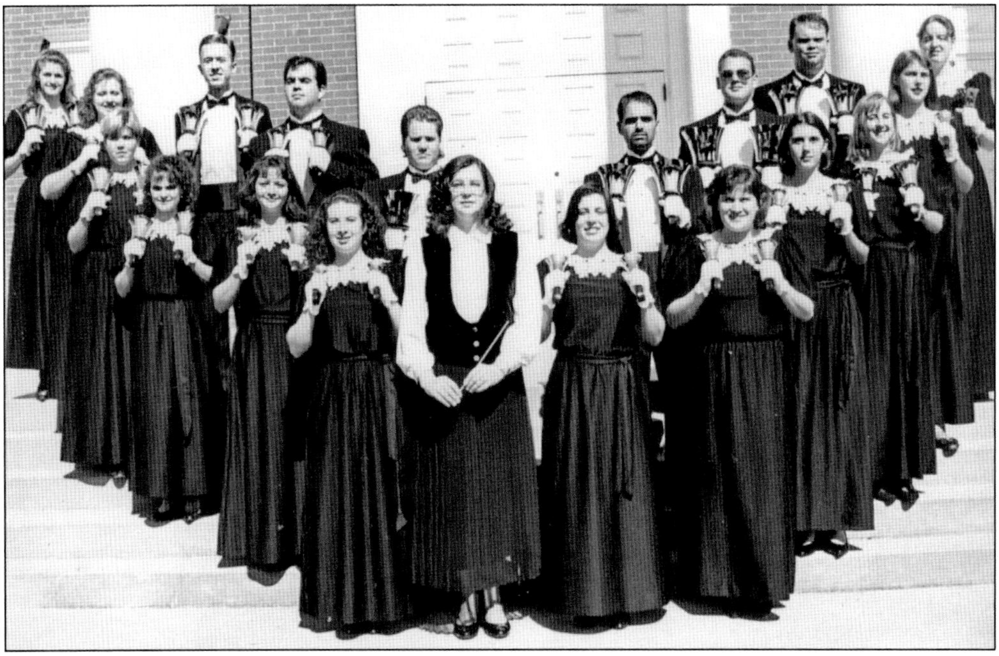

With the establishment of a handbell choir in 1979, Campbellsville College became one of the few institutions in the country to have such a unique musical organization within its School of Music. The choir has been under the direction of Nevalyn Moore (center) since 1981.

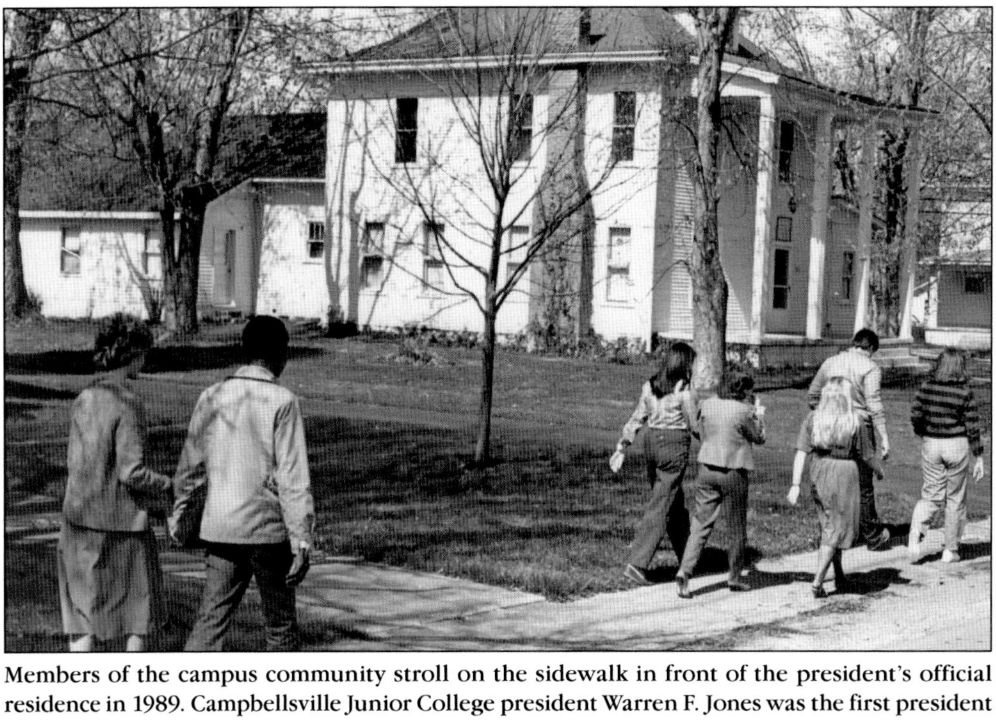

Members of the campus community stroll on the sidewalk in front of the president's official residence in 1989. Campbellsville Junior College president Warren F. Jones was the first president to reside in the building. He began living there in March 1941. The building was razed during the 1990s so that the property could be used for the construction of a new residence for future Campbellsville University presidents.

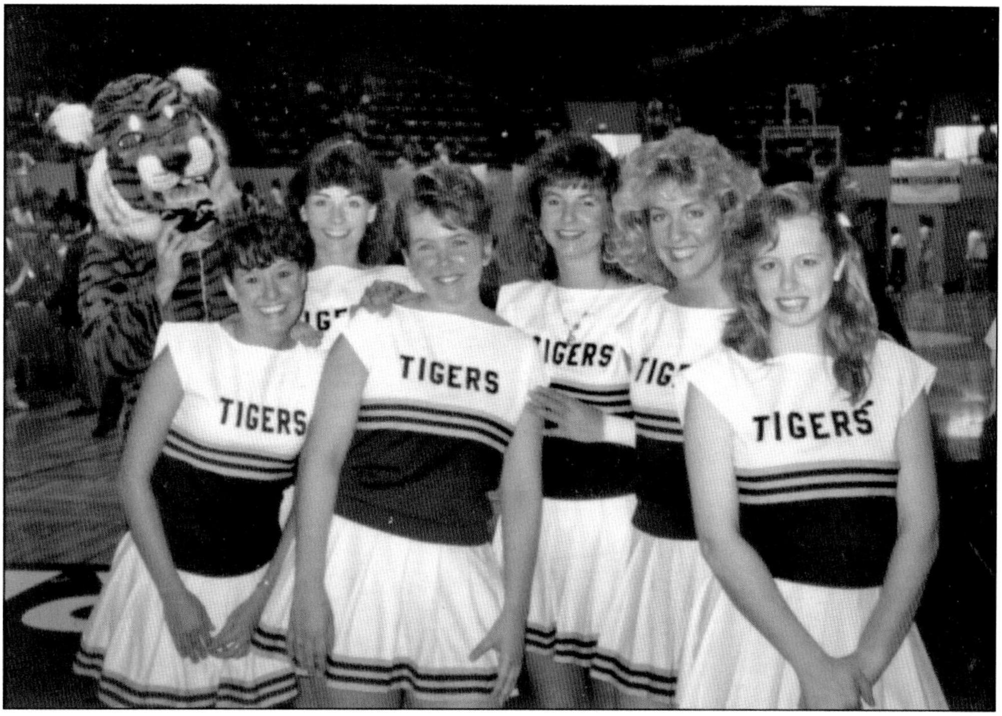

Campbellsville College's cheerleaders enjoy the festive atmosphere at the National Association of Intercollegiate Athletics (NAIA) national men's basketball championship tournament in 1990.

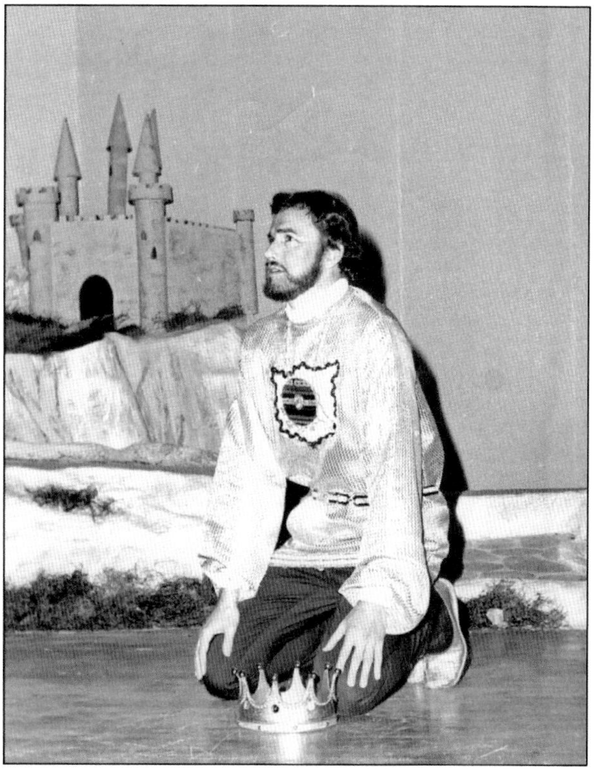

Russ Mobley portrays King Arthur during a spring 1990 production of *Camelot*. (Photograph by Stan McKinney.)

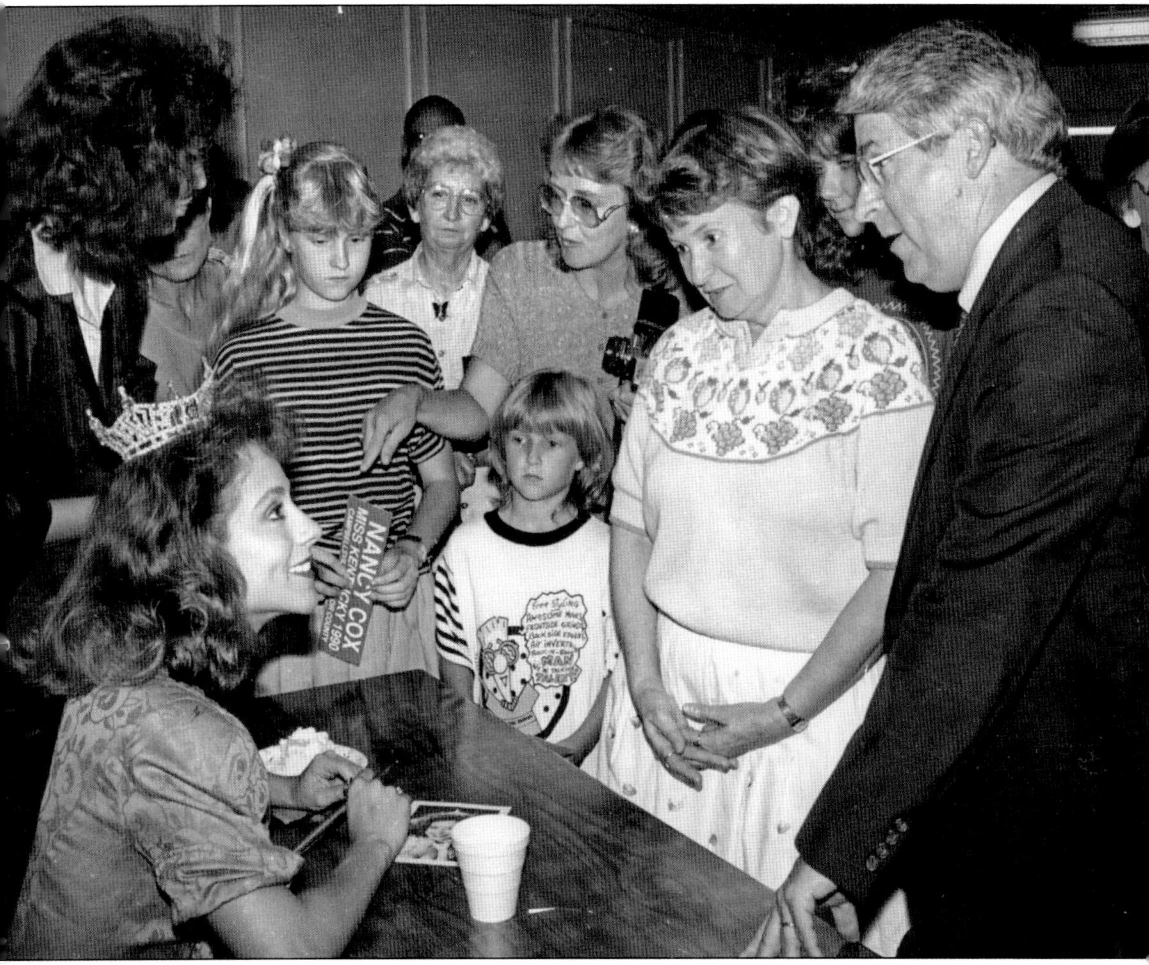

Nancy Cox, Miss Kentucky 1990, is shown at an autograph session conversing with Pres. Kenneth Winters. She was the second Campbellsville College student to win the Miss Kentucky competition. Nanci Bowling won the title in 1962. (Photograph by Stan McKinney.)

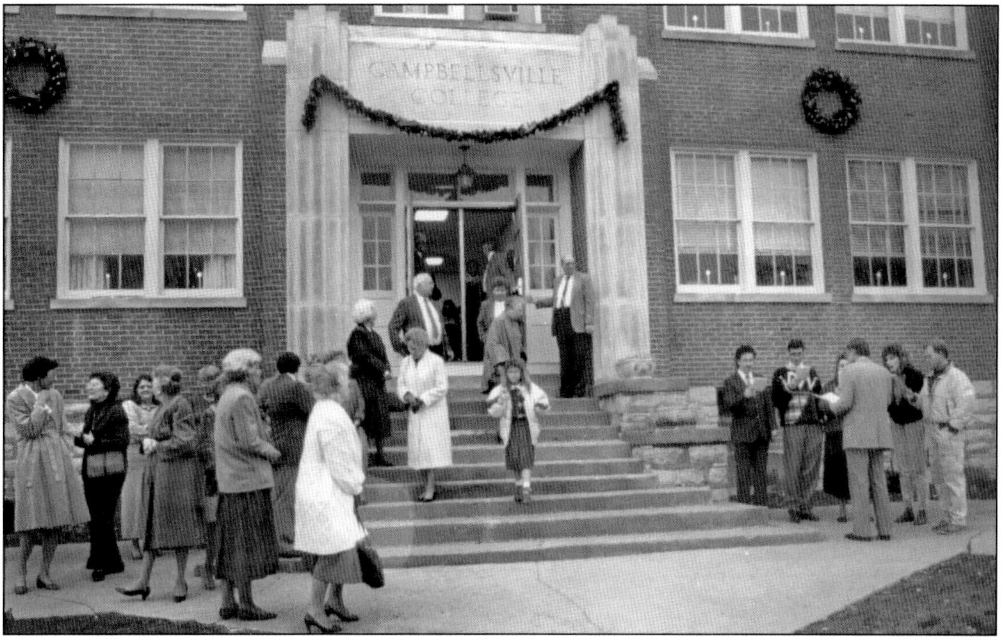

Following the Christmas Home Tour held on December 16, 1990, a reception was held at the Administration Building to celebrate the holiday season. Dr. Forest Shely, a longtime trustee of Campbellsville College and Campbellsville University, holds the door open. A small vocal group from the music department can be seen serenading the guests with Christmas carols.

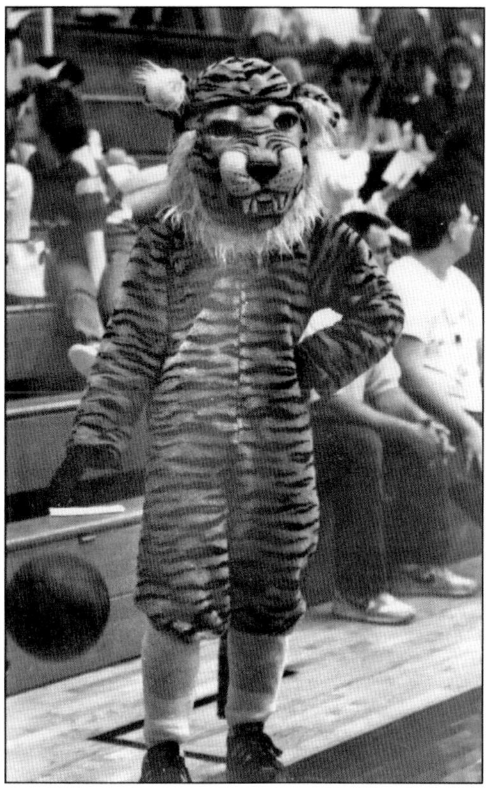

The Campbellsville College tiger mascot is dribbling a basketball while watching the action on the court. (Photograph by Sandy Cribbs.)

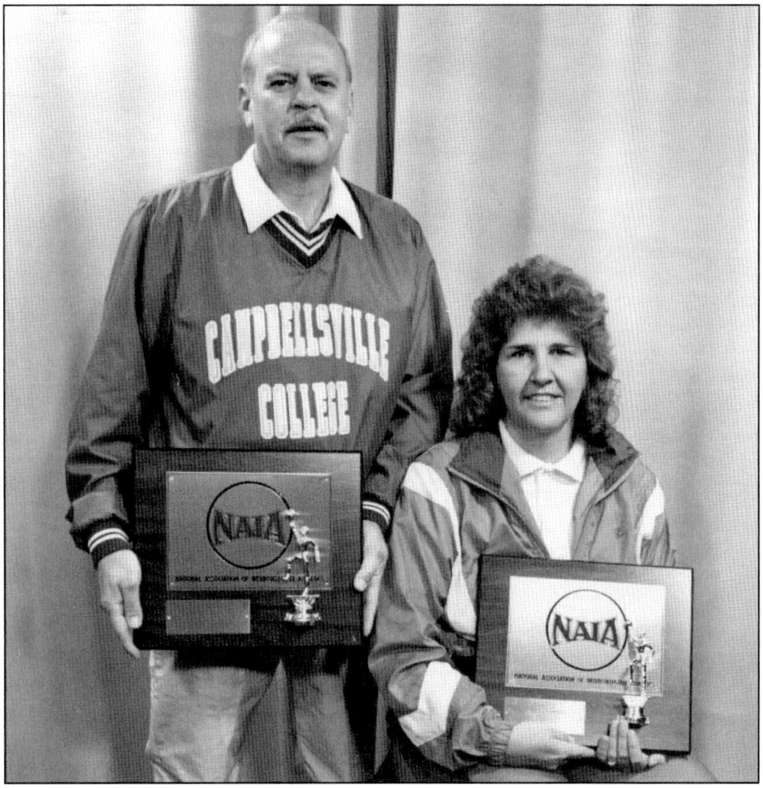

Coaches Lou Cunningham and Donna Wise hold the plaques that their respective basketball teams earned by qualifying for the NAIA national tournaments in 1991. (Photograph by Joan McKinney.)

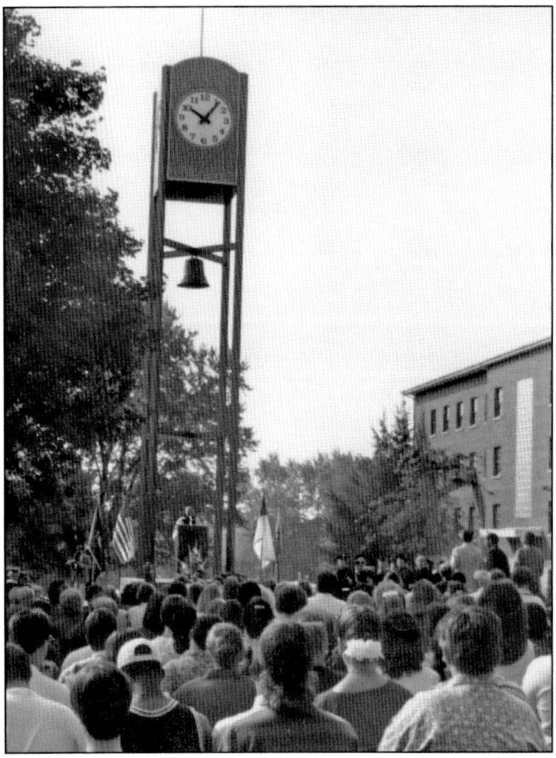

The Carillon Clock Tower was dedicated as part of the Founder's Day celebration on September 16, 1992. Standing 60 feet tall, the Carillon Clock Tower is a campus landmark that was donated to Campbellsville College by Schulmerich Carillons and Dr. Jerry Bennett in 1992. An image of the clock tower became the centerpiece of the Campbellsville College, and later Campbellsville University, logo when it was redesigned by Dr. Bennett in 1993.(Photograph by Joan McKinney.)

Tiger tennis player W. D. McCubbin serves during a practice session.

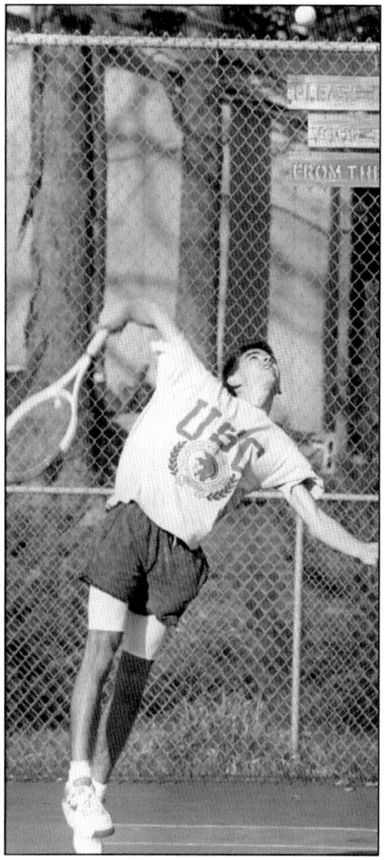

Campbellsville College sponsored the 1,924th Kentucky historical highway marker erected in the Commonwealth of Kentucky. Dedicated on Founder's Day 1993, it honors both the founding committee of the Russell Creek Academy and the men who raised the funds during 1913 and 1914 to keep the academy a private Baptist educational institution. (Photograph by Jamie Mings.)

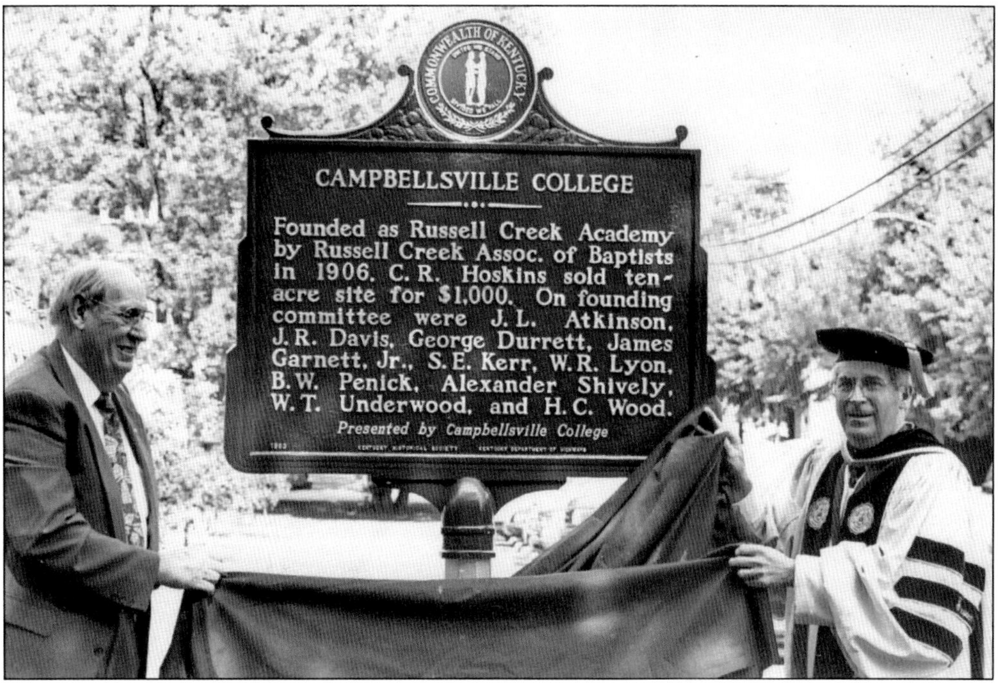

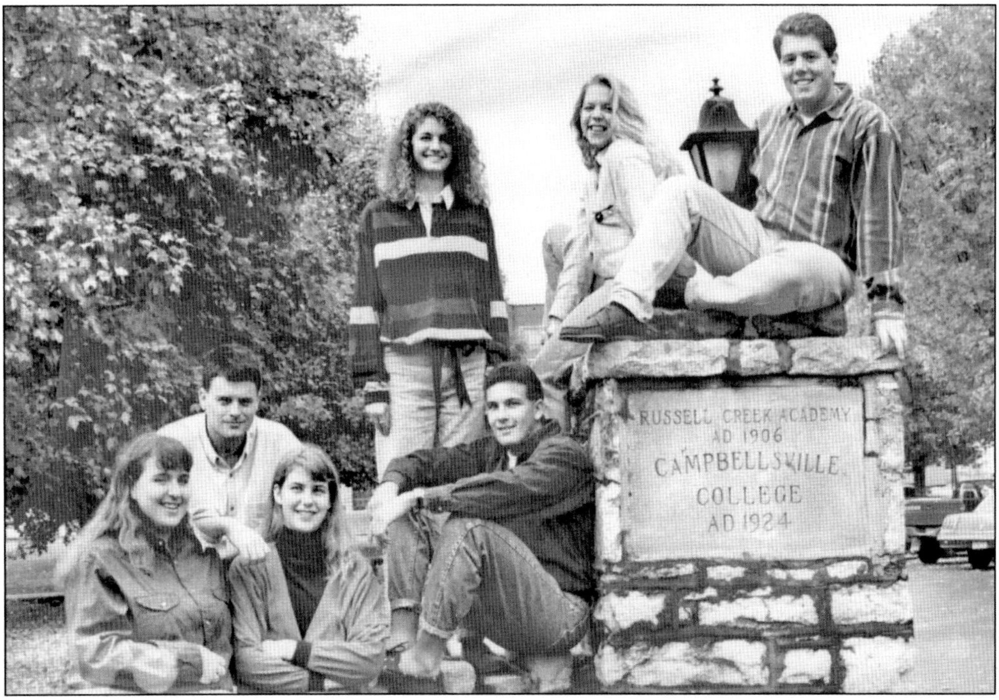

The Campbellsville Singers are, from left to right, Jennifer Shoemaker, Mike Richard, Bonnie Moore, Rick Clapp, Cicely Maggard, Valerie Owens, and Brian Clifford. (Photograph by Tamara Marsteller.)

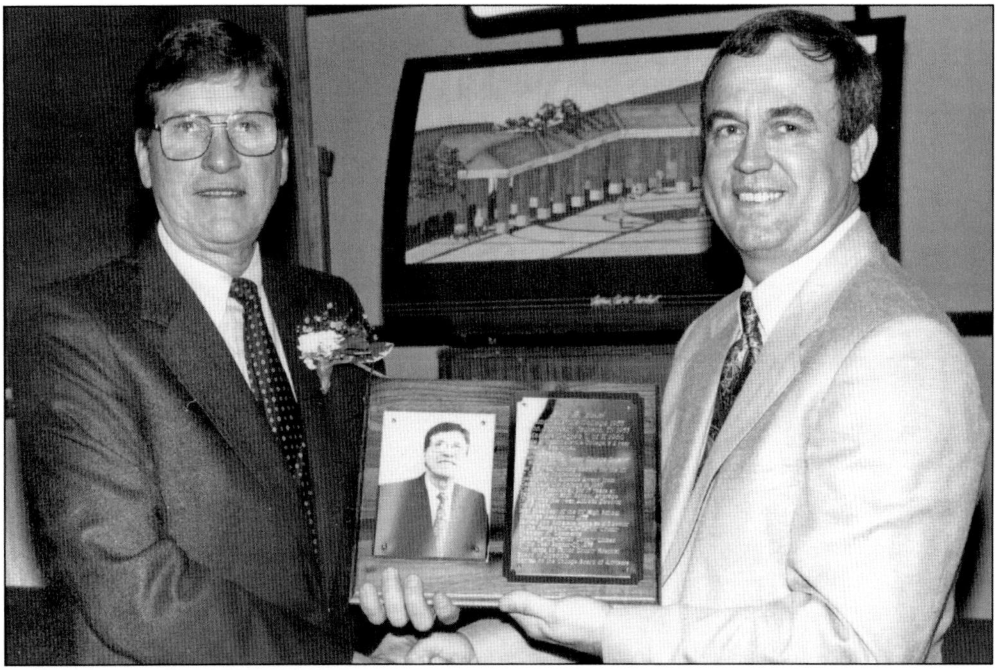

Ronnie Hord (right) congratulates Billy B. Smith on his induction to the Campbellsville College Athletics Hall of Fame on February 19, 1994. Smith, who starred on the basketball team from 1951 to 1953, was part of the hall of fame's inaugural class. (Photograph by Joan C. McKinney.)

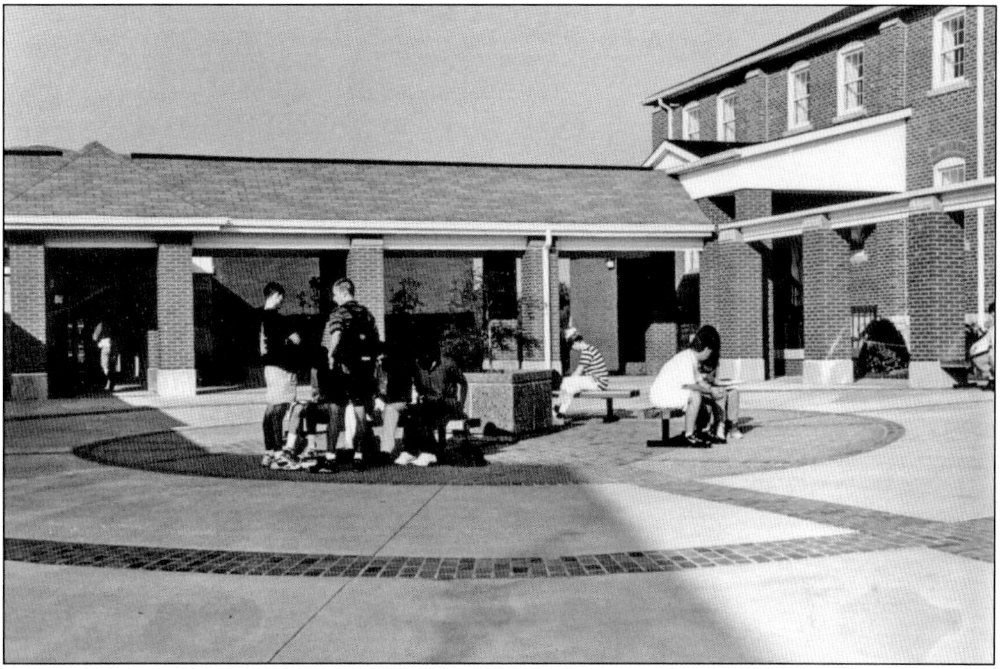

The College Courtyard was dedicated on Founder's Day in September 1994. The courtyard, located between the Student Union Building and the Science Building, also includes a covered walkway. The celebration was the last under the name Founder's Day, which was renamed Heritage Day. (Photograph by Bogdan Ratiu.)

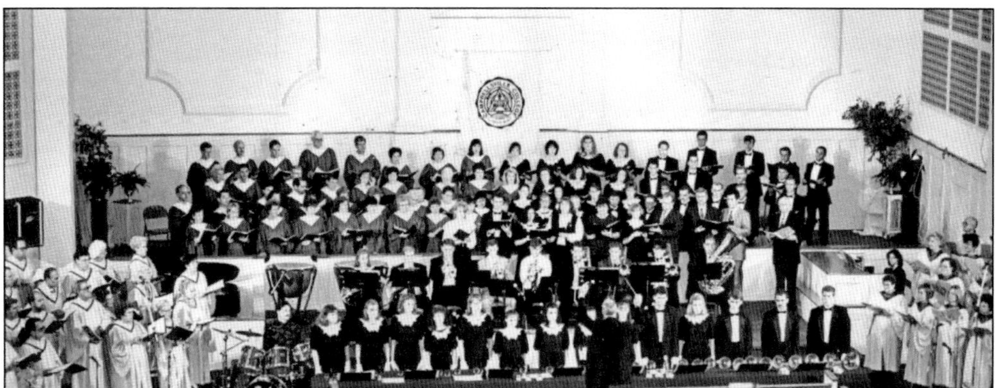

Dr. Kenneth Martin directs the members of a number of choral and instrumental ensembles from the School of Music at the Heritage Day Choir Festival held September 19, 1995. The festival celebrated 150 years of Southern Baptist history. (Photograph by Michelle D. Towles.)

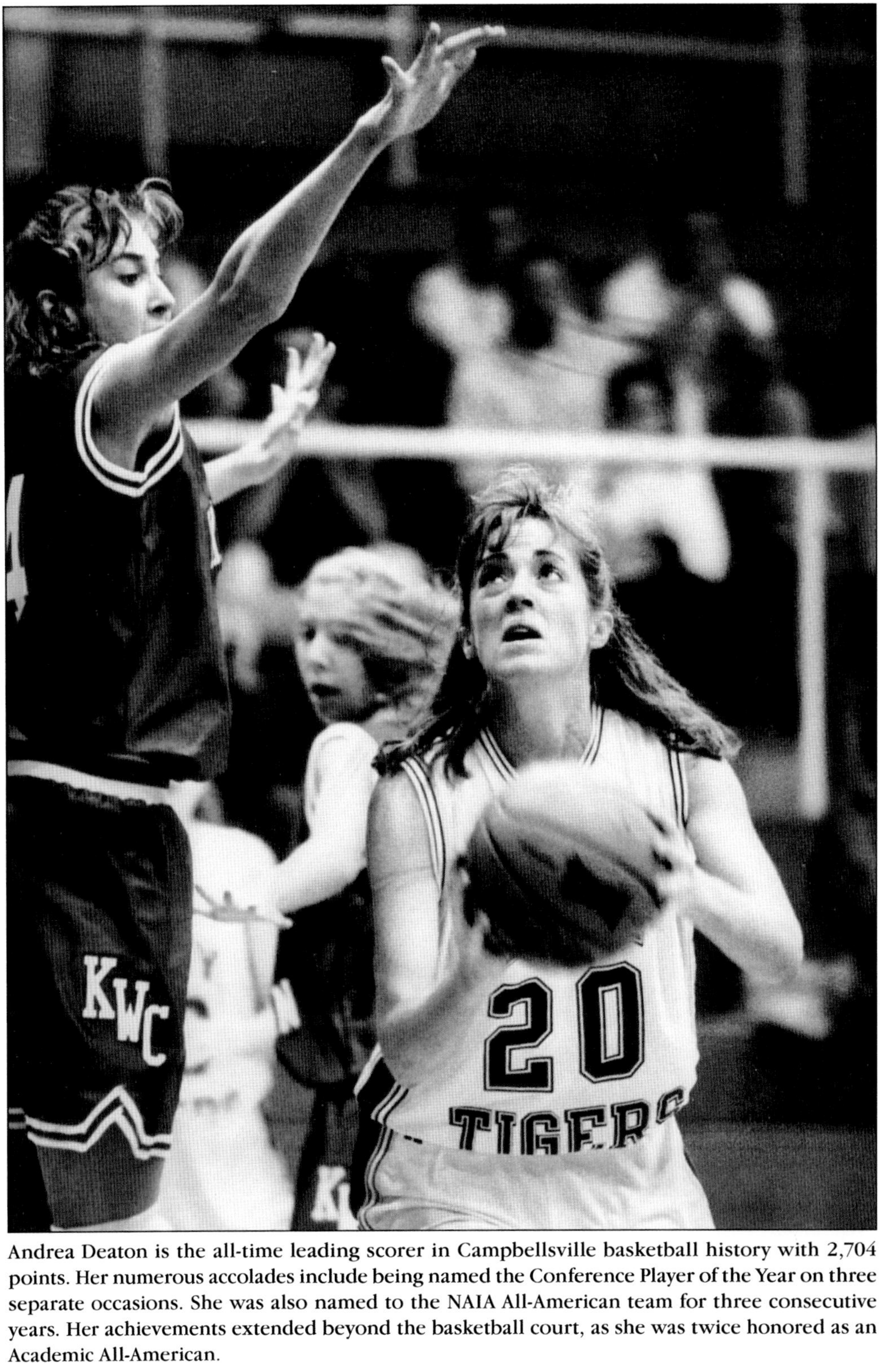

Andrea Deaton is the all-time leading scorer in Campbellsville basketball history with 2,704 points. Her numerous accolades include being named the Conference Player of the Year on three separate occasions. She was also named to the NAIA All-American team for three consecutive years. Her achievements extended beyond the basketball court, as she was twice honored as an Academic All-American.

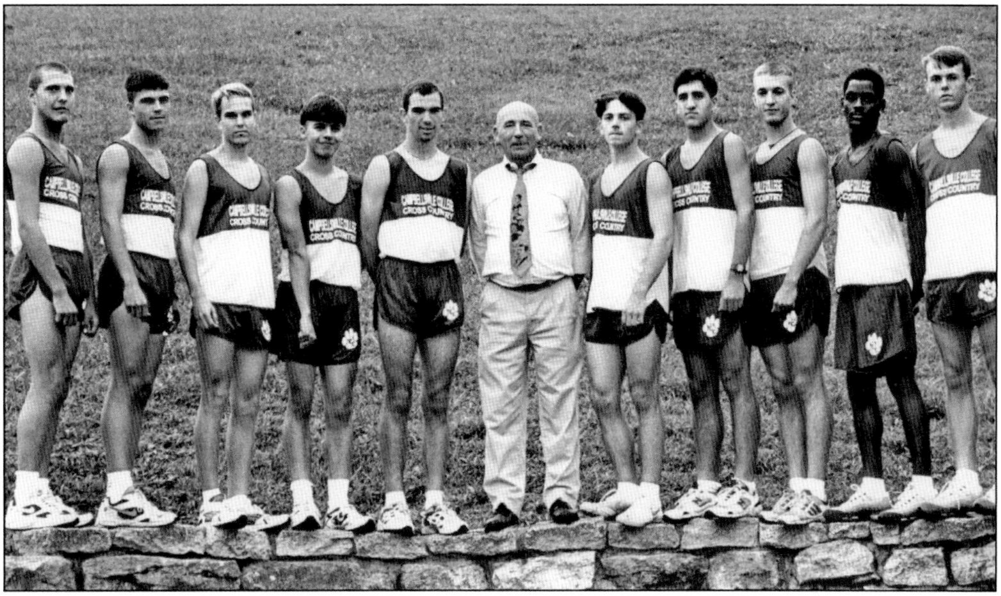

Coach Tom McDowell is flanked by the members of the 1995–1996 men's cross-country team. Pictured from left to right are Steve Helbig, Josh Skillman, Jason Clark, Chavi Muniz, Ryan McDowell, Tom McDowell, Adam Wiley, Jason Holland, Aaron Harbolt, Willie Stewart, and Darren Childers. (Photograph by Michelle D. Towles.)

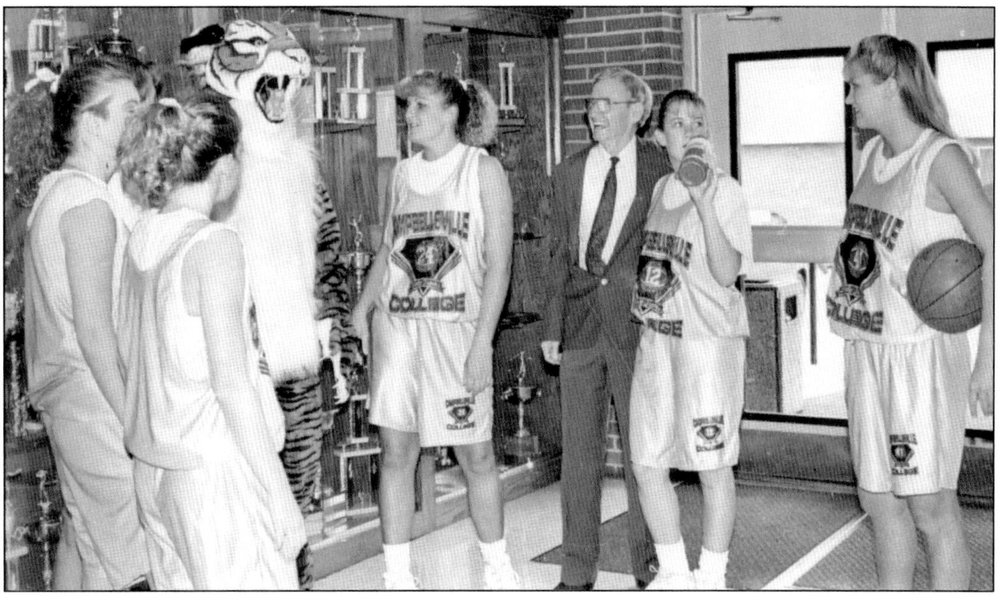

Bobby Himes and members of the Lady Tiger basketball team admire the mascot's spiffy new stripes in 1996. The mascot's new outfit was donated to Campbellsville College by Himes.

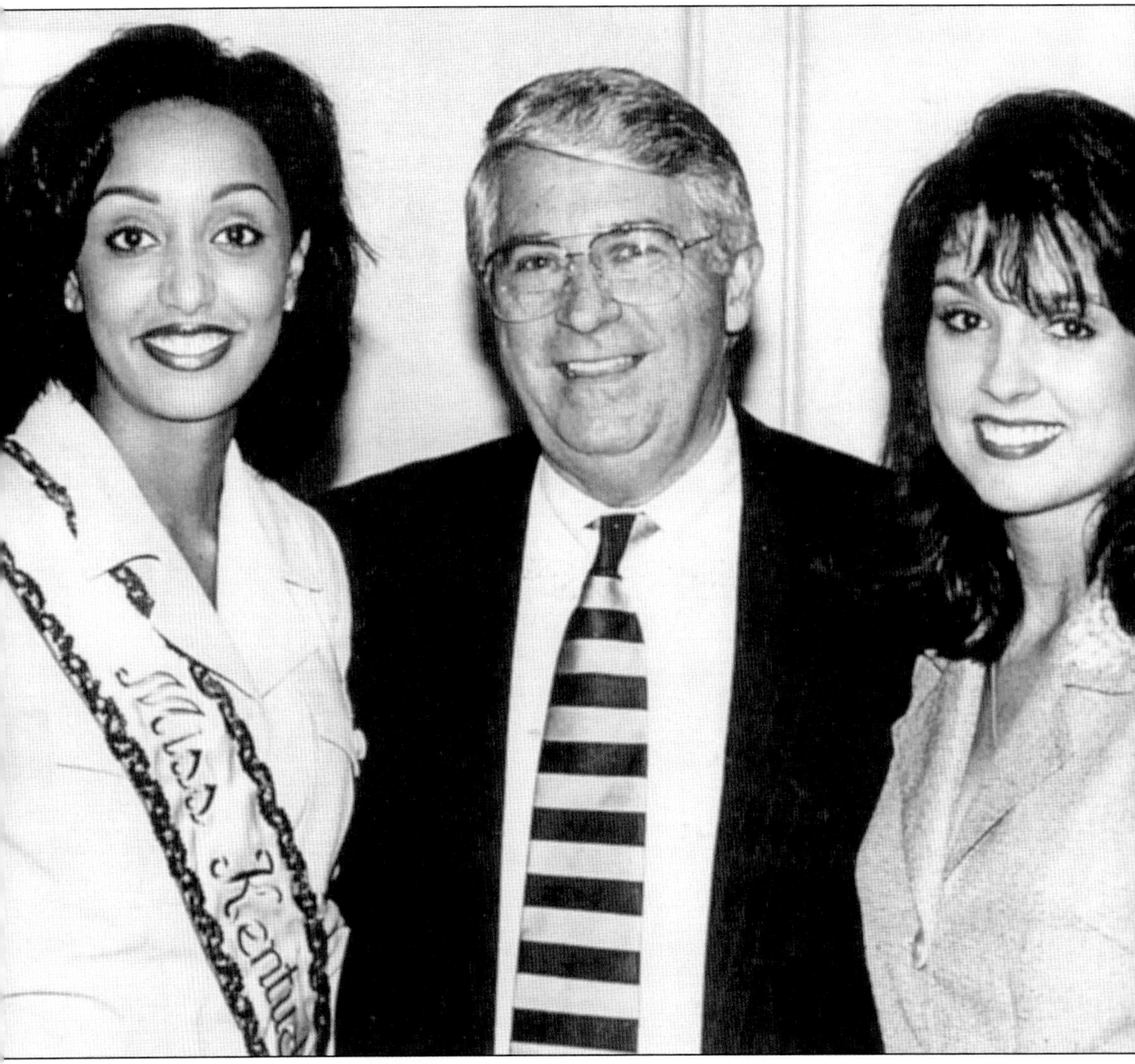

Pres. Kenneth Winters is flanked by two Campbellsville students who won the Miss Kentucky title. On the left is Veronica Duka, Miss Kentucky 1996, who finished in the top 10 at the Miss America Scholarship Pageant. Laura Sue Humphress was Miss Kentucky 1994. (Photograph by Joan C. McKinney.)

Four

CAMPBELLSVILLE UNIVERSITY 1996–2007

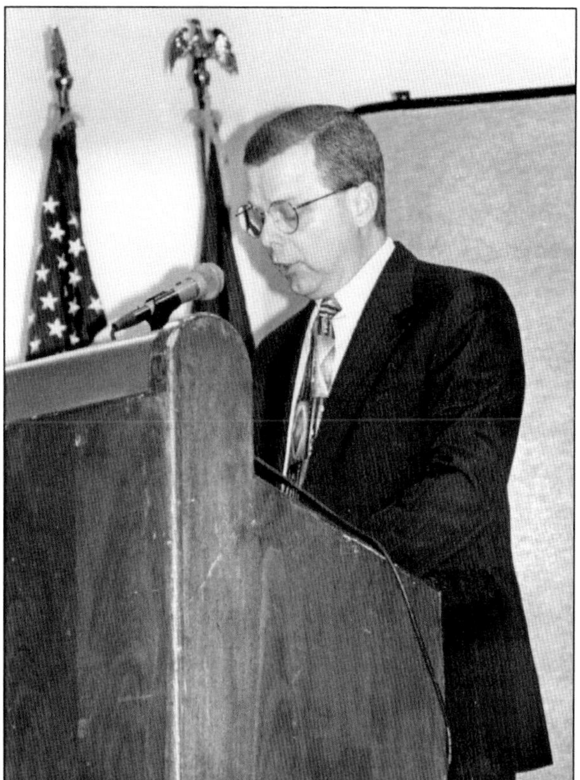

A new era in the institution's history was launched when Rev. John Chowning, chairman of the board of trustees, announced on April 11, 1996, that Campbellsville College had become Campbellsville University. (Photograph by Michelle D. Towles.)

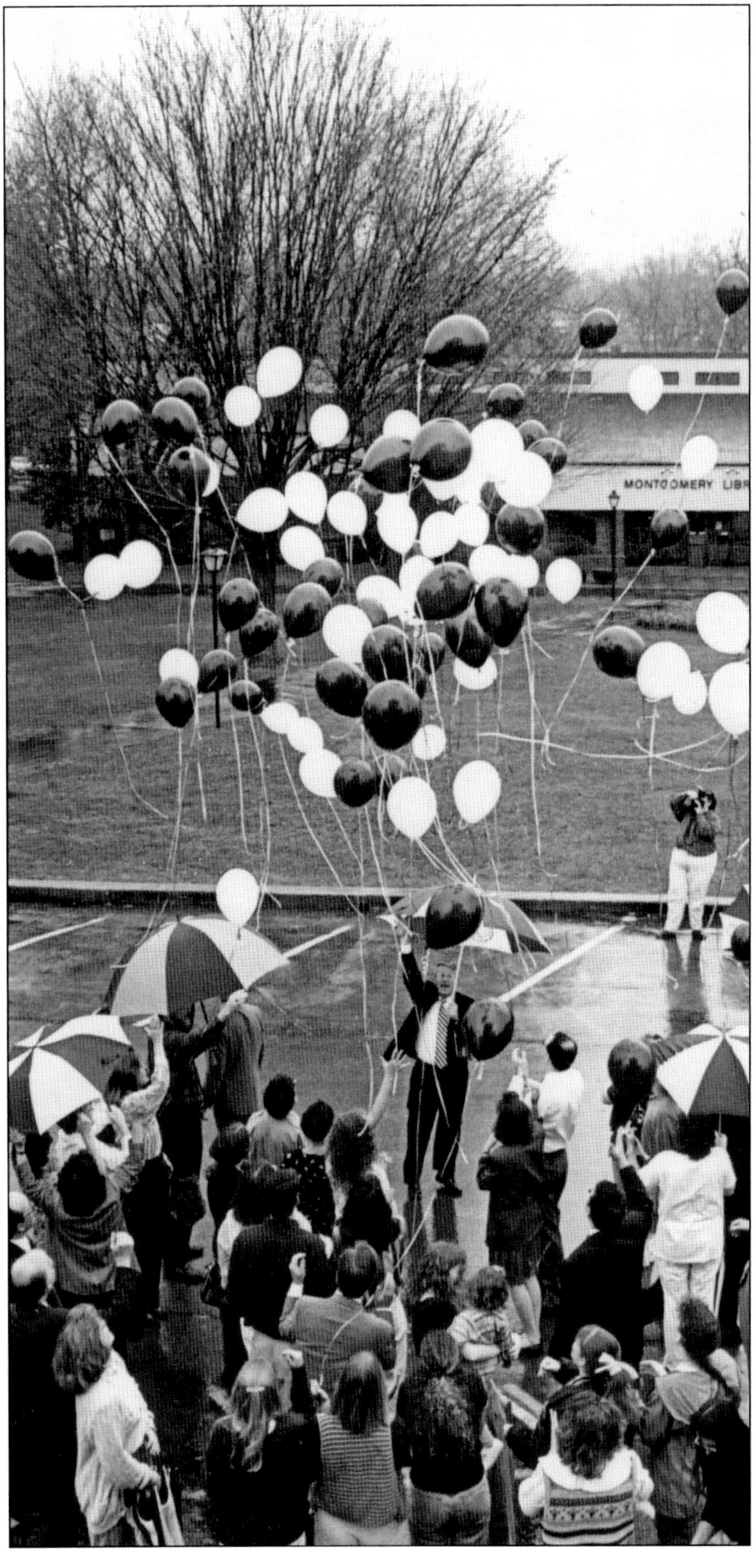

To celebrate the establishment of Campbellsville University, 90 maroon and white balloons, each representing a year of the institution's history, were released in front of Montgomery Library.

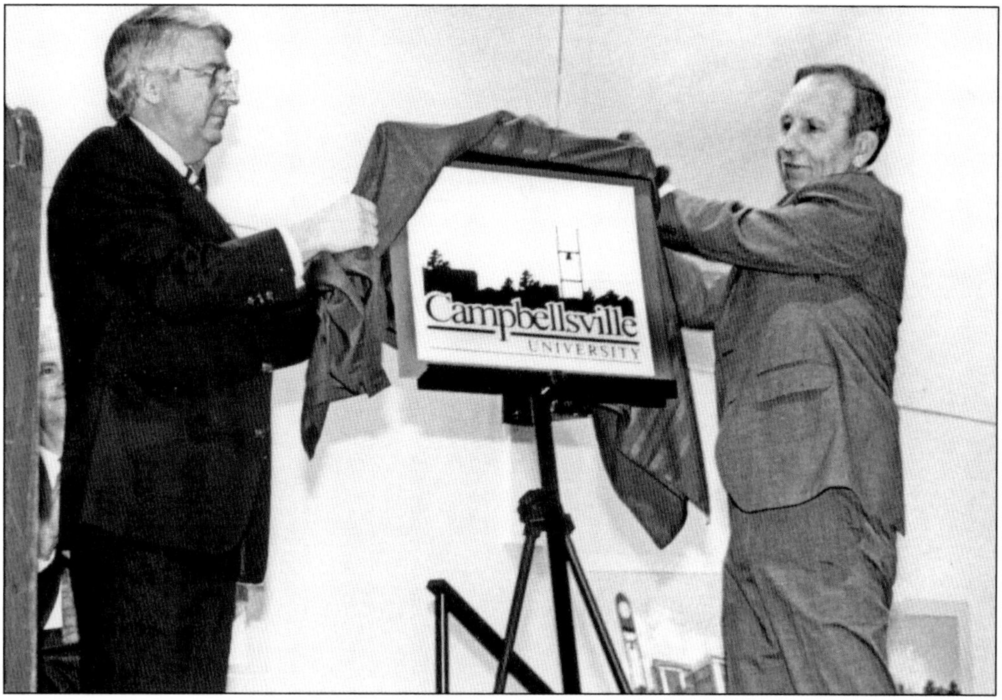

The change to university status necessitated a new logo, which is unveiled by Pres. Kenneth Winters (left) and Roger Davis.

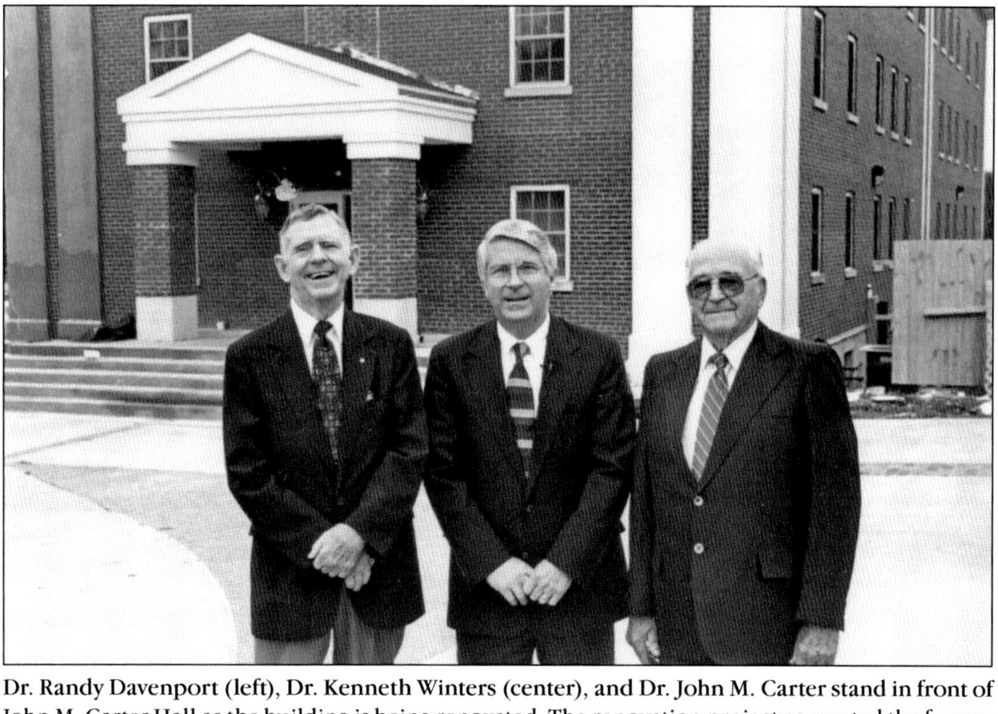

Dr. Randy Davenport (left), Dr. Kenneth Winters (center), and Dr. John M. Carter stand in front of John M. Carter Hall as the building is being renovated. The renovation project converted the former dormitory into an educational building. The redesigned structure contained eight classrooms, two meeting rooms, several laboratories, and a significant number of office spaces.

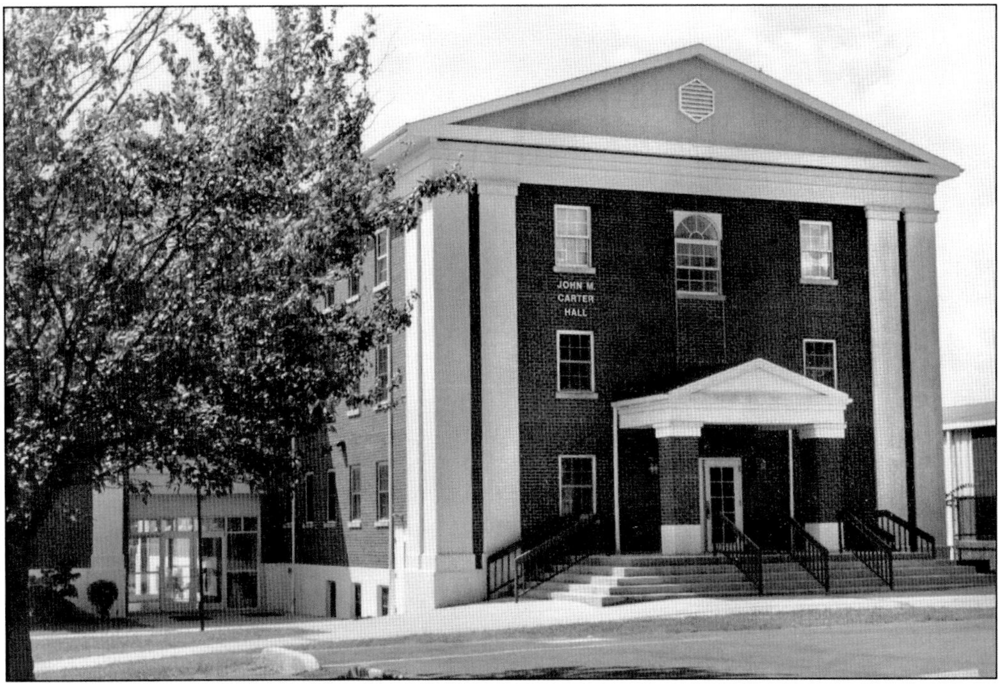

John M. Carter Hall was rededicated on Heritage Day 1996. The keynote speaker was the building's namesake, Dr. John M. Carter.

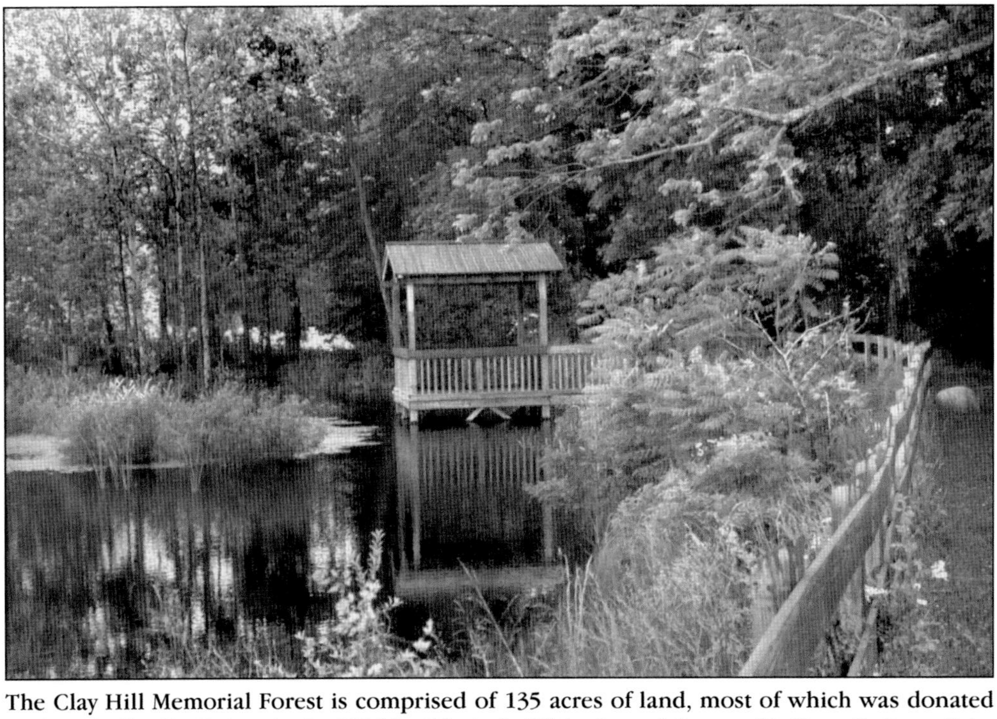

The Clay Hill Memorial Forest is comprised of 135 acres of land, most of which was donated to Campbellsville University in 1996 by Edwin L. White Jr. and George W. Howell. One of the more popular features of the facility is the forest's numerous hiking trails, which are open to the public.

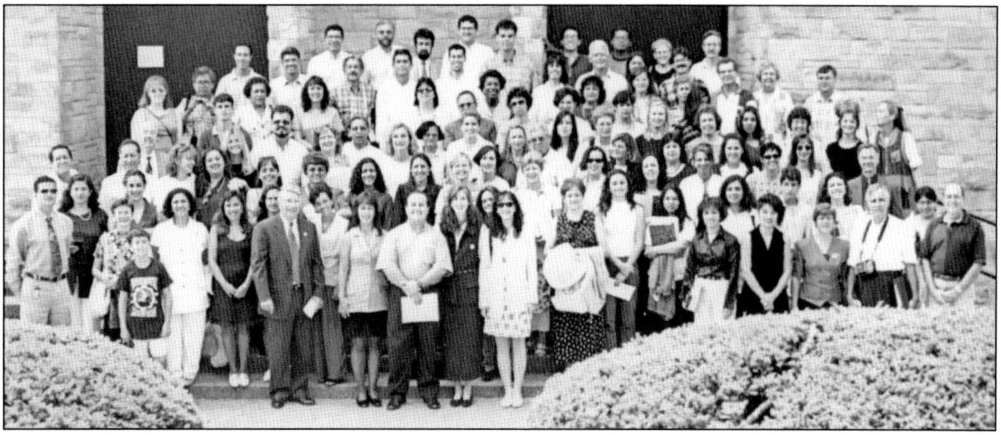

Dr. Kenneth Winters (left foreground, in suit) stands with the Brazilian members of the campus community in front of the Alumni Building in 1997. (Photograph by Joan McKinney.)

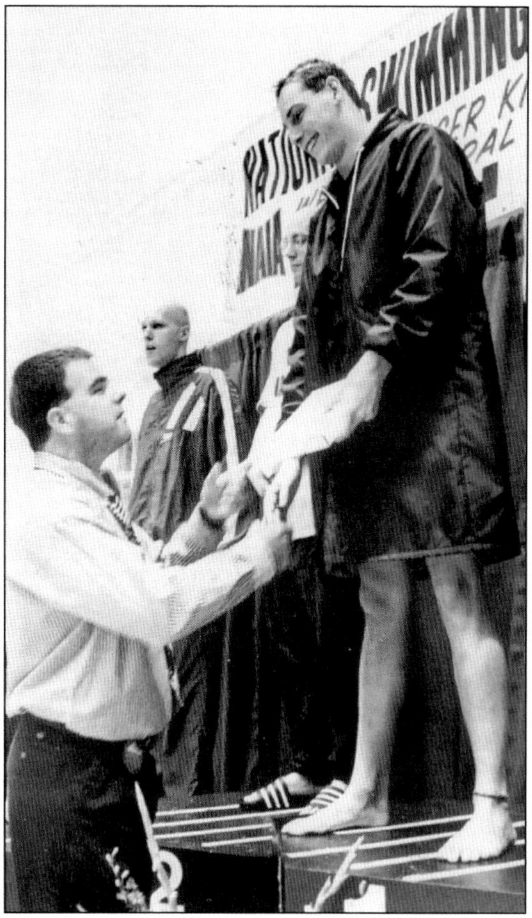

Brendan Ward (right), a student from Zimbabwc, is congratulated by coach Dean Brownley after winning the 100-yard butterfly at the 1997 National Swimming and Diving Championships held in Tacoma, Washington, on March 7, 1997. His national title was the first in any sport in the history of Campbellsville athletics. Erica Grammell, from Canada, finished third in the women's 100-yard backstroke and sixth in the women's 200-yard backstroke. Both Campbellsville University swimmers were named All-Americans. (Photograph by George Allen.)

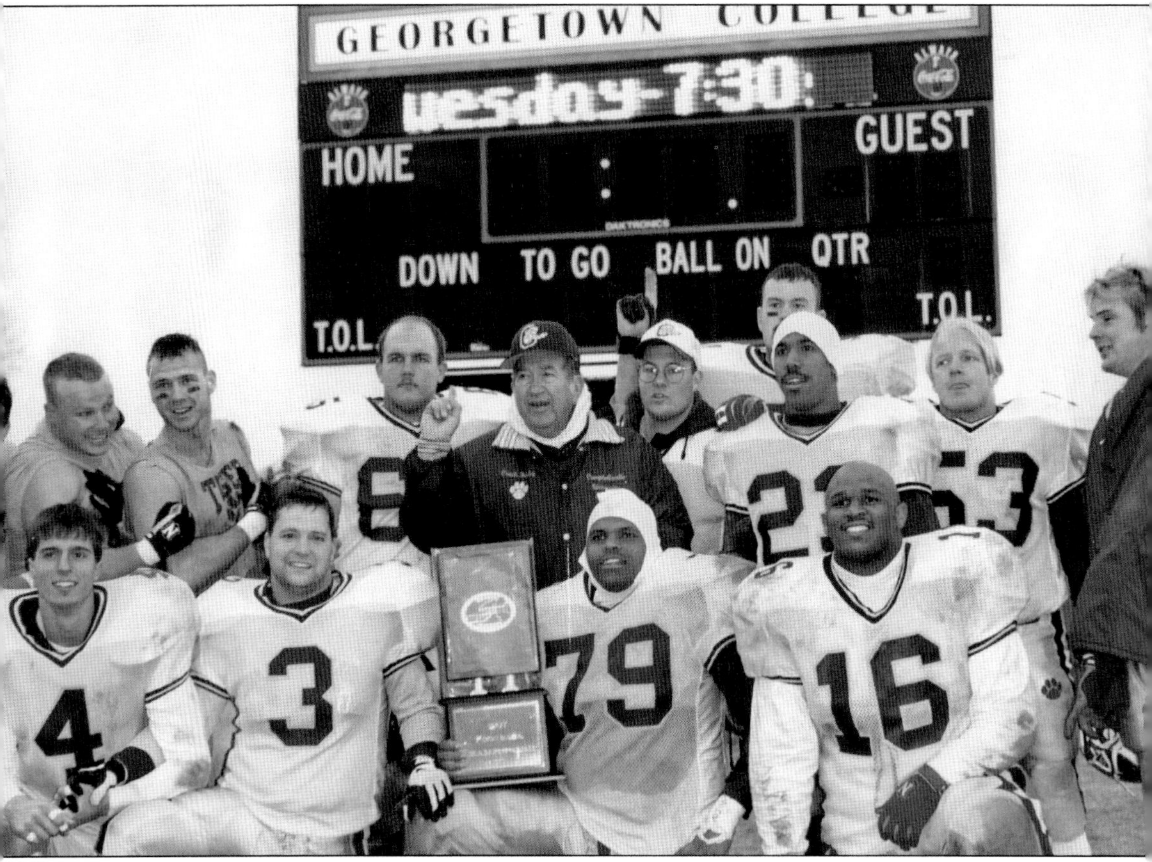

During the 1997 season, Tiger football players hoist their Mid-South Conference Football Championship trophy after defeating rival Georgetown College 38-21. Following the successful season, which included Campbellsville University's first appearance in the NAIA playoffs, head coach Ron Finley was named Mid-South Conference Coach of the Year. Thirteen players on the team were named either First or Second Team All-Conference. Twelve players were named to the Academic All-Conference List.

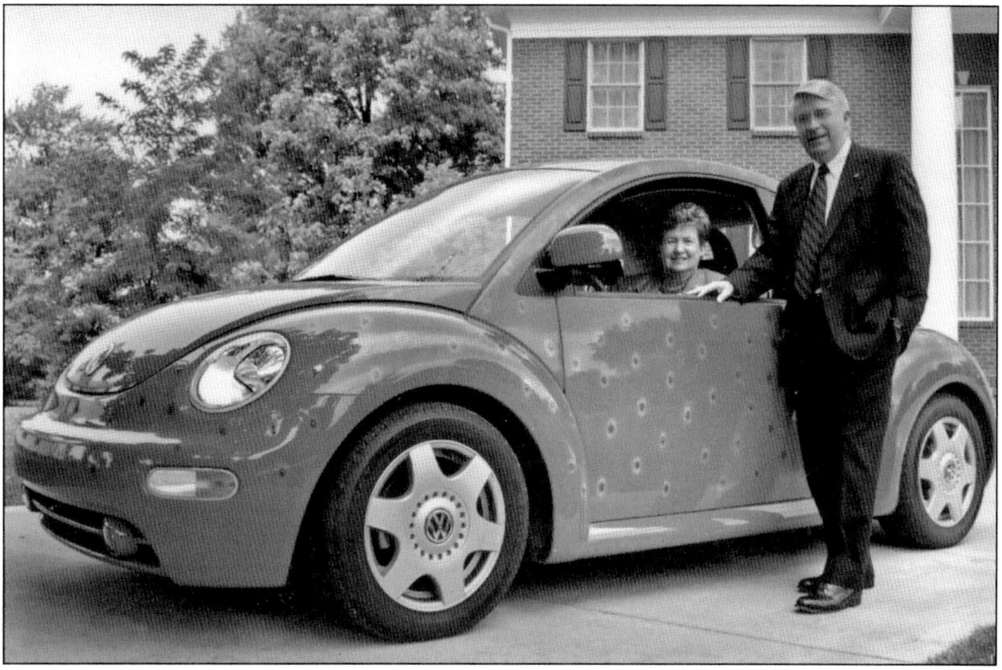

Dr. Kenneth Winters and Shirley Winters are pictured with the Strawberry Bug in September 1998. Shirley, who is known as the Strawberry Lady, always served strawberries to guests who attended social functions at the president's home. Her creativity in using strawberry motifs for decoration provided widespread publicity for the institution, including articles in the *Lexington Herald-Leader* and *Good Housekeeping*. (Photograph by George Allen.)

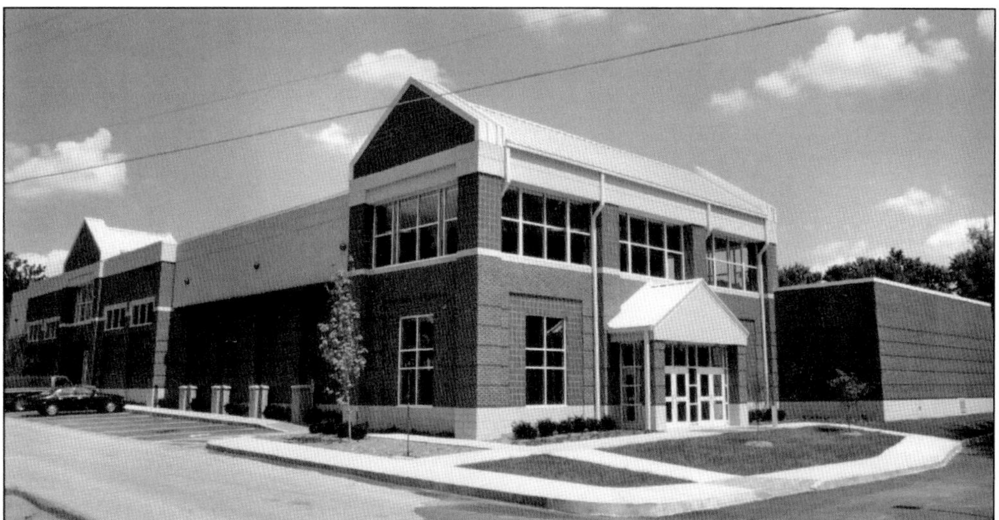

The Gheens Recital Hall was the centerpiece of an expansion to the Gosser Fine Arts Building. Dedicated on Heritage Day 1998, it has proven to be an excellent venue for performers to display their musical talents.

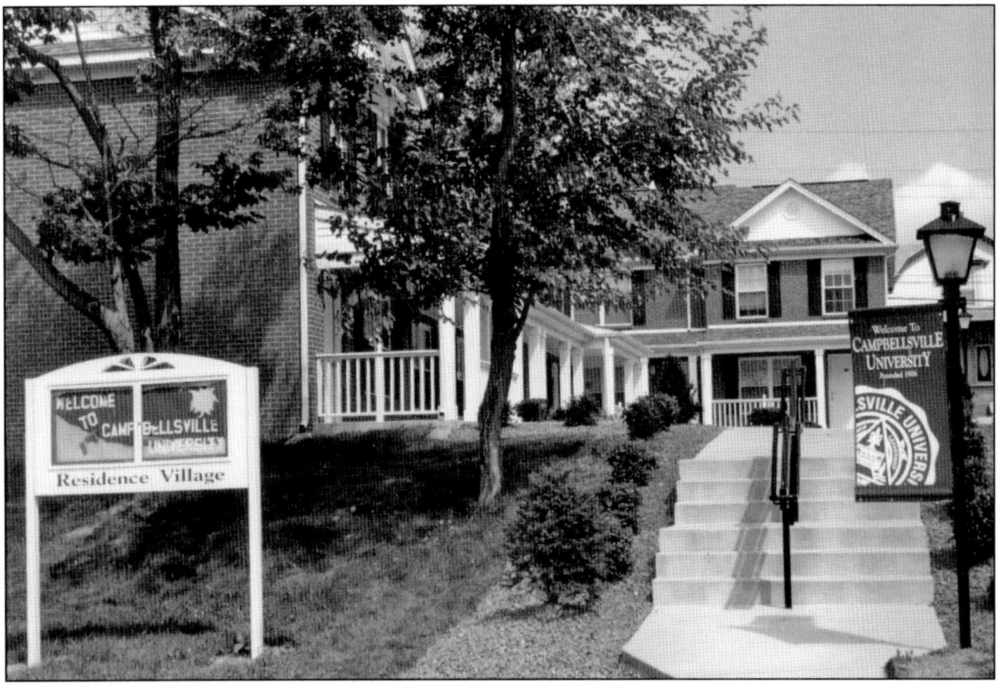

Eschewing traditional dormitories, the ladies in the Women's Residence Village live in town house–style accommodations. The village has proven so popular among students that additional buildings continue to be constructed in order to keep up with the demand.

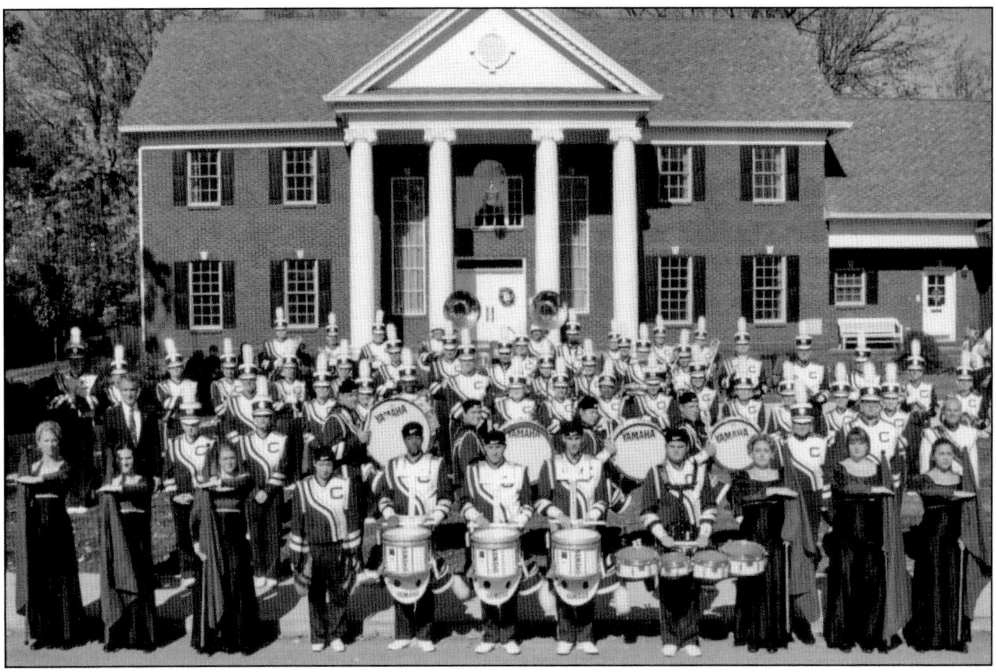

The Campbellsville University Marching Band, under the direction of Dr. David McCullough, prepares to perform in front of the Betty Dobbins Heilman President's Home at the dedication of Tiger Way on October 30, 1999. (Photograph by Crystal Anderson.)

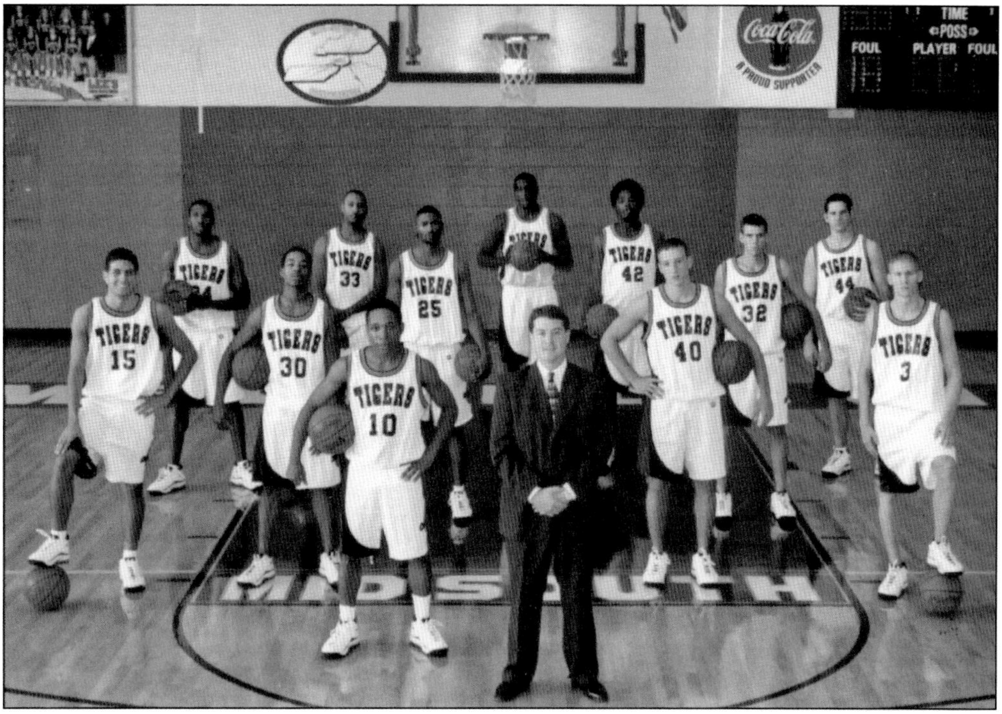

Head coach Travis Ford stands in front of the 1999–2000 men's basketball team. Ford, in his final year at Campbellsville University, led the team to their third consecutive berth in the NAIA national tournament.

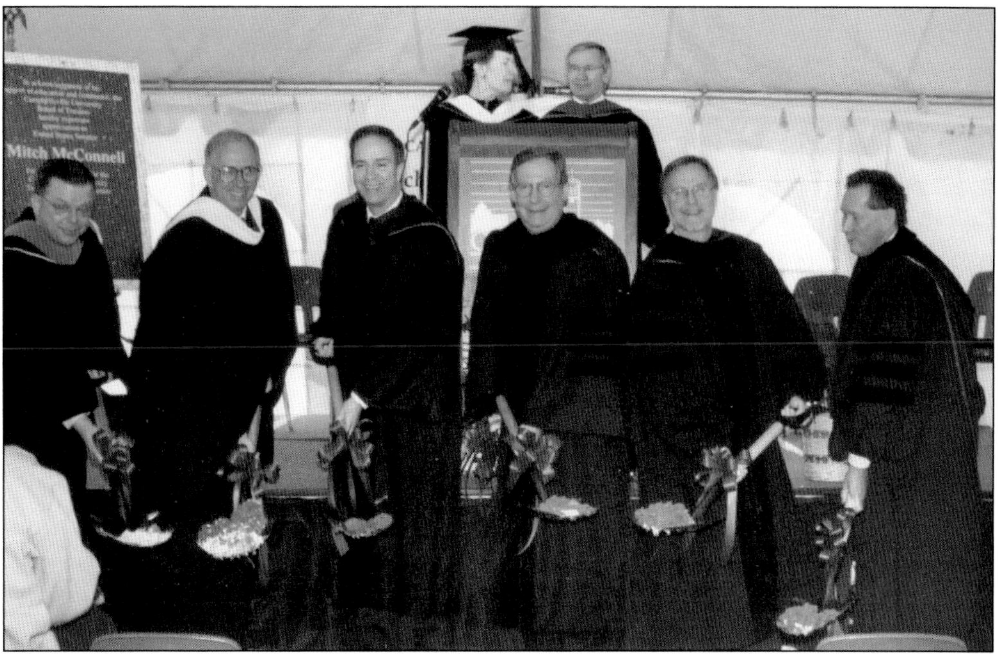

Shown from left to right in the foreground, John Chowning, Dr. Larry Noe, Pres. Michael V. Carter, Sen. Mitch McConnell, Dr. Paul Conco, and Dr. Frank Cheatham break ground on the Technology Training Center on February 17, 2000. (Photograph by Cheri Glass.)

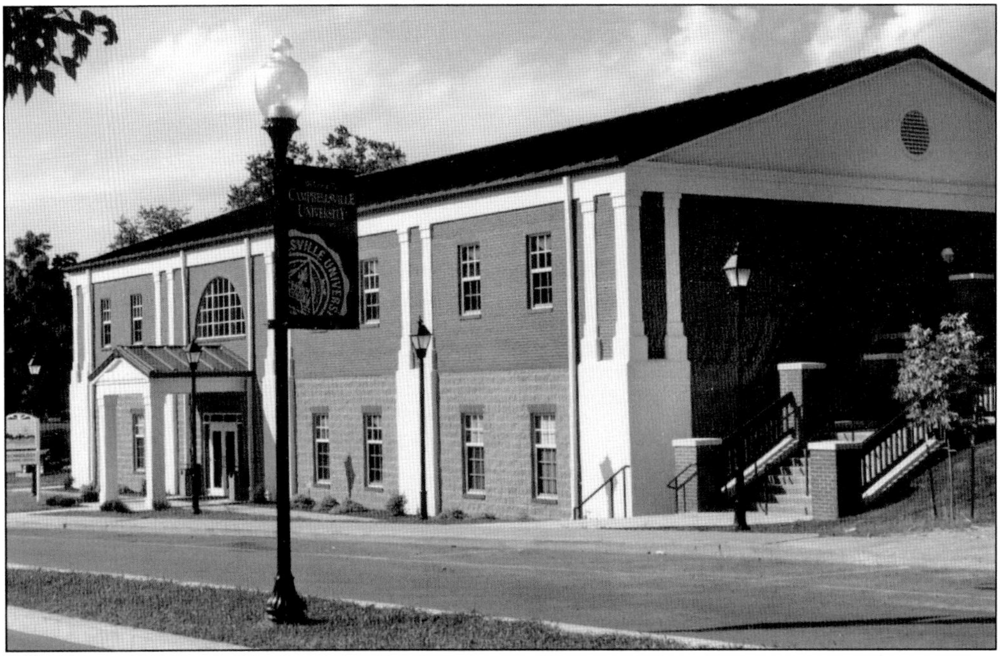

The Campbellsville University Technology Training Center is a unique facility used by the university, government officials and agencies, regional economic development groups, local schools, and businesses. The building includes videoconferencing facilities, classrooms, conference rooms, and several computer labs.

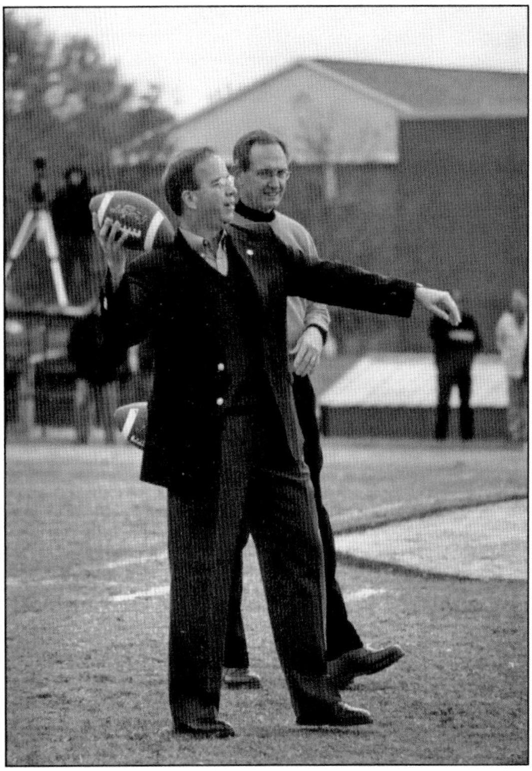

Georgetown College's president, William H. Crouch Jr. (right), watches as Pres. Michael V. Carter prepares to pass the football down the field. This lighthearted moment preceded the annual grudge match between the two rival institutions.

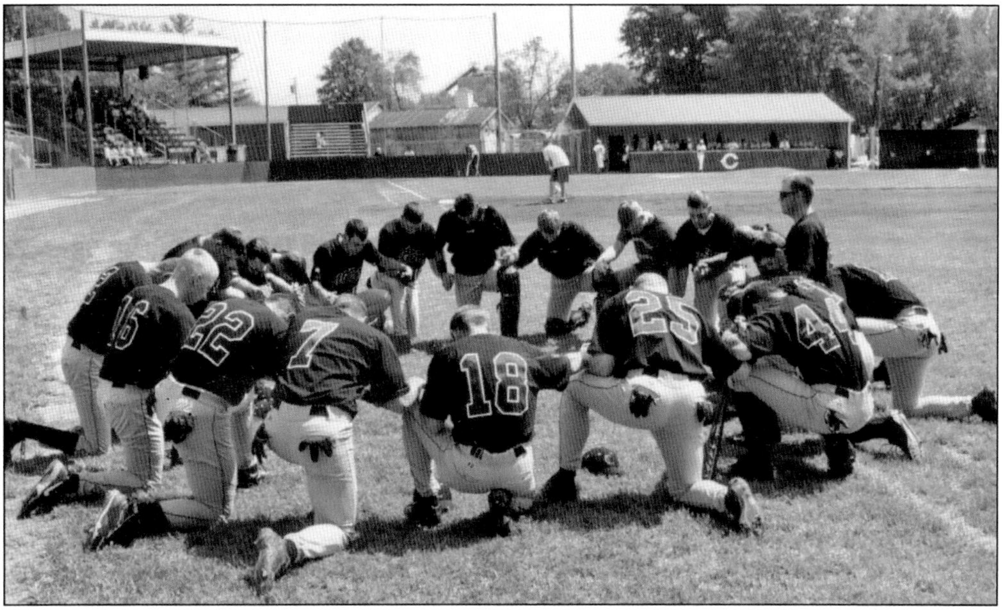

The members of the 2000 baseball team pray together before taking the field to play for the Mid-South Conference championship. The Tigers defeated Union College 7-3 to claim the conference crown.

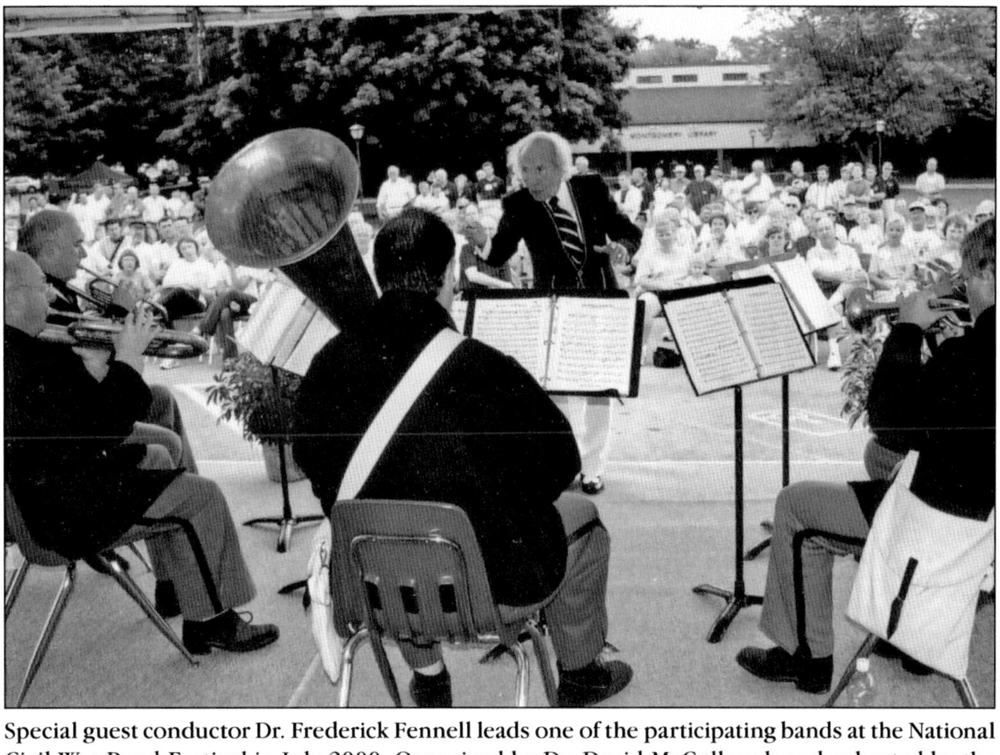

Special guest conductor Dr. Frederick Fennell leads one of the participating bands at the National Civil War Band Festival in July 2000. Organized by Dr. David McCullough and cohosted by the American Civil War Institute and the Campbellsville University School of Music, the festival featured Civil War bands from 11 states. The event was held a second time in 2003.

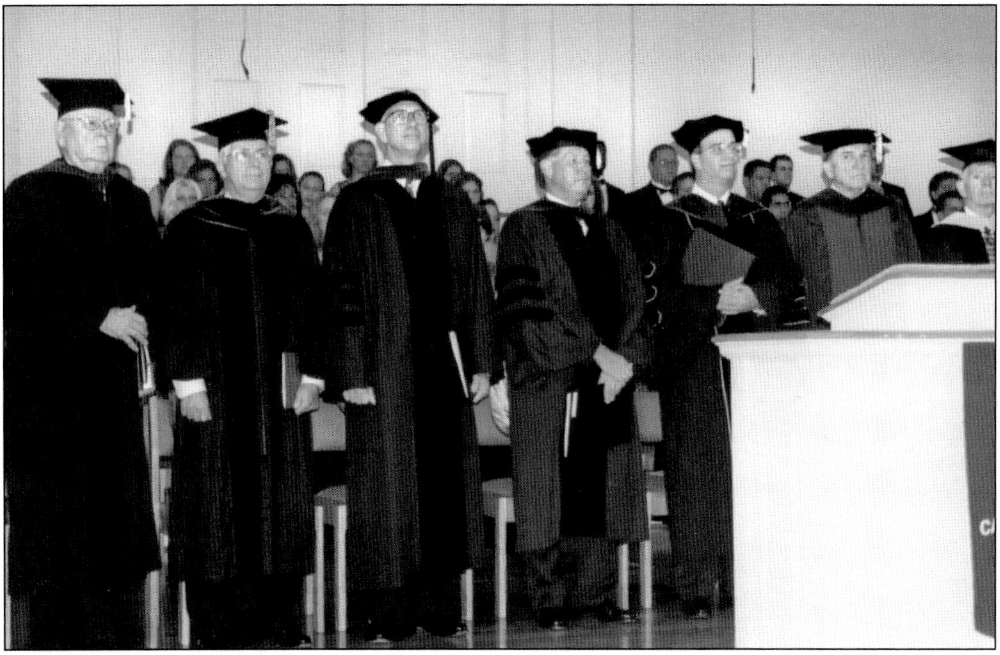

On September 15, 2000, Dr. Michael V. Carter was inaugurated as the 10th president of Campbellsville University. Pictured on the stage are, from left to right, Dr. A. B. Colvin, former president Dr. Kenneth Winters, Dr. Larry Noe, Dr. Frank Cheatham, Carter, Dr. E. Bruce Heilman, and former president William Randolph Davenport.

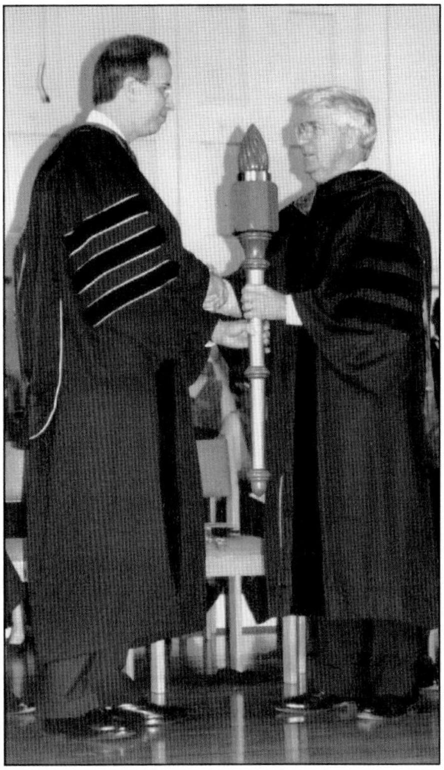

Dr. Kenneth Winters (right) passes the academic mace to his successor, Dr. Michael V. Carter. (Photograph by George Allen.)

Dr. Larry Noe, chair of the board of trustees, places the presidential medallion around Dr. Michael V. Carter's neck. (Photograph by George Allen.)

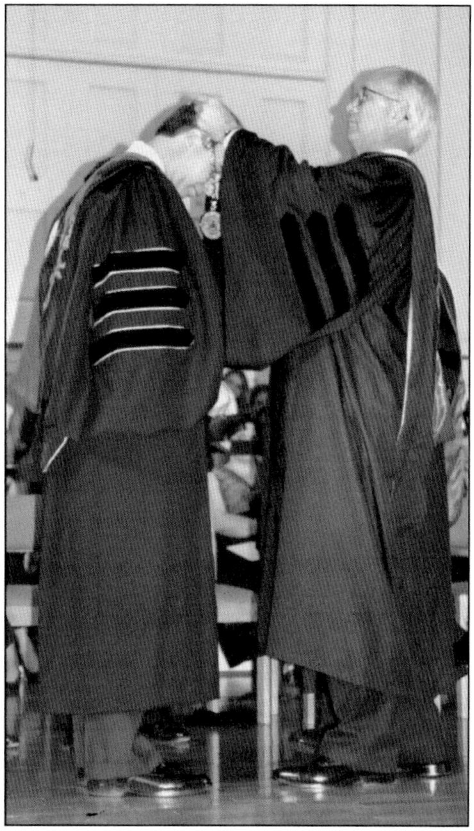

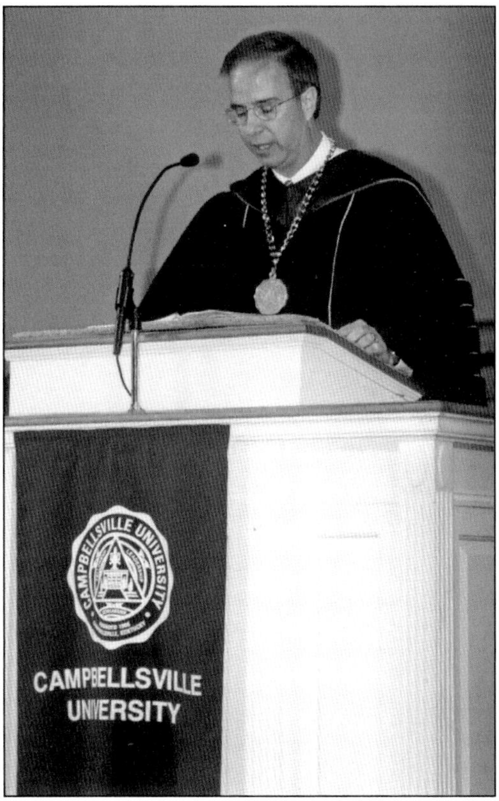

Pres. Michael V. Carter uses his inaugural address to unveil his vision of Campbellsville University's bright future.

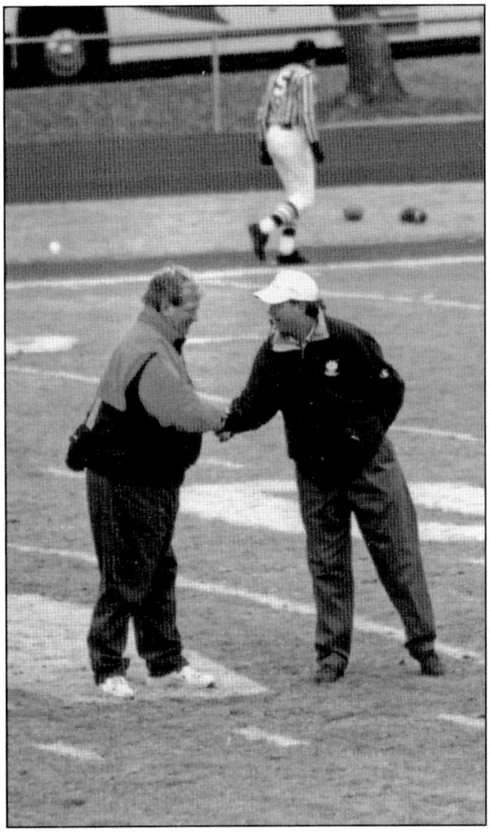

Pres. Michael V. Carter (right) greets Baker University's president, Daniel M. Lambert, prior to kick-off of the KWTO Bowl on December 2, 2000. The bowl game was held on Plaster Field at Southwest Baptist University in Bolivar, Missouri. (Photograph by Bryan Blair.)

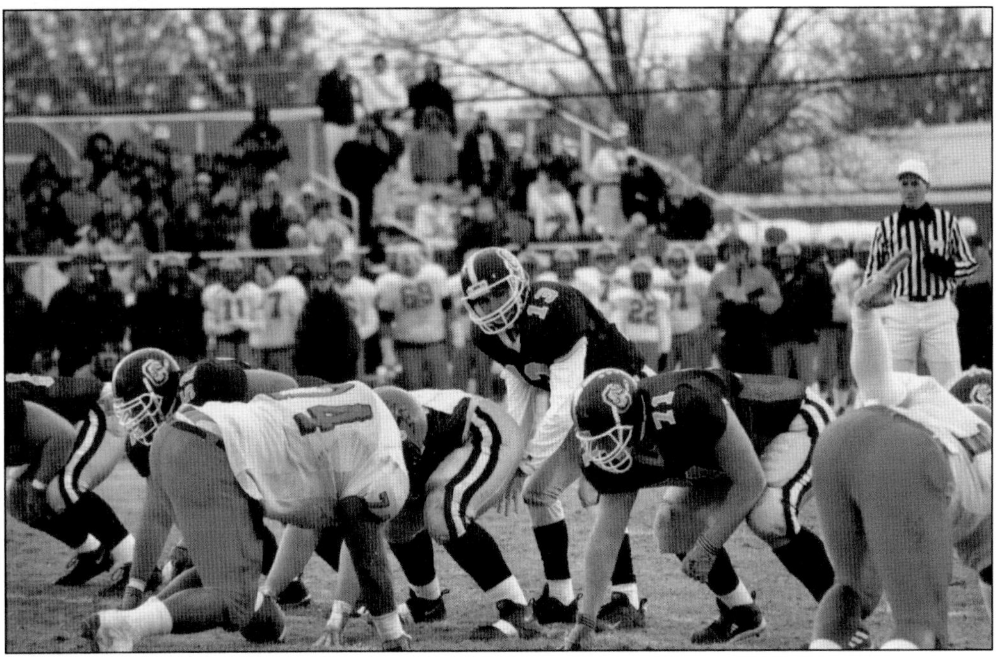

Despite their superior offensive output, the Campbellsville University Tigers fell to the Baker University Wildcats in a hard-fought game 27-23. (Photograph by Bryan Blair.)

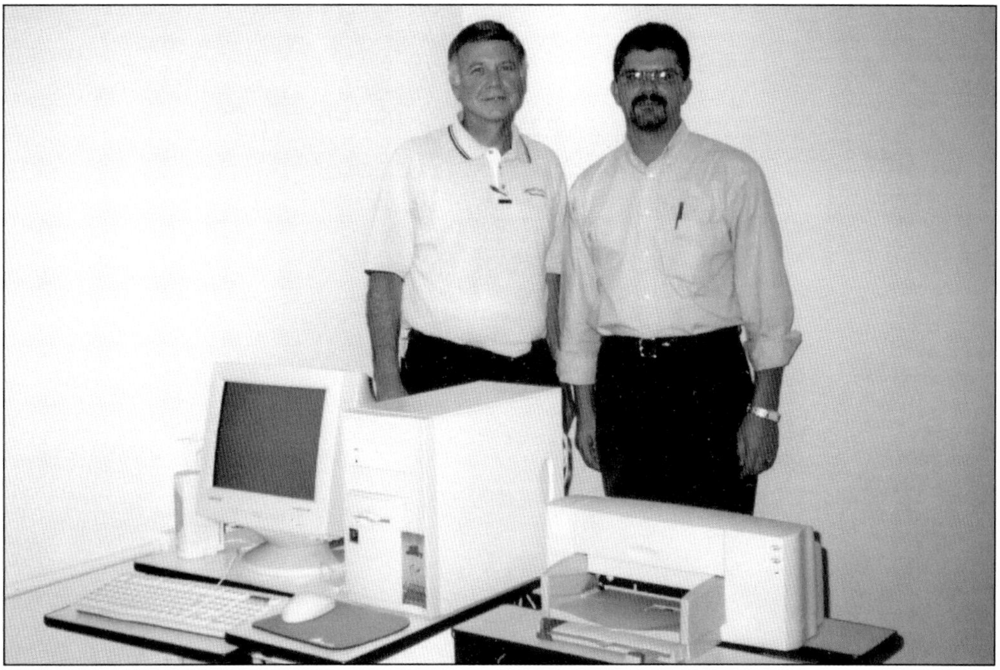

Dr. J. Robert Gaddis (left), dean of the Campbellsville University School of Music, and Dr. Alcingstone "Tony" Cunha stand together in Recife, Brazil. Dr. Gaddis helped lead the initiative that created a partnership agreement between Campbellsville University and the Seminario Telogico Baptista do Norte do Brazil to establish a satellite campus in Recife, Brazil, in July 2001. Dr. Cunha served as the director of the Campbellsville University Brazilian Partnership from July 2001 to December 2006, when he accepted a position as assistant professor of music at Campbellsville University.

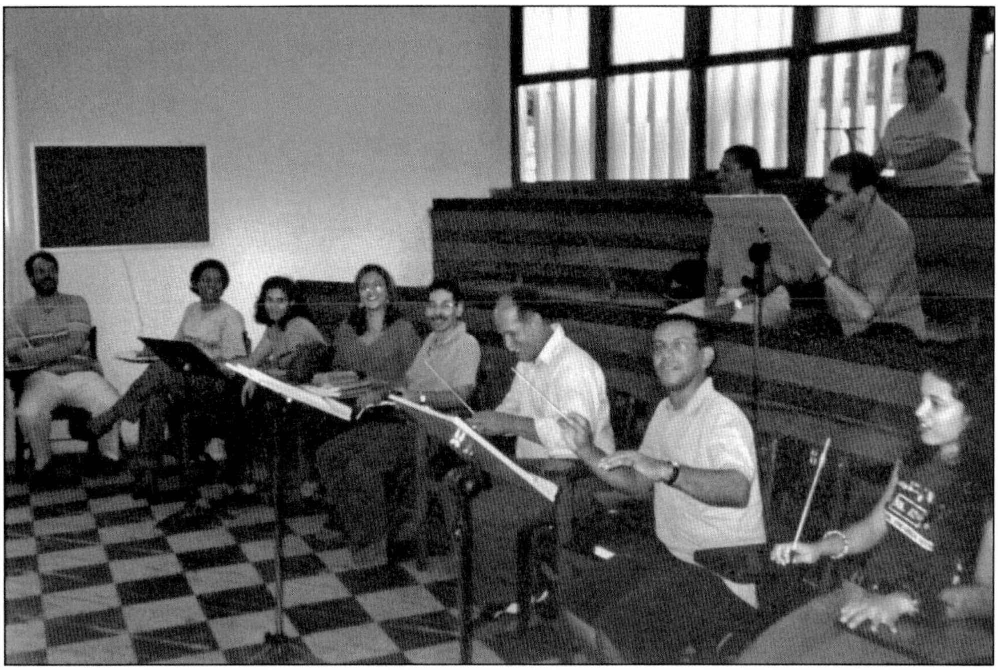

These music students are participating in an advanced conducting class in Recife, Brazil.

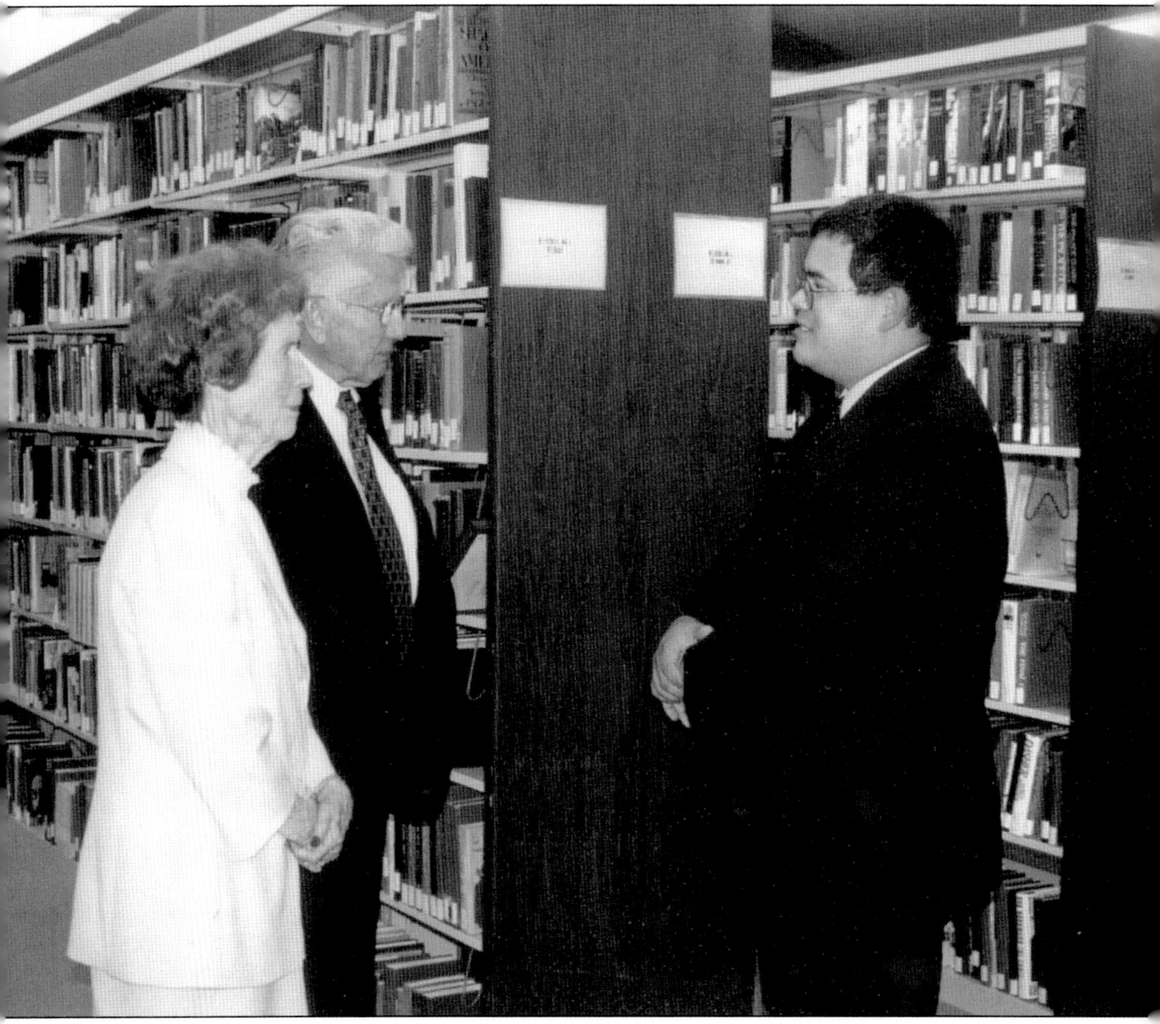

Dr. Ed and Ovaleta Montgomery (left) are pictured discussing the ongoing renovations of Montgomery Library with Dr. John Burch (right), director of library services, in 2001. The Montgomery family's continued dedication to library services at Campbellsville University resulted in significant improvements to the physical structure of the building, as well as technological improvements. The improvements in information technologies made it possible for library services to be extended outside of Campbellsville, Kentucky, to students in such distant locales as Recife, Brazil. (Photograph by Joan McKinney.)

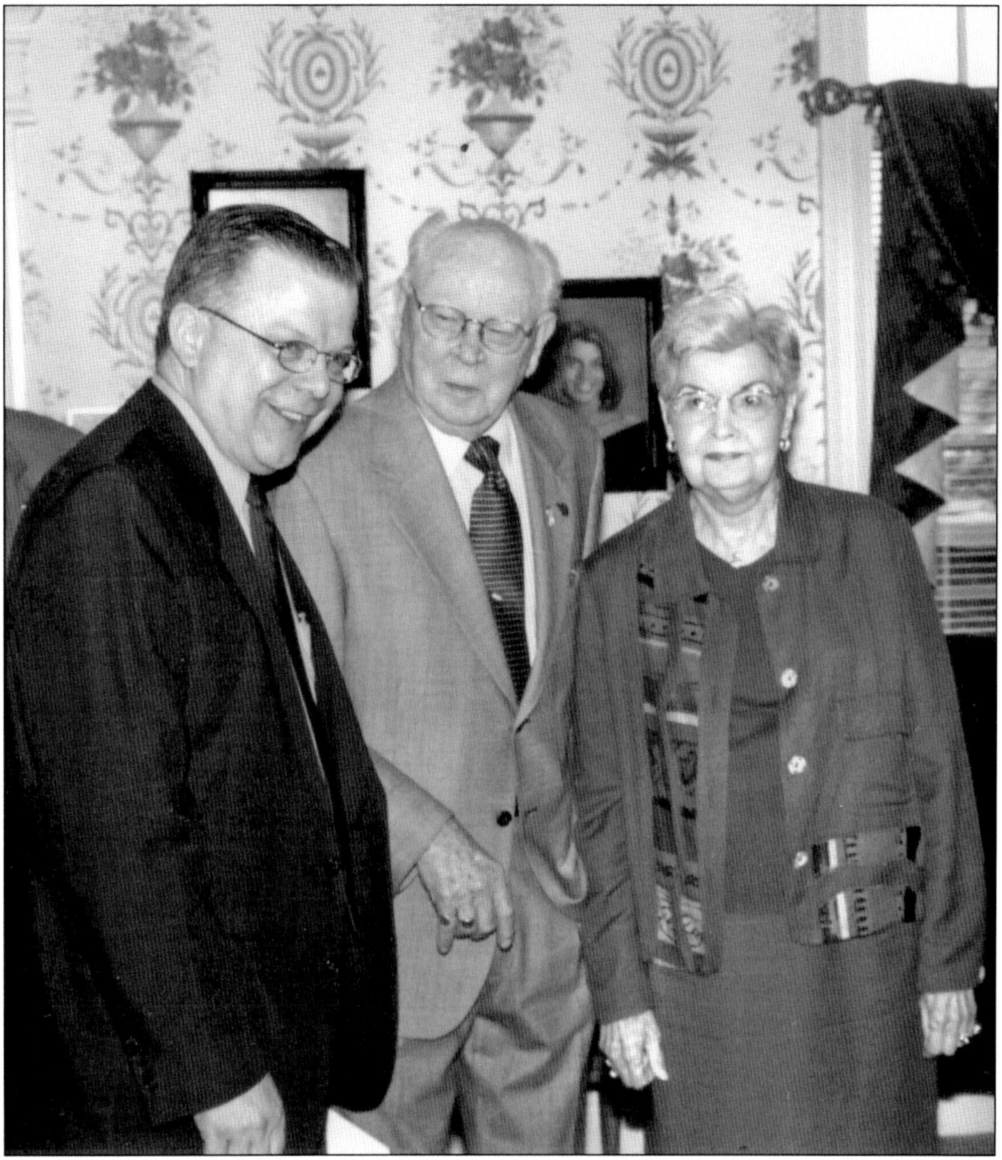

Rev. John Chowning (left) shares a humorous moment with Dr. A. B. Colvin and Irene Colvin. Dr. Colvin, affectionately known as "Mr. Kentucky Baptist," donated his Baptist history collection to Campbellsville University's Montgomery Library. The collection consists of more than 30,000 books, periodicals, and manuscript materials. Not surprisingly, it is particularly strong in the area of Kentucky Baptist history.

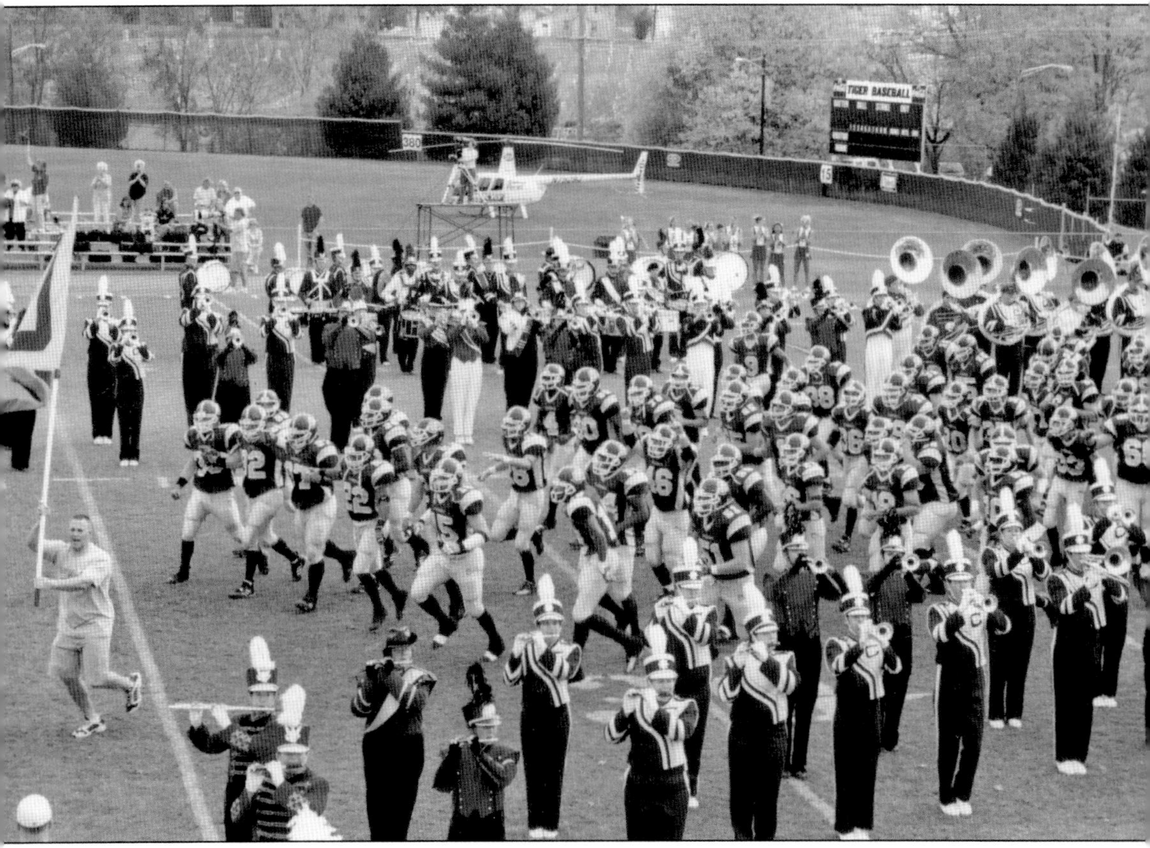

The football team charges the field as the marching band plays the fight song. Joining the festivities are members of high school marching bands that are guests of the Campbellsville University School of Music. (Photograph by Bryan Blair.)

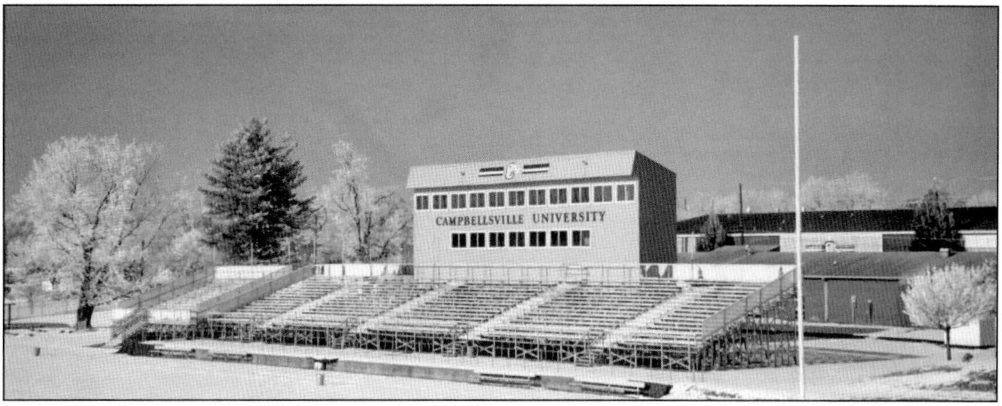

This picturesque view of the football stadium was captured on a snowy winter day. (Photograph by Bryan Blair.)

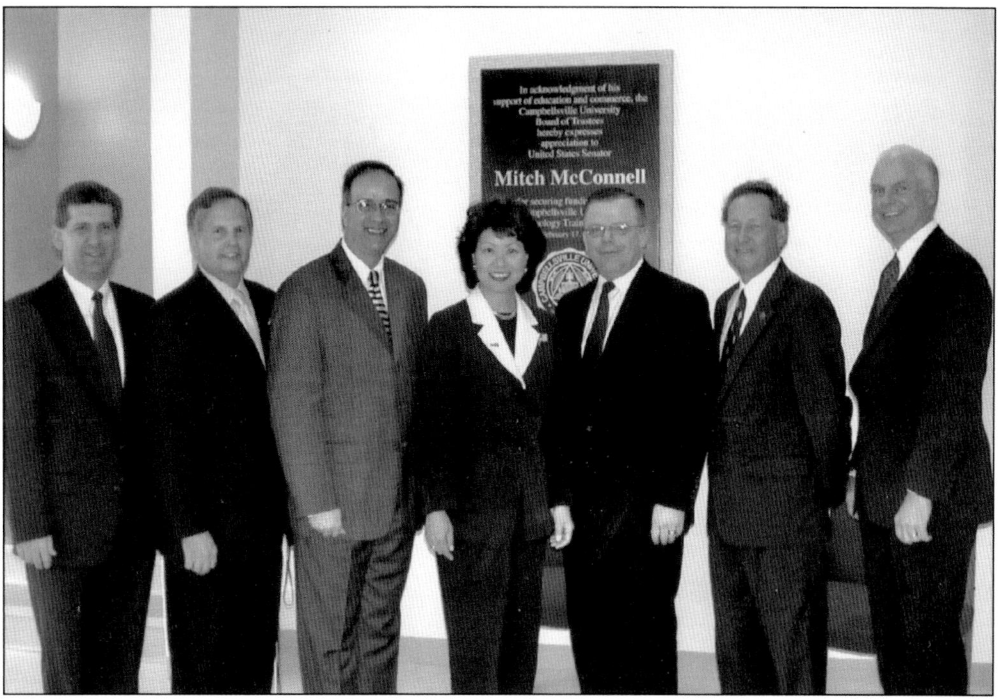

U.S. secretary of labor Elaine Chao (center) is joined on May 11, 2002, by, from left to right, Dr. Alan Medders, Otto Tennant, Dr. Michael Carter, Rev. John Chowning, Dr. Frank Cheatham, and Marc Whitt. They stand in front of a plaque in the Technology Training Center honoring Chao's husband, U.S. senator Mitch McConnell. (Photograph by Joan McKinney.)

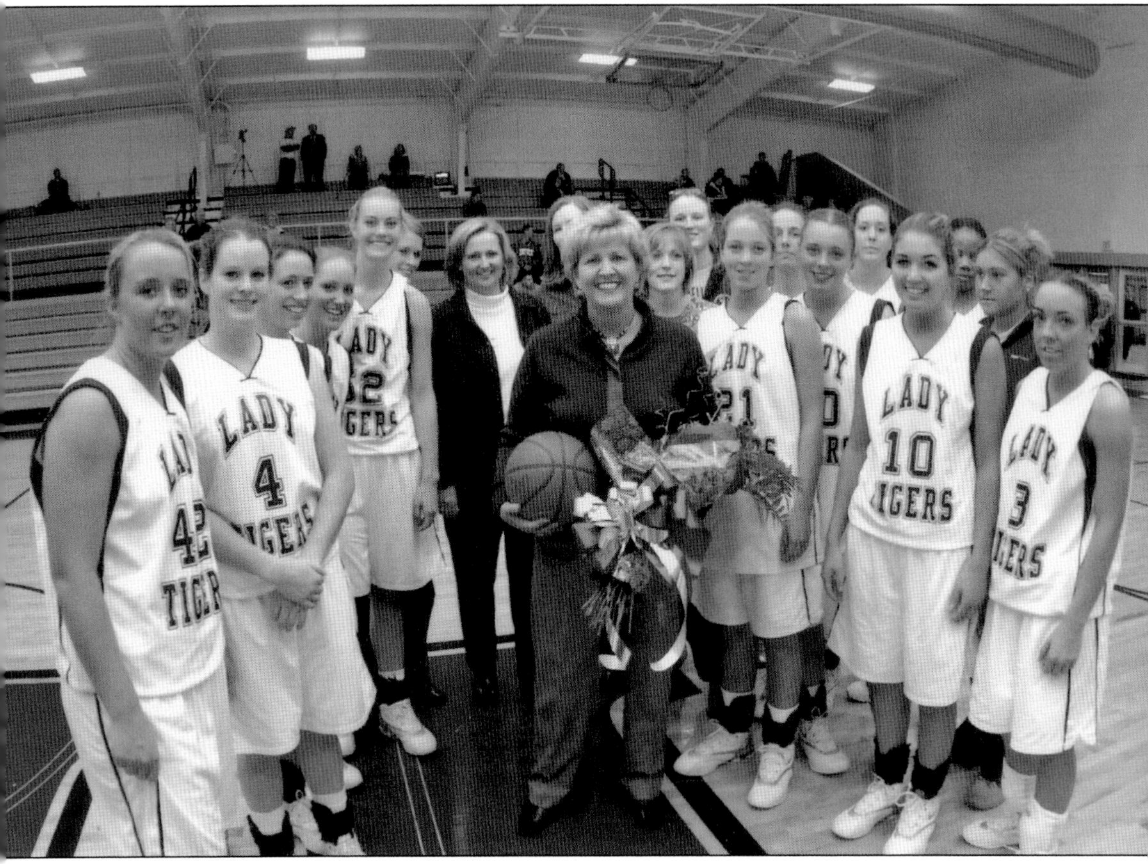

Coach Donna Wise is surrounded by current and former Lady Tiger players after earning her 600th career victory on December 11, 2003. Among her many accolades was her selection as a member of the NAIA Basketball Hall of Fame in 2000. Coach Wise retired after the 2006–2007 season, which marked her 32nd season as the coach of the Campbellsville Lady Tigers. Her final career record was 660-281. (Photograph by Crystal Anderson.)

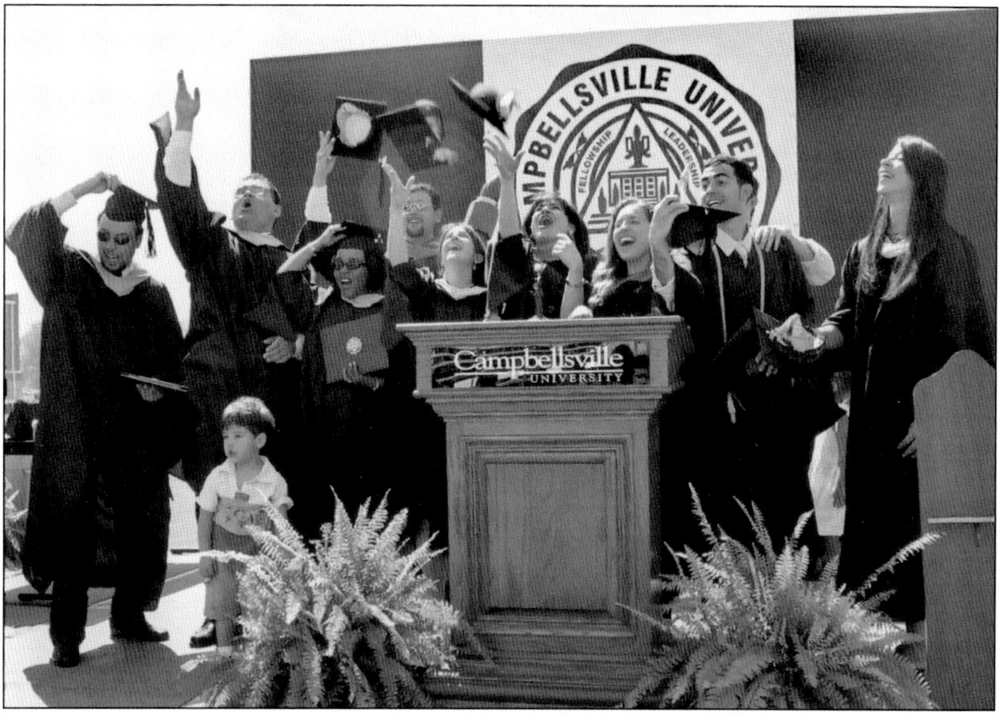

A group of international students from Brazil celebrate their graduation on May 8, 2004. (Photograph by Silvia Campelo.)

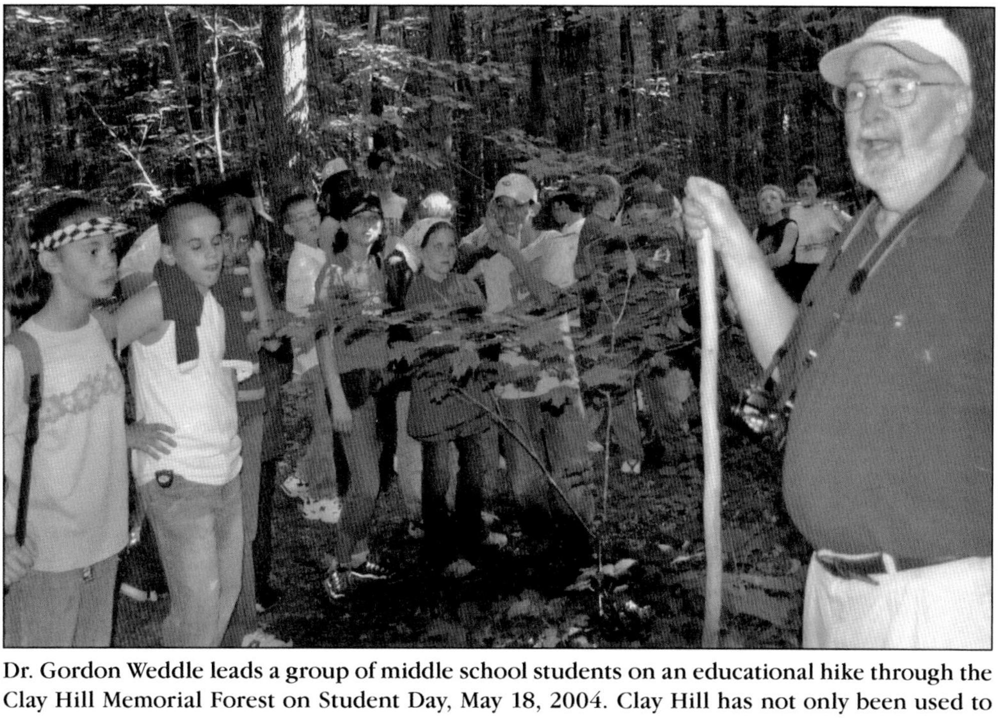

Dr. Gordon Weddle leads a group of middle school students on an educational hike through the Clay Hill Memorial Forest on Student Day, May 18, 2004. Clay Hill has not only been used to educate Campbellsville University students, but also thousands of elementary, middle, and high school students from throughout the surrounding region.

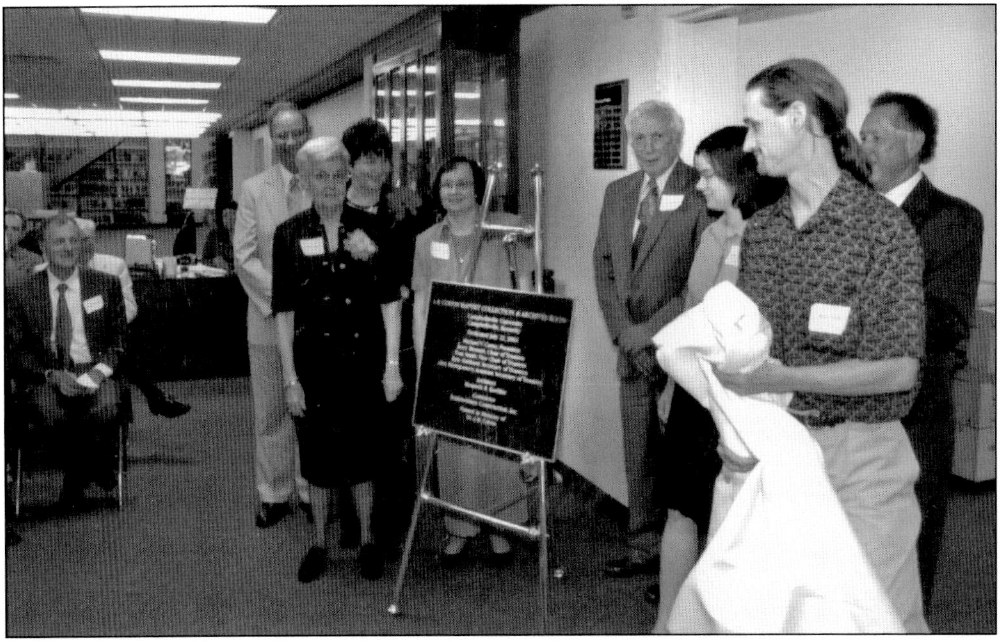

The Colvin family unveils the plaque honoring the late Dr. A. B. Colvin at the rededication of Montgomery Library. Through the generosity of Dr. Colvin and his family, the A. B. Colvin Baptist Collection and Archives was constructed within the library to house Dr. Colvin's exquisite Baptist collection, as well as other historically significant collections. Research space was also constructed so that scholars and students could comfortably utilize the resources provided by Dr. Colvin. (Photograph by Joan McKinney.)

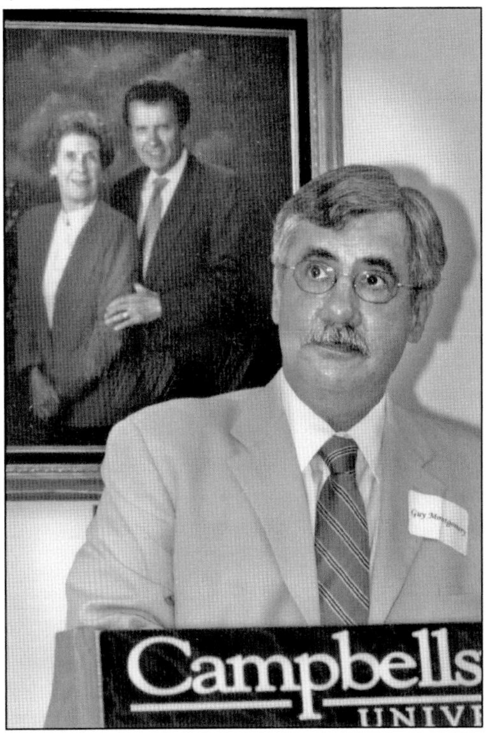

Guy Montgomery stands beneath a portrait of his parents, the late Dr. Edwin and Ovaleta Montgomery, at the rededication of Montgomery Library on July 22, 2004. Thanks to the generosity of the Montgomery family, generations of Campbellsville students and faculty have had, and will continue to have, their educational endeavors greatly improved by the quality library resources that the Montgomerys have provided to Campbellsville University. (Photograph by Joan McKinney.)

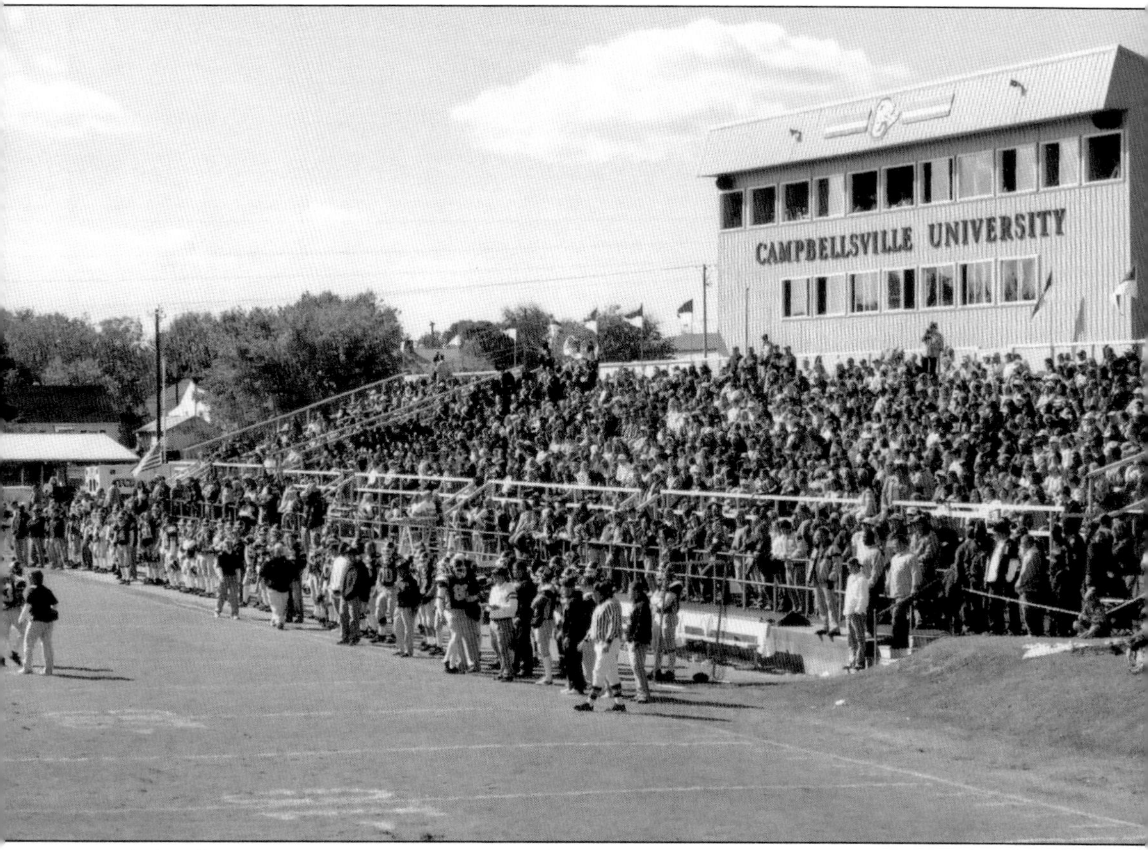

Campbellsville University's fans enjoy a football game on a beautiful fall afternoon. (Photograph by Tiago Pinheiro.)

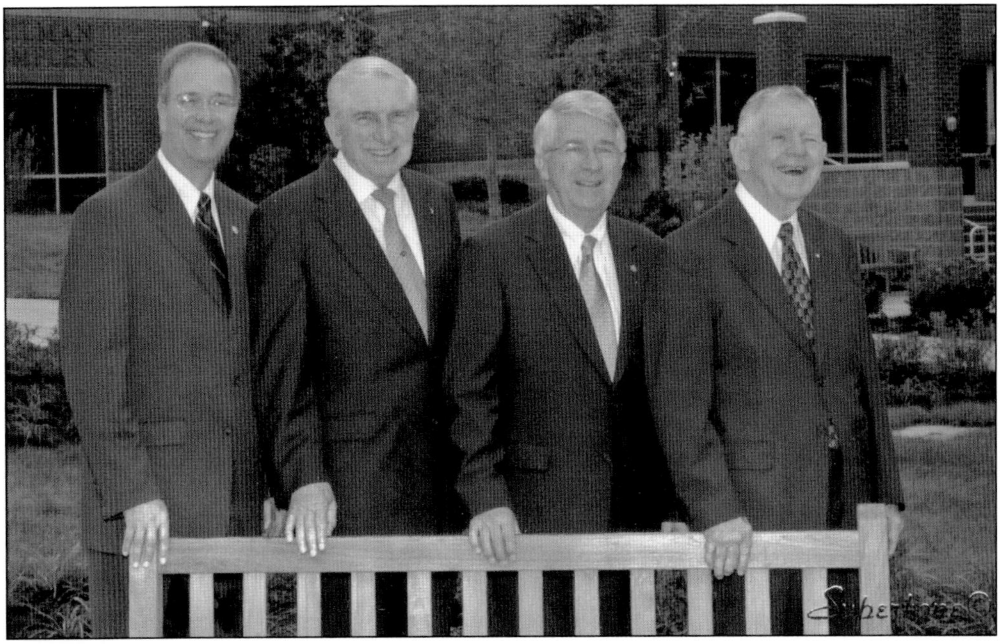

From left to right, Dr. Michael V. Carter, Dr. E. Bruce Heilman, Dr. Kenneth Winters, and Dr. Randolph Davenport stand in front of the E. Bruce Heilman Student Center Complex. Dr. Heilman graduated from Campbellsville Junior College in 1949 and has served multiple terms on the board of trustees. His distinguished academic career includes service as the president of several institutions, including the University of Richmond. Contained within the student center are the Winters Dining Hall and the Davenport Student Commons, which honor two of Campbellsville's former presidents. (Photograph courtesy of W. D. McCubbin.)

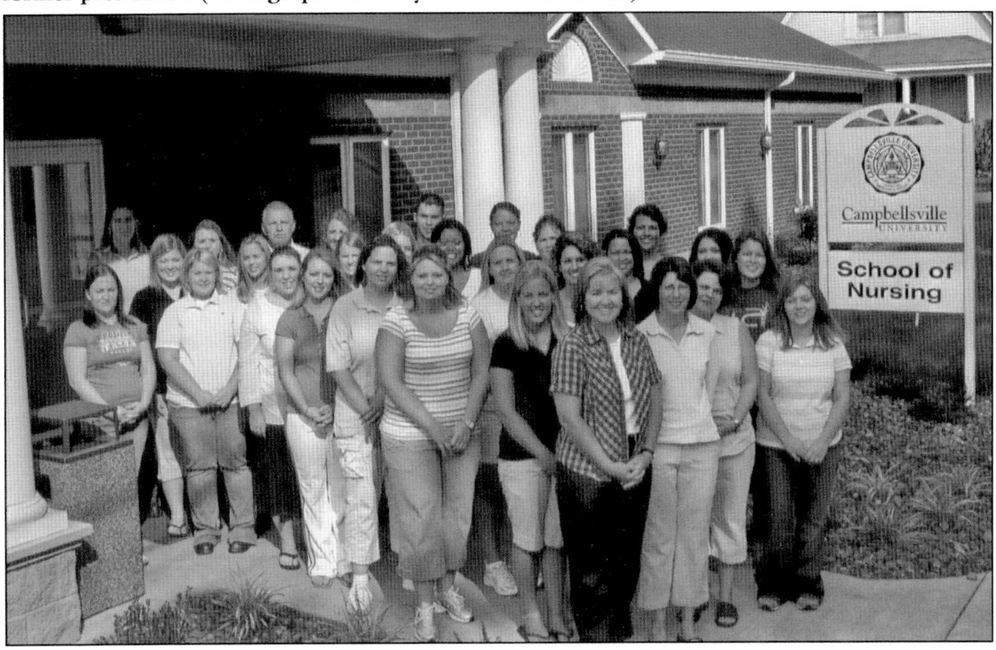

Dean Jo Ann Wever's inaugural class of nursing students stands in front of the new School of Nursing building in August 2006. (Photograph by Tiago Pinheiro.)

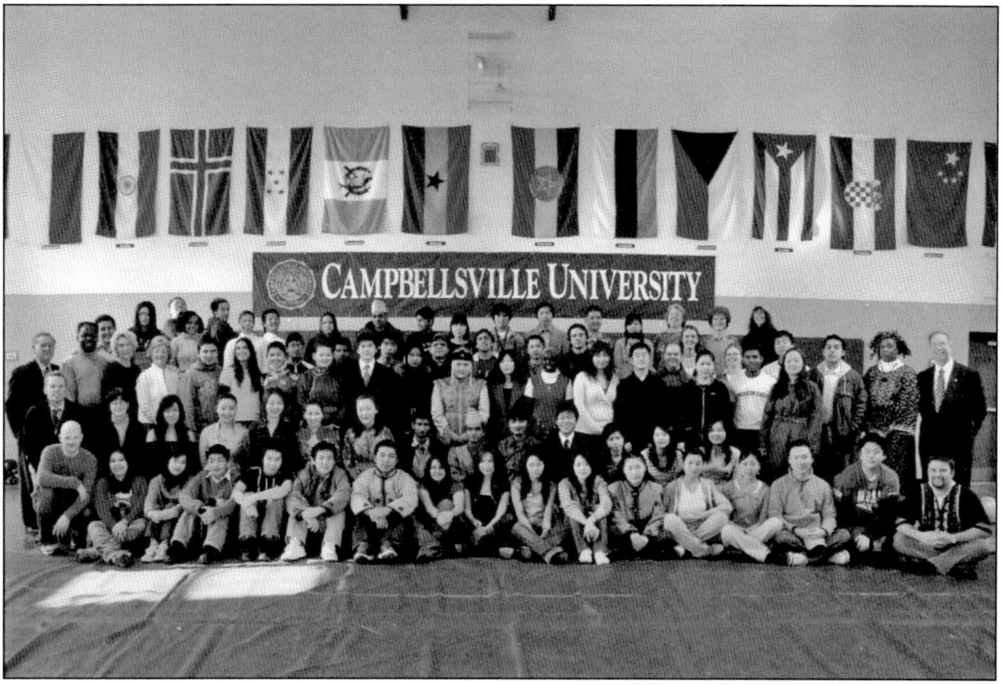

The diversity of Campbellsville University's student body is evident at the International Education Fair.

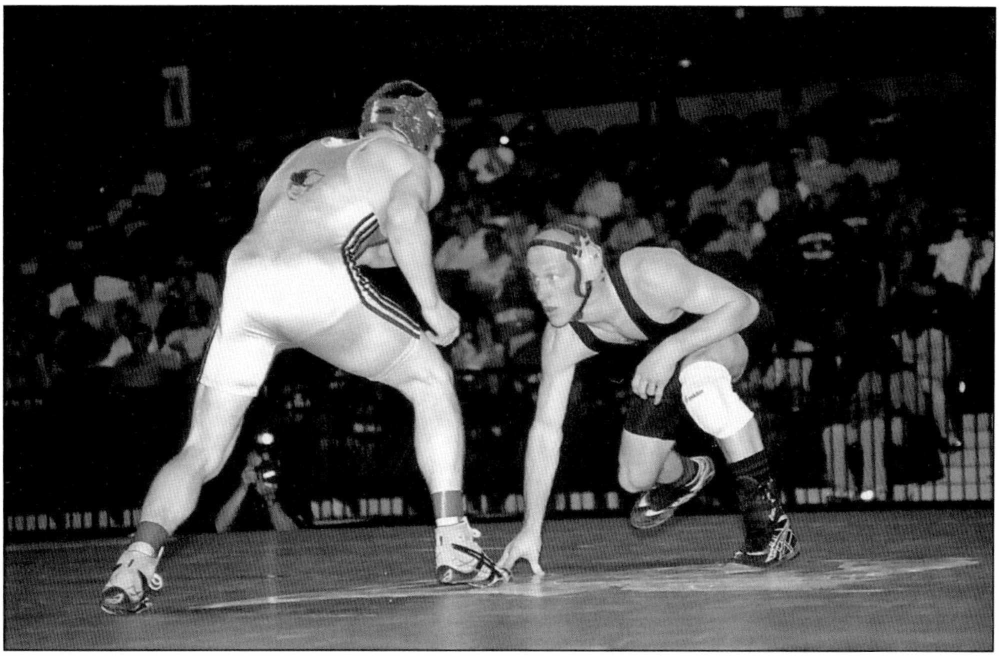

The wrestling team, coached by Franky James, finished the 2007 season ranked seventh in the nation. This is a remarkable achievement considering this was only the third year of the wrestling program. Another milestone was achieved when Tiger wrestler Zach Flake defeated the University of the Cumberlands' Brad Cooper at the NAIA national wrestling tournament to win the national championship in the 141-pound weight class.

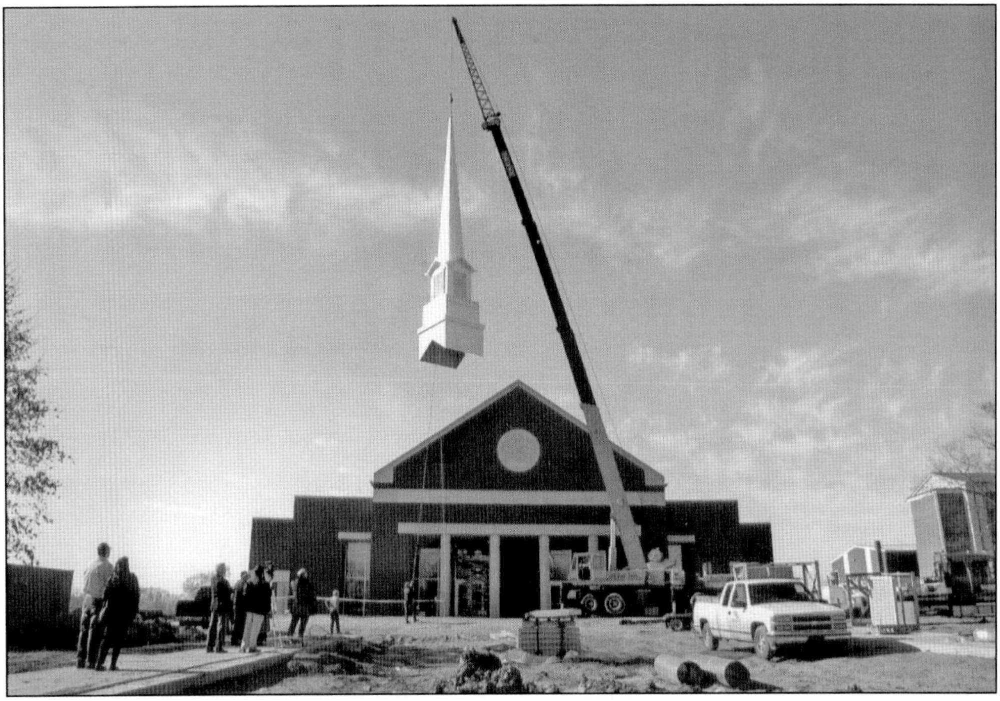

The steeple designed by Dr. Jerry Bennett is lowered onto the George W. and Marie T. Ransdell Chapel.

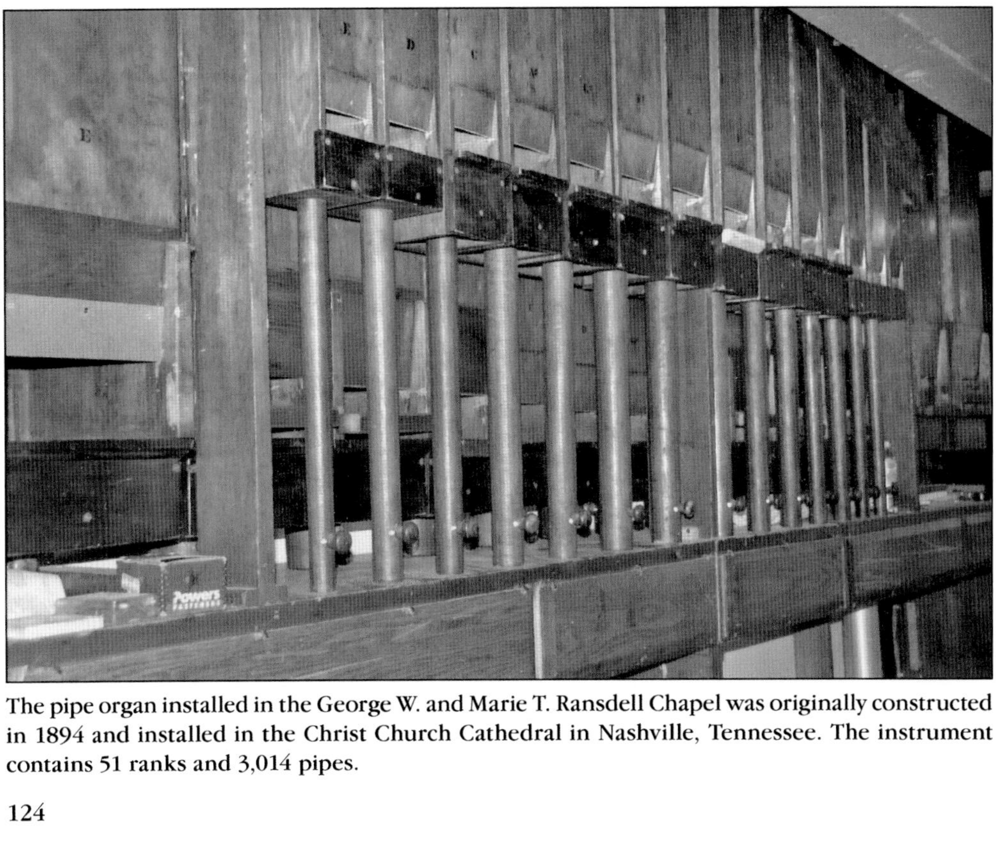

The pipe organ installed in the George W. and Marie T. Ransdell Chapel was originally constructed in 1894 and installed in the Christ Church Cathedral in Nashville, Tennessee. The instrument contains 51 ranks and 3,014 pipes.

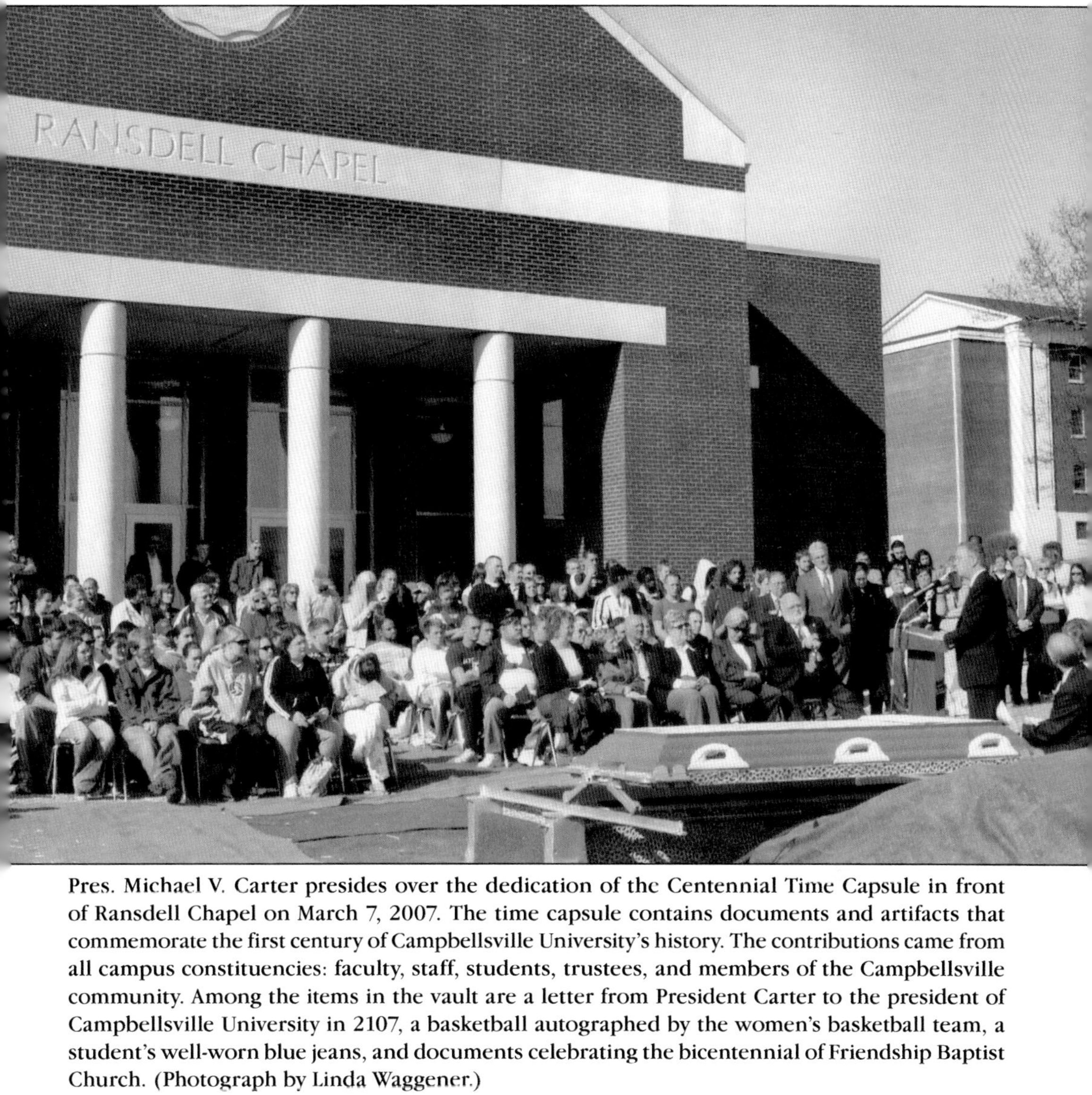

Pres. Michael V. Carter presides over the dedication of the Centennial Time Capsule in front of Ransdell Chapel on March 7, 2007. The time capsule contains documents and artifacts that commemorate the first century of Campbellsville University's history. The contributions came from all campus constituencies: faculty, staff, students, trustees, and members of the Campbellsville community. Among the items in the vault are a letter from President Carter to the president of Campbellsville University in 2107, a basketball autographed by the women's basketball team, a student's well-worn blue jeans, and documents celebrating the bicentennial of Friendship Baptist Church. (Photograph by Linda Waggener.)

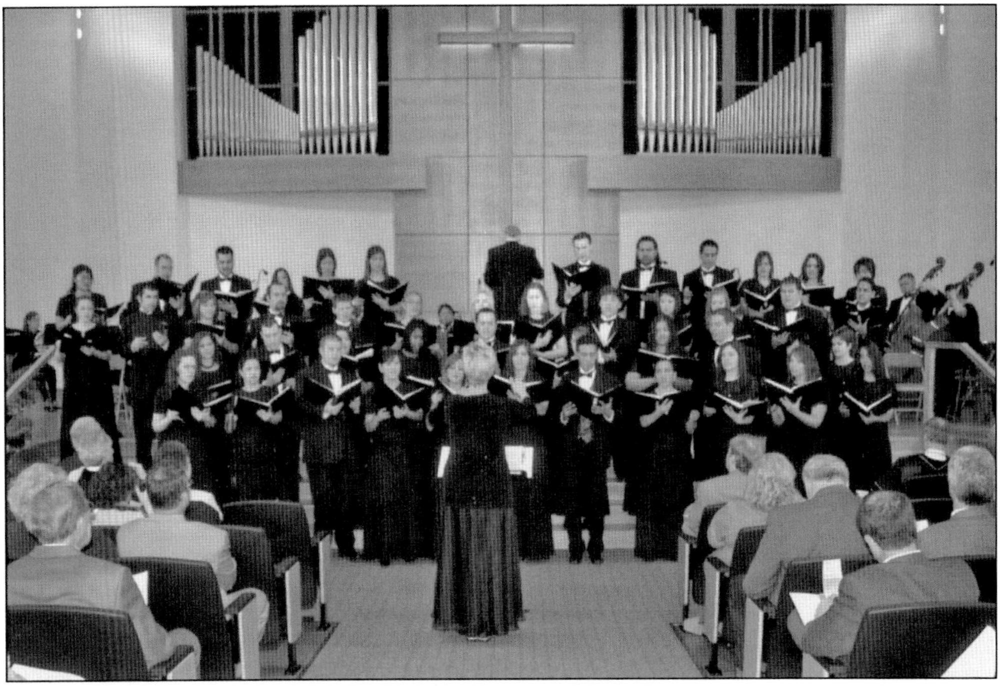

Dr. J. Robert Gaddis conducts the premiere public performance of *The Ephesian Trilogy* at the dedication of the George W. and Marie T. Ransdell Chapel on April 18, 2007. Commissioned from Jeff Cranfill, the work for choir, orchestra, and organ was composed in honor of Campbellsville University's centennial. (Photograph by Heather Campbell.)

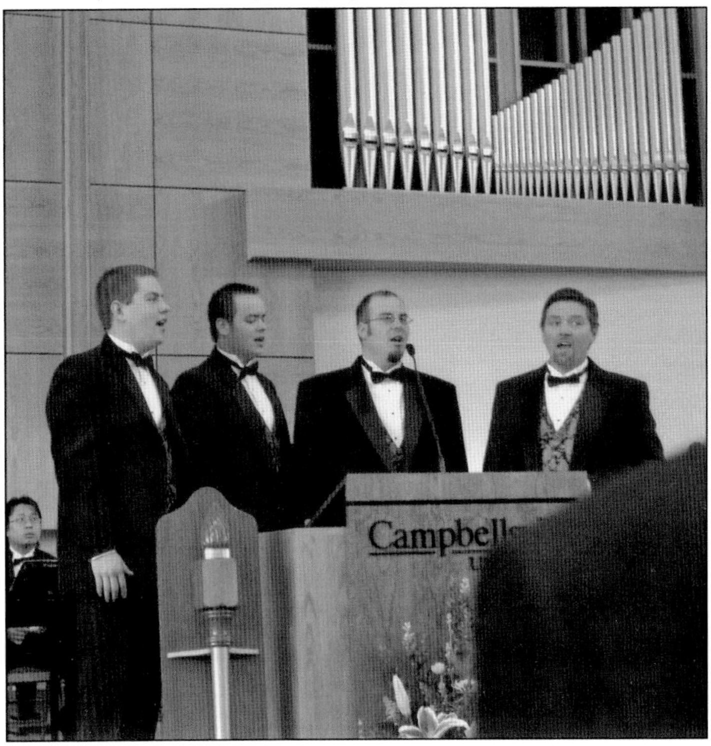

From left to right, David Rodgers, Joshua Hensley, Jason Logan, and Tim Hooper, collectively known as the CU Sound, lead the congregation in the singing of the alma mater at the Ransdell Chapel dedication. (Photograph by Heather Campbell.)

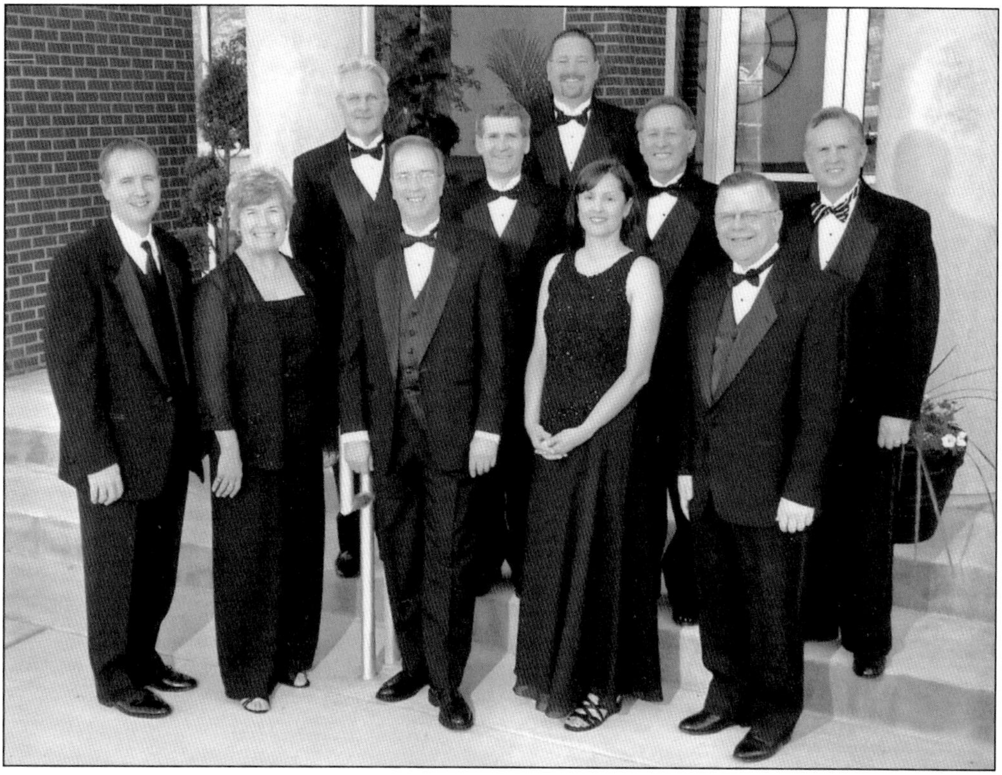

The administrative council posed for this picture at the Black-and-White Centennial Gala. The members are, from left to right, (first row) Tim Judd, Virginia Flanagan, Dr. Michael V. Carter, Dr. Jeanette Parker, and John Chowning; (second row) David Walters, Dr. Alan Medders, Rusty Hollingsworth, Dr. Frank Cheatham, and Otto Tennant. (Photograph courtesy of Bramel Photosource and Photography Services, Lebanon, Kentucky.)

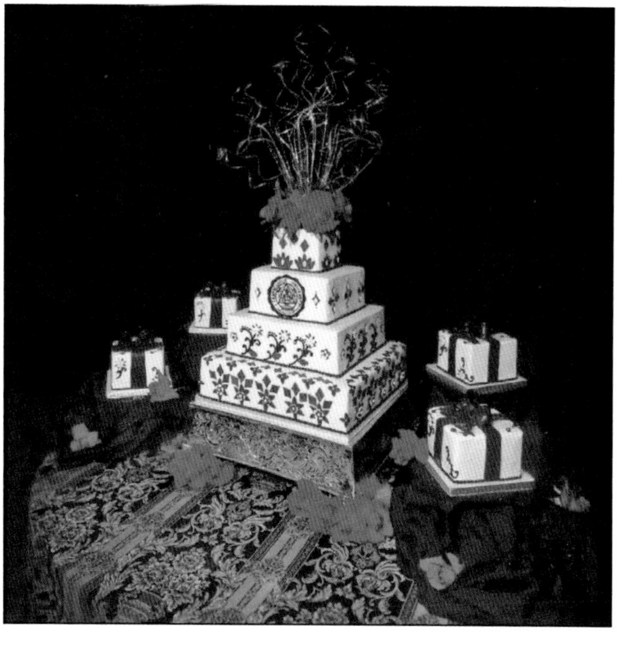

Happy 100th birthday, Campbellsville University! (Photograph courtesy of Bramel Photosource and Photography Services, Lebanon, Kentucky.)

Across America, People are Discovering Something Wonderful. *Their Heritage.*